A Miraculous Life!

By Perry Arbogast

Dedication and Gratitude

I dedicate this book to the glory of God and the kingdom He is creating, through His son Jesus, and to my wife Michelle, thank you for your constant support throughout our marriage.

A special thanks to all who helped in making this book so much better.

Sherry Baerlocher, Dr. Bruce Hitchcock, Karen Dale, Dr. Steven Lennertz, General Randy Ball, David Ruch, Josh Ruch, Dylan Ivan, Gennie and Tom McAferty, Marilyn Powell, and Wanda Young. The insights and improvements you provided were invaluable.

Contents

A Miraculous Life!

By Perry Arbogast

Everything you are about to read, actually happened. Names have sometimes been changed, to protect the identity of certain individuals. It is not my intent to harm anyone's life. This is a true story of my life. It has been one of the most amazing and miraculous lives. Shootings, stabbings, falling out of cars, off cliffs, and so many more, I should be dead many times over! The mathematical probability of still being alive is so astronomically small, that there had to be a Living God directing, protecting, and overseeing my life. You say you don't believe in a God! I challenge you to read this book and keep that belief.

I am a journal writer. Every morning, my routine includes writing my most intimate thoughts, in a prayer journal. I have kept meticulous records. I have five filing cabinets filled with important papers about my life. Much of what you read was journaled at the time it happened. It has been an amazing ride. I wanted to record some of the miracles God did in my life.

One last thing, some of the stories are so remarkable, that you may wonder if they are true! I want to state, emphatically, that they **are** absolutely true!

Family Legacy

My story starts before I was born. What happened back then, directly impacted my life. We are a product of our parents. Their experiences, their prejudices, their values, and their dysfunction.

I will start with my mother, Evelyn Marie Owen. She was born into abject poverty. Such extreme poverty, that she and her many siblings occasionally lived in tents. Tragically these tents burned down and they lost everything they did own. Because of the wood stoves, and the embers that would pop out, it was only a matter of time before they inevitably caught the tents on fire. No pictures or heirlooms survived. The only thing that was passed onto my generation, was the torturous brutality.

To keep food on the table, Virginia, (Marie's mother, my grandmother), would frequent the bars and seedy places and was known in the community as a lounge lizard. Her choice of men was abysmal. Men of high character are not normally found in the local bar. Some of the men Virginia brought home were sick and depraved individuals.

When my mother was a skinny twelve-year-old, one of the "customers" wanted two for the price of one. So, when Virginia was gone, he came in and had his way with Marie. Raped and enraged, Marie waited until her

1

mother returned and told her mother what had happened. Her mother screamed at Marie and claimed she was lying. What happened next is so unbelievable, that I interviewed others siblings who claimed they witnessed it, just to verify its truth.

Virginia was very sadistic; she stripped Marie naked and tied Marie to a post. Virginia then took a whip and beat Marie, till she could no longer stand. She was left hanging on the post all day. When the scum-bag-of-a-man returned that night, Virginia told him the "lie" Marie had fabricated about him. They both went out and brutally beat her again until she was unconscious. They untied Marie, carried her back into the house, and threw her on a bed. They then poured salt into the raw wounds. The pain and exhaustion were too much for Marie to handle and she would pass out. Every time Marie would become conscious, they would do it again and again. Virginia passed her sick brutality onto Marie.

That incident spawned a hatred for men in Marie. Marie grew up with an underlying rage towards men, that manifested itself when I was born. Marie told me many years later, that being raped and the subsequent betrayal by her own mother, triggered a sadistic level of anger in her. She said, "Something snapped in me that day."

It would be many years before psychiatrists would diagnose her as manic depressive with sociopathic tendencies. She got some twisted delight in killing animals. It made her feel powerful over life and death. She delighted in inflicting pain and torture because it made her feel in control. As a little boy, all I knew was the brutality it spawned.

You may be wondering how, with her hatred of men, did I come about? This is how Marie told it. Marie and her siblings lived in poverty and brutality. It was so severe, that when Marie was in high school, she and her sister Terra met two brothers, Bud and Jerry Arbogast, and saw a way out.

The Arbogast boys couldn't have been more different. Jerry was outgoing, the life of the party. Terra and Jerry soon became an item. The other brother "Bud" was a passive, quiet, introverted type. He wasn't the sharpest pencil in the box. He was somewhat simple-minded. Marie saw she could dominate and manipulate him. She was so desperate to escape her mother's house, that when she saw the opportunity, she jumped at it. She said, "I saw a way out." Both couples married and this is where my story begins.

Marie told me many times, that she had long before decided she would never have kids. Having been raised in a household of over ten children, and she, the oldest, she had no interest in children. Yet to her utter dismay she became pregnant on her wedding night. My older sister was born, and eleven months later, I was born.

When my mother saw that she had given birth to a boy, with that disgusting penis, (her words not mine) she decided to kill it. All that rage

2

and anger that had built up over the years would be avenged on this sacrificial baby boy. She was deeply mentally disturbed. So, when she got home with me from the hospital, she had already worked out how she would carry out my murder.

We lived in a logging camp in the mountains of Oregon. Marie waited until Bud boarded the crew van the next morning. When it pulled out, she set her plan into action. She drove me deep into the mountains, far from civilization. She hid the car off the dirt road and grabbed me and headed into a very remote canyon. She hiked far from the road and down to a secluded creek. She liked to kill things with her bare hands. When she killed chickens or dogs, she didn't use an axe. She preferred to feel the intimacy of snapping its neck and feeling the life drain away. She had planned to hold my head under the water to kill me.

This was the first miracle! God had already set circumstances in play that defy probability. On that exact morning, a man was hunting in the remote area, and saw Marie hiking, carrying a baby. He was aware of Marie's mental challenges and was prompted to follow her to see what she was up to. To him, it didn't make sense that a mother, who had just given birth, would be out in the mountains with her newborn. He kept out of sight and was standing nearby when he saw her begin drowning me. He screamed out for her to stop. She was startled to see another human so far from civilization. A Divine appointment for me. God was watching out for me and protecting me long before I was old enough to know about a Heavenly Father who loved me.

This incident spawned some legal action, but I never heard the details. What I did hear was that Marie spent time in a mental hospital, but eventually she was released. Back in the 50s and 60s, in the remote wilderness of Umatilla County, there were no checks and balances. Not like we have today. Law enforcement and Child protective services, were none existent in the remote logging community.

Marie was released to continue her quest to kill me. One morning she waited for Bud to leave for work, then she took me into the kitchen. She took the time to fill the sink with water. She was determined to drown me with her own hands. She decided to carry it out in the privacy of her own home so no one could thwart her. She believed she could lay my dead body in the crib and claim that I died of crib death.

She told me she put her hands around my neck and was putting me under the water when she heard a male voice cry out, "Marie NO! Don't do this wicked thing." She jerked her head around but could not see anyone. She was not religious in any sense of the word but knew it could only have been God. For me, it was another Divine intervention.

She was so terrified by that experience, that she began to dabble in the mystical cults. From that time forward, she was drawn to the wildest extremes of the religious fringe. She became a religious cultist, but only when it suited her.

Often when cultists want to practice bizarre life practices, they become reclusive and socially distance themselves. Marie and Bud became reclusive and outcasts within the family. There were several reasons. Partly because Marie didn't want them around and made it abundantly clear. But there were lots of other reasons as well.

Marie and Bud got into snakes and had them all over the house. Bud's mother was deathly afraid of snakes and Marie knew it. Many family members were aware of her mental condition, and her sadistic brutality and they wanted no part of it. I think mostly though, it was because she was considered a religious nut case. All this was just fine for Bud and Marie; it made it a lot easier to hide broken bones, lacerations, bruises, and the swollen faces of their children.

The Accident

What I am about to tell you, I don't remember. Everything I know has been told to me by everyone who was there when it happened. I have talked to the other family members who were present and witnessed it. In addition to my own family, who were there, I spoke to the doctor who was part of the medical team.

When I was two years old, we were riding in Mrs. Wachter's car, on our way to Pendleton Oregon. (Marie and Mrs. Wachter were part of the same cult.) We were on highway 395 when I somehow fell out of the car. Behind us was a Chip truck driver who saw it unfold before his eyes. He says when we began to round the corner, the door came open on the right rear of the car and he saw a baby hit the pavement at highway speed. It bounced up and slammed into the rock embankment beside the highway, and rolled back into his lane. He was already on his breaks as he entered the corner and pulled into the oncoming lane, to miss hitting the baby. When he came to a stop he jumped out of the truck and ran back and picked me up off the highway. I have jokingly said that this gives new meaning to bouncing baby boy!

By this time Mrs. Wachter had turned around and returned to the scene. The driver put my bloodied and unconscious body on Marie's lap. They sped off, to the nearest hospital, some 70 miles away.

When the doctor saw my condition, he notified the family that if I lived, I would be a vegetable. My brain was so full of sand and gravel that it took them over three hours in surgery just to clean it out. He told the family my head was so smashed up that I would not survive the night, and even if I did, I would never be able to hear or see again. The doctor told those in the waiting room; "I don't want to give anyone false hope. He will be a deaf, blind, vegetable."

4

Evidently, God didn't get that memo! Divine intervention again! They called it a medical miracle at the time. Not only did I survive the night, but I also defied all medical odds, and lived.

In addition, not only did my eyesight come back, I had been given an extraordinary gift. I had the ability to see, with crystal clarity, detail at extremely long distances. Ophthalmologists have examined the concave and convex curvatures of my eyes, and have marveled at their perfection.

My hearing was exceptional as well. What shocked everyone though, was the mental acuity. My IQ was above average. Who knows but that God did use that accident, to trip something in my brain?

One would think that after a miraculous recovery, a mother would grow even closer to her child. Not in my case. Marie rationalized in her mind, that it was because of this accident, that she never bonded with me.

She defended herself with the rest of her family saying, "When the Doctor told me he was going to die, I shut down. It was because of the dire prognosis, that I never bonded with him!" But the family knew better, because, I was already two and a half years old at the time. She had never bonded, nor would she.

When I was a little older, she blamed me for their poverty. The accident caused a financial hardship for the family, and Marie held me personally responsible.

We not only lived in abject poverty, we lived in horrendous squalor. This is another reason we never had visitors. The filth was so bad, we even had animal feces in the house. Marie even had ducks living in the house, so you had to step around the droppings. We reeked of body odor. Marie would only allow one bath a week; "…because we can't afford the water" she would say. That was a lie! We received our water from a spring!

Marie hated housework, so if there were dishes to be washed, we kids did them. She saw us as her slaves. She actually told us she was a queen, and we should address her as "your highness." She perceived herself as privileged and entitled. She saw herself as superior, and far smarter than "ordinary" people. She saw herself as royalty, and we were her subjects.

We were to obey her or be severely punished. We were never allowed to question her. If we hesitated at all, she perceived that as insubordination, and that warranted a beating. If we dared to complain, she would become enraged. Oh, how she loved to inflict pain. She would use hoses that left welts, that would swell up and bleed. She had a board that she would beat us with. Belts, willow switches, she wasn't afraid to use anything at her disposal.

Marie was especially irritated by noise. She suffered from migraine headaches. If I made a noise, in her twisted mind, that was deliberate disobedience and justified a beating.

5

Mrs. Walkter, watched one day, as a comical incident played out. When I was about four years old, I was in the back of our little mobile home and evidently making some noise. This infuriated Marie. She opened the front door and screamed my name. I couldn't see her, but I assumed she was at the front door, so I ran around toward the front of the trailer. She, thinking I was still at the back of the trailer, ran to the back of the trailer. She screamed my name again, so I turned around and returned to the back of the house. Unfortunately, she did the same and returned to the front door. She thought I was deliberately avoiding her.

When I finally ran up to her, she was in a fit of rage. In her mind, she had been defied, and that would have to be punished most severely. She grabbed my hair and tossed me around like a rag doll. When my hair came out, she became even more enraged. When it was done, blood was everywhere.

Now Bud wasn't there at the time, but Marie told him how I had defied her and concocted a hellacious lie, which she did often. She delighted in manipulating Bud to rage against me. He not only knew of the torture and abuse; he allowed it to happen. He was a complicit accomplice. He was spineless. He would do almost anything to appease her rage.

Marie would come up with a lie, and get Bud to whip me, and Marie would be grinning at me the whole time. Bud never tortured me, like Marie, but he knew of her torture and never intervened. When she was ranting at him, she often threatened him, that if he ever crossed her, she would wait till he was asleep and smash his head in with a cast iron frying pan. She was dead serious and he knew it. He was also fearful of her brutality and knew full well the depth of her depravity.

The Bully

Marie was the quintessential bully. She would mock and belittle me, then get within half an inch of my face, and dare me to flinch. If I backed off, she would beat me, so I had to stand firm, as she spit in my face. She would often become angry and start verbal tirades, and if I dared smile, she would beat me. "Are you laughing at me?" she would scream, "Do you think something is funny, well I'll give you something to laugh about!"

Sometimes she would get in my face and slap me and dare me to get mad. She would taunt and goad me until I would make some look that would justify a beating. She would say things, like "That hurt, didn't it?" "I'll bet you're mad, aren't you?" She would mock…. if I dared say anything, she would scream "Don't talk back to me" and the beating would occur.

There were times I would be standing in the kitchen, and she would walk up behind me and take a can of canned food and smash it onto my head. It would cut my head open, and leave a semi-round arching scar. What was my offense? It could be as little as I was in her way. She would cut my scalp open with a can and yell, "Get out of my way!" Years later, my wife was cutting my hair for the first time, and she asked me, "What are all these half circles in your scalp?" So, I told her.

One time she broke my eye socket when she threw a solid piece of glass at my head. Marie never needed a reason to go off in a tirade. One of the worst beatings I remember was over a dirty comb. I remember that well because I was around 12 years old when it happened. Imagine getting severely beaten, because there was something between the tines of a comb. Sometimes it was a look that she deemed was defiance. Perhaps it was the way I walked away. If she detected any hint that I was angry, it would set her off. Needless to say, I grew to hate her with every fiber of my being.

Marie would later admit, that all the hatred she had for me, was because I was male. I had a penis, (her words, not mine). Therefore, I was in the same wicked company as her attacker. In her mind, the injustice she endured after the rape, must be avenged. I was the whipping boy. She would exact her revenge on "it".

She couldn't even stand to hear my voice. Throughout my childhood, I heard the same mantra, "Your voice is so irritating." "I don't want to hear a word out of you all day." "You should be seen and not heard." She would say, "Why don't you go play on the highway, and if I'm lucky you will get hit by a car."

Some of you reading this may think to yourself, "No mother hates her kid that bad!" I wish it were true, but we are seeing more and more mothers, who are killing their children. I have spoken to many, who endured even worse, at the hand of a sexually deviate father. As bad as my torture was, at least I was never raped by my father. My heart goes out to those women, who had to suffer the indignity of incest. They had it so much worse.

Mean and Powerful

Marie was a big heavy-set woman, well over 200 pounds. One afternoon, in the trailer court, some women were getting mouthy with Marie. So, she invited them, all three of them, to bring it or keep their mouths shut! All three women came at Marie, all at once.

What happened next, was forever known in the community, as a warning, not to mess with Marie. When she was angry, she was out of her mind. In one blow she hit the first woman so hard, she fell unconscious at Marie's feet. She then began mercilessly beating the other two. Marie was a street fighter. She pulled hair; took bites out of the skin, gouge at the eyes, and would strip their clothes off. She even took one of the women and tossed her like a rag doll. When it was finished, she stood over them daring them to stand and get some more. She had so completely whipped them, that they

7

wouldn't even move or sit up. It was a savage beating, and they were afraid of more, so they played possum.

When one of their husbands tried to come to their rescue, Marie picked up a weapon and chased him away. He ran and called the police, but they never came.

Marie later worked at the Edward Hines Lumber mill. They instantly took a dislike to her. Yet instead of firing her, and having to pay unemployment; they put her on the Green Chain. (For those of you, who are not in the lumber industry, let me explain: Pulling "Green Chain" is one of the most physically exhausting jobs in the mill. Lumber is wet when it is green, and extremely heavy when freshly cut from a log. Long strips of lumber, some twenty feet in length, fall on the Green Chain. Someone has to pull, sort, and grade it. This is normally done by the stoutest men at the mill.)

Marie knew precisely what they were trying to do. She seethed with inner rage and determined she would never be shown the door. She worked the Green Chain for years. She was not only mean and stubborn; she was strong as an ox.

The Shame of Poverty

I didn't understand the meaning of poverty until I entered first grade. We lived far out of town and had to catch a ride into Ukiah Oregon. The school was the same one Bud, Marie, Terra, and Jerry had graduated from. It was a small community, so everyone knew everyone else. I was an outcast before I ever walked into the school for the first time. No one in the community liked Marie. Not even her sister Terra.

The community only knew me as, "The filthy child!" "That's the child of those nutcases, live'n up the highway." I was the offspring of the mentally unstable! We were the outcasts! We lived in isolation, in a mobile trailer, miles from prying eyes.

When I was six, I didn't know or understand, that our family had a reputation. That first day of school I learned a lot, but not from the curriculum. I was oblivious. I hadn't even considered my clothes when I dressed for school on that first day. Yet when I sat there at my desk, I looked at all the other kids in their new clothes, and I felt self-conscious.

We were too poor to afford new clothes. The kids referred to my pants as high waters. I had no idea what that meant. Marie had always ironed on knee patches where the holes were. I was so skinny that I wore the same pants, even as I grew. I remember those pants, dark green bell bottoms that rode a third of the way up my shins. I only had two pairs of pants in the drawer.

That afternoon when I left school, I had a list of supplies I was expected to bring to class. Pencils, paper, a box of crayons, an eraser, and a bottle of

Elmer's glue for crafts. All the other kids evidently got the memo, but we had not. So that first day of school, I learned that Bud and Marie were not up with the times.

When I arrived home, I gave the list to Marie, she naturally went into a rage. I was costing her good money. I wasn't worth all the expense.

The next day I arrived with a tiny box of five crayons. Other kids had boxes of 64 crayons with a built-in sharpener. I had never been around other kids, but that day I learned the social shame of poverty. I was not only socially backward, I was extremely scared and shy. I remember that I walked with my eyes focused on my feet. I learned very fast that I was a social outcast. I was so skinny that I was the natural target for the bullies in school. I hated school. In fact, it got so bad, that in the mornings before school, the dread was so overwhelming, I would become physically sick, and vomit in the toilet.

My redemption was my brain. I was a quick learner. I might have been poor, but I was not stupid. I might have been dirty, but I learned quickly to clean up.

In our little grade school, at the end of the week, there was a tradition of bake sales. Everyone was expected to bring a treat from home, and at the beginning of lunch hour, the teacher would conduct a bake sale. The other kids would spend nickels, dimes, and quarters, and purchase treats. Of course, I never participated, because Marie would have nothing to do with this. The idea of giving me loose change was out of the question. Yet another layer of humiliation.

Week after week I longed to eat the sweets that the other kids were enjoying. But I sat at my desk empty-handed. Other kids noticed and often mocked me. Even at a young age, I wondered why Bud and Marie were so different! Other parents gave their kids money, why had mine never given me any change, even a penny?

Birthday Presents

As a child, I remember my birthday gifts well. Because we never got gifts. We didn't practice Christmas. Marie hated the idea of having to buy gifts. So, when I received my first birthday gift it was amazing. Only later would I realize the lack of care or love behind them.

I was celebrating my 5th birthday and we were sitting at the table when my mother brought in my gift. It was a can of half-used shaving cream. Bud protested but Marie insisted. She told me I could spray the old stumps outside with it, but not inside.

I thought it was pretty special, that she gave me a present. It was the first nice thing I could remember. Only upon reflection, did I realize she had no intention of wasting good money on a real present. So, she went to the

9

bathroom and grabbed a used can of shaving cream, and presented it to me as if she had gone to great lengths. Her hatred of me had no bounds.

The next year I was old enough to know that I should expect a present. She grabbed a magnet off the refrigerator and handed it to me, "Here this is your birthday gift." I had great fun with that magnet. Thinking back on it now, I realize once again how little forethought she took in these gifts. She would have been disappointed to know, how much fun I had with that insignificant magnet.

The Puppies

When I was just a little child, I knew instinctively that Marie was unstable, different, and odd. Several things that she did, struck me as disturbing even as a small boy.

It was an exciting day for the three of us children. Our dog was in labor and the birth of her puppies was imminent. We were mesmerized as we watched each new puppy being born. We would gleefully scream out the number as they kept coming one by one. We kept wondering how many she would deliver. To our utter delight, it turned out to be a large litter. I was personally amazed at the tender care, of the mother, for her newborn pups. She cleaned each one and carefully nudged it close with her nose, keeping it near her body to keep it warm.

The next morning when I woke, I rushed out to see the new arrivals. Bud had just left for work and Marie was standing at the kitchen sink. She had placed the box with all the puppies up on the counter. Our dog was sitting by her side, looking intently up at the box that housed her newborn. The mother dog was whining. Marie then picked up each puppy one by one, and with a quick jerk, snapped its neck, and tossed it into the garbage can. She looked as carefree as if she were snapping carrots in half.

I had witnessed her killing other animals all my life. The intimacy in which she killed each puppy, with her bare hands, was yet another clue of her disturbed mind.

The Birthday Gift

The best birthday gift, I ever received was a surprise from Bud. As a small boy, I was always asking for my very own pet. Bud brought home a tiny kitten and presented it to me. My brother and sister joined me, as we spent the whole evening crowded around the cute little ball of fuzz. The honor I felt was amazing, for the first time, I had something that was mine alone. I needed something to love, to care for, to watch over.

That night I could hardly sleep. Early the next morning I rushed out to greet my new pet. Marie was tossing something into the trash and I walked up and looked down into the can, and there laying on the trash was the lifeless body of my kitten. She did not know I saw her toss it in the can. As the tears welled up in my eyes, Marie simply stated it was an accident; she accidentally sat on it, was her story. Her hatred for me had cost that innocent kitten its life. The loathing in my heart for her was intensifying.

The Snakes

Because we had snakes in the house, I was not afraid of them. This would prove to have horrible consequences. I was playing down near the creek when I came across a bunch of baby snakes. I grabbed a hand full and walked to the trailer to show my sister. When I entered the house, Marie had a horrified look on her face, and I was terrified I was in trouble. Yet to my great surprise she said in the most gentle but firm voice, "Perry, take those back outside immediately, they don't belong in the house."

I had come across a den of rattlesnakes. Once again God had a Divine Intervention. Tiny rattlers are far more deadly than adult rattlers. Partly because the venom is so concentrated and toxic, but also because they have not learned to give dry bites, so they inject the full load.

God closed their mouths and not one bit me. Perhaps it was because I had no smell of fear. Perhaps it was because I spoke in such cheerful tones when I was playing with them. I may never know, but what I do know is that God was watching over his little boy long before I ever knew of Him.

Marie later told me, that she did not scream at me, for fear that I would squeeze or drop them in the house. She did not punish me though, and that was all I was thankful for at the time.

The Warning

I had an older sister and a younger brother. Early one morning, I was awakened by Marie's loud ranting. She had Sherry, Carl, and I, come out to the back porch of the trailer. She had a pistol in her hand and shot our pet cat in the head, and as it flopped around dying, blood splattered on my legs. She screamed, "This is what is going to happen to you if you don't get out of my house, and I better not see you till it's dark." I ran up into the hills to a fort I had constructed. Needless to say, I spent lots of time there. This was fine with Marie, just as long as she didn't have to see me or hear my "irritating little voice."

The Betrayal

Marie treated my little brother differently. Because she had me as the whipping boy, (she would later confess), and had so completely transferred her loathing towards me, that she gave Carl a pass. He became the baby of the family. Carl and I shared a bedroom throughout our childhood. My sister had her own room and got privileges for being the oldest. Carl and I shared old military bunk beds. At night he would often put his feet on the springs, and bounce me, to irritate me. When he got older, he would wait

11

till I was half asleep, and he would sling me off the bed. This would drive me to great anger, but I could never do anything for fear of the beating I would receive. Carl knew this of course and milked it.

One night he was relentless, for several hours he continued to bounce me. I begged him to stop and he just giggled with evil delight. I then began to threaten him, he was delighted all the more that he was getting my goat. Finally, I had reached my limit and retaliated. When Marie came in and saw I was in a fight with Carl, she flew into me and gave me a severe beating. She never even asked Carl what had precipitated the fight.

Carl got off scot-free, and in so doing, he learned a valuable lesson. He could deflect his punishment to me! Whenever he was about to get a whipping, he would quickly distract Marie by telling her something I had done. She would turn her attention towards me, and forget all about Carl.

When I was young, very young, perhaps in first or second grade I came to believe Marie was insane. She was peculiar and odd. I was very observant and could see she was unstable. Other kids would say "My mom, says your mom, is crazy". Just being around her gave me the creeps. Even as early as third grade I thought she was incredibly stupid. Her rational and reasoning skills were ridiculous to me.

One night I shared my insights with Carl. I wanted him to see what I saw. I shared all the odd behaviors we had seen. I told him I was convinced she was mentally disturbed.

What a mistake that was. Carl later snuck into Marie's purse and stole a quarter. She caught him and was whipping him with the board, Carl screamed out "Perry believes you are Mentally Disturbed!" Marie turned to me and in a flash began to whip me. Even though she turned her rage on me, and whipped me, I was even more deeply wounded by the betrayal of my brother.

Randle, Washington

I told you already how much I hated school. Yet when we moved to the rain forests of Randle Washington, it got even worse.

The school year was nearly half over and Bud got a new position with the forest service. I transferred to Randle elementary. The principal walked me into Mrs. Griggs's classroom. She was gray-haired and had a stern angry scowl. I took an instant dislike to her, she reminded me of Marie.

I sat in the back of the room at an empty desk, trying to become invisible. Mrs. Griggs had everyone stand and say the pledge of allegiance. In my first school, we didn't do the Pledge! I had never seen it done or heard it before. I was looking around, wondering why they all stood, and why they were putting their hands on their hearts. I was surprised as they all spoke in unison.

Mrs. Griggs saw me sitting at my desk, stopped everyone, and called me to the front of the classroom. I was terrified. Everyone was staring at me.

She took a paddle off her desk, and as she stood over me, she grabbed my arm and started whipping me with the paddle. She was yelling, "So you want to start off being a defiant little brat, well we will just see about that. I'll show you who's boss. When I tell you to stand and recite the pledge, you will do as I say!"

I had only been in her classroom for several minutes and she was already giving me a whipping. She told me to sit at the desk right in front of her desk, so she could keep a close eye on me.

I learned that in life, some people are just cruel. Mrs. Griggs was one of the nastiest people I ever knew. She was just like Marie, and I hated her with all my heart.

The Shootout

I hated those four years we lived in Randle Washington. It rained all the time. It was depressing. Marie and depression were not a good mix. Some of the most horrific memories happened there. The worst of it was, we lived in a filthy trailer court, out in the middle of the woods. Our neighbors were drunks, prostitutes, thieves, and dope addicts.

One night, I was awakened by sirens and gunshots. It sounded like a war. Bullets were flying everywhere. Men were yelling and screaming, it was terrifying. One of the men that lived next door was firing a pistol and was right under my bedroom window. I was on the top bunk and watched him crouching behind a stump. At one point in the gun battle, he looked back at our trailer and then up at me. I was frozen in fear. I was sure he was going to pull the trigger because I had seen him, and could identify him. Then he ran into the brush at the back of the trailer and more gunfire. I kept waiting for the bullets to come through the flimsy side of the trailer. At one point I saw a bullet spark as it ricocheted off our propane tank.

I have no idea how many bullets were fired. The shootout lasted quite a while. It seemed to me to have lasted perhaps 20 minutes, but maybe it was only ten. It seemed like hours at the time. In the end, only one person was shot in the hand. Everyone got away, not one arrest! We found out later, that a group of drug dealers were making and selling drugs out of their mobile home. The police had come fully armed, but somehow everyone got away. Randle Washington is a small town, and I think the police were just outmatched. The drug runners were well-armed.

Once again, I look back and marvel that no one was seriously wounded. Not one of the bullets actually went through our trailer, even though they were surrounding it and using it as cover. Even before I knew Him, God was protecting my life.

13

The Peace Offering

When I became a teenager, I hated Marie. By then, I fully realized how dysfunctional she was. Despite all this, I decided to try and appease her hatred of me. It was Mother's Day and I had never bought Marie a gift. So, I decided to go all out and buy her a Mother's Day card and a gift, a beautiful pendant. I took the time to write a personal note and wrap the gift.

I presented both to her with the best smile, I could muster. She opened the gift and saw the pendant. She threw it on the floor and stomped on it! She began yelling at me for, "Being so stupid! You know I don't wear jewelry!" She mocked, then promptly ripped the card in two and threw it in my face, and stomped off.

I reached a new level of visceral hatred that day. She had hurt me for the last time. I was so full of rage, all I could think of was killing her. I could not sleep; all my waking hours were spent going over how I would torture her slowly, and remind her of every injustice she had done to me.

I wanted Marie to suffer, she could not die quickly. I wanted her to beg for mercy and I would spit in her face, and laugh that sadistic laugh. The same sadistic laugh, I had been forced to endure, all my life. I was going to exact my revenge on the bully. Oh, how I relished her torturous death. A blackness entered my soul and I nurtured it with delight. I planned very carefully, every detail of her agonizing death. Day after day I seethed with inner rage. I was just waiting for the opportunity.

My daydreaming became obsessive. I would sit in class at school and my mind was constantly working out details. I was captivated by the thought of her hideous death. I would lay awake at night and devise the most painful ways I could imagine. I feared that she would die too quickly, so I devised ways to prolong her agony.

The Stabbing

I spent months planning every detail of the witches' just rewards. I was standing in the kitchen, when for some reason, Marie went into an uncontrollable rage. She grabbed a butcher knife and lunged at me. I was very athletic and dodged her first attempt. She had me pinned in the corner of the room and began swinging wildly slicing through the air, trying to cut me up. I ducked to the side and realized that she had not seen me do it. She was still coming forward stabbing at where I had just been; simultaneously she let out a guttural scream, one I had never heard before. She had gone totally blind in her rage. I dived under the table and escaped.

Bud had seen the whole thing from the living room. He had been yelling at her to stop! He continued to plead with her as he ran into the kitchen.

She kept screaming, "Where are you? I'll kill you! I'll kill you, you &%#%@#$"

Bud kept yelling at her to put the knife down. He explained to her, that I had left, and was no longer in the kitchen. Only then, did she scream out to Bud, that she was blind!

Once again God had a divine intervention. Doctors will tell you; she experienced a retinal blackout due to extreme blood pressure in the eye. But I tell you, it was the only time in her life that she went blind in a rage, and she was in a rage daily. Doctor, I disagree! I respectfully submit that God caused it that day, to save a young boy.

It took a while for her to settle down and for her blood pressure to stabilize. But as it did, her eyesight began to return. That was probably the first time I seriously began to wonder if there was a God, and if He was watching over me.

Going for a Ride

My brother and I had a couple of friends, Wally and Louis. One day we were hiking in the hills above the trailer court. There was a gravel pit they used to build the highway system years before. It wasn't being used, and we would go there and sit on the rim of the pit, and throw rocks down into the bottom. On this particular day, we discovered a recently abandoned old car. Someone had stripped it down including the seats. It still had tires and we got the great idea to push it to the edge, jump in, and ride it to the bottom. The car was a four-door, so each of us took a door, and opened it. We easily pushed it to the edge. We all agreed, we would start it over the edge, then all jump in at the same time.

As it started over the edge, suddenly a powerful warning came over me and I jumped aside. The others saw me and did the same. Just then, the front tire dug deep into the gravel and caused the car to roll. It flew down the mountainside, tumbling and cartwheeling, flying into pieces. When it came to rest in the bottom of the pit, it was a crumpled heap of metal, hardly recognizable. We looked at each other and without a word, we each knew that if we had jumped in, we would all be dead. We hadn't anticipated how soft the embankment of the gravel quarry would be. That split-second decision, to jump free, had saved my life. I had fully intended to jump in. But a strong thought of "Don't do it" at the last second, kept me from following through.

God was protecting me from my own stupidity. He protected me from my own self-sabotage. He was always there, even though at the time, I didn't recognize His voice. There were other times, I could clearly see His intervention.

Hanging by a Thread

A friend invited me to go with him on a woodcutting expedition. The Deters used wood for their kitchen stove and the fireplace. Leroy Deter and his father needed my help. So, one Saturday morning we all piled into his farm truck and headed deep into the mountains.

We loaded several cords of wood into an old single-axel cattle truck. The wood slats towered eight feet over the flatbed. We stacked it to the top and then threw even more on top until it created a large dome. The truck was extremely top-heavy.

All three of us piled into the cab after a very long day, of hard work. We were coming up the old Poison Creek grade, a steep dirt road. On the left side was a sheer drop-off of several hundred feet down to the river. Just as we started the trip out of the canyon, it started to rain. The old truck was laboring to climb with the full load. We were barely plugging along when the truck started to slide in the mud. Mr. Deter came to a stop, but the heavy truck started to slide backward. I was sitting on the passenger's side, next to the door. Leroy was in the middle and his father was driving. When it started to slide toward the edge of the cliff, I quickly opened my door and jumped. I looked back, as the truck started over the edge. My heart stopped, as I watched the underneath of the truck come into view.

Time slowed down; I was watching my friends going over the edge to their deaths. Suddenly the truck stopped! It was tipped so far that the top of the load was falling out and tumbling in the air and crashing into the river at the bottom of the canyon. I stood there, wondering why it was not going on over. It was inexplicably suspended in a rollover. It was perfectly balanced over the edge. It looked as though it was defying gravity.

I ran towards them. I could hear Mr. Deter in a controlled voice telling Leroy not to move!" They were both pinned up against the driver's door. I couldn't see them; all I could see was the underneath of the truck. I kept waiting for it to topple into the ravine.

I didn't want to touch the truck, for fear that the movement would send it on over. Slowly, with deliberate orders, Mr. Deter told me to take off my belt. He then told me to very carefully see if I could open the passenger's door and put something in it to prop it open. He then told me to feed my belt up over the seat and hold on with all my might. Then he told Leroy, to slowly reach up and grab hold of the end of my belt. I held on with all my strength, as Leroy ever so slowly, began to climb up the belt. When he was up high enough to put his hands on the upper side of the seat, I took hold of both of his arms, and he took hold of mine. We gently worked together and he slid out. Then we hooked Leroy's belt to mine and the two of us tossed it to his father. We duplicated the same procedure until we got Mr. Deter out. We stood there looking at the truck. It made no sense, why it had not gone on over.

There was a lot of nervous laughter as we recounted our near-death experience. We stood there in the rain and waited for it to slide on over, but it never did. Eventually, we started to hike towards the highway and hitched a ride back to Burns. They actually saved the truck later with a bulldozer. We found out that the back wheels had caught a stump over the edge. That stump saved their lives. Again, my life was spared.

I was becoming much more aware of God's protection.

The Summer Job

When I was 12 years old, I worked constantly. I mowed lawns, babysat, house sat, or any number of odd jobs. One of them was painting a service station. It was located on Highway 395, near the trailer court. It was an old gas station made of cement blocks. The owner was a crusty old man who was often drunk.

He asked me if I would spend my summer scrapping off the old paint with a hand scraper and repaint it. I was thrilled to have a summer job. I spent that summer meticulously scraping each block one by one. Row by row, I made my way around the entire building. When I could no longer reach high enough, I climbed a ladder and circled the building, working my way to the top. It was some of the hardest work I had ever done.

When I had finished the scraping, I took a brush and hand-painted the entire building white. Then I went back and painted the middle two rows bright red, and the top two rows a brilliant royal blue. It took all summer, but it looked fantastic.

The old guy was thrilled with how it had turned out. He was always bragging to the other customers about what a hard little worker I was. I took pride in what I was doing.

Unfortunately, because I was so young, we never agreed on how much I was making. I trusted adults, and I guess I figured it depended on how good a job I did. When I finished the project, the owner paid me 20 dollars.

Because of the way I was raised I never argued with adults, so I went home feeling pretty low.

When Bud came home from work I told him, I had finally gotten paid for my summer job, but I was disappointed that I had made only 20 dollars. He shouted "HOW MUCH?" I repeated myself and I saw him turning bright red. He was as angry as I had ever seen him. He started shouting threats, got in the car, and took off.

It was the only time in my life, I could remember Bud ever defending me. I don't know what he did or said, but when he got home, he handed me a wad of cash. He didn't talk to me, but I could hear him shouting at Marie in the bedroom, about some of the threats he had leveled at the old guy. I just remember how good it felt, that he had rectified an injustice on my behalf.

The Gruesome Death

It was during that summer, that I was confronted with the reality of death.

One day a hippy on a three-wheeled motorcycle, with gorilla handlebars, pulled in to get fuel. When he was reentering the highway, he drove around a pickup and camper, right into the path of a logging truck. He went under the back set of doolies and got pinned. The trike burst into flames. His body was mangled in the wreckage, and he was screaming for someone to help him. A number of people rushed to help but the flames were too intense. We watched in horror, as he burned to death. It was the first time in my life, I had watched someone die.

Hearing him plead for his life, and being unable to do anything was agonizing. He was alive one minute and dead the next. One moment I'm cheerfully painting a wall, and the next moment, a man lies chard to death. Life can end in a single moment. It occurred to me that we can never know our last second on this earth.

That incident taught me that life is fragile. When that man climbed out of bed that morning, he didn't realize he would never see his pillow again. When he ate his lunch, little did he know that he had experienced his last meal! He had no idea when he pulled into the gas station, his life would end there. When he kicked started that motorcycle and put his hand on the throttle, he didn't imagine that within 60 seconds he would be dead.

We are all just one heartbeat from death. It can come at any instant. That young man thought he had his whole life out before him. Watching him die so quickly, woke deep in me, the realization of my own mortality.

Granddad and the Family Legacy

If you have ever watched "All in the Family" you already know my grandparents. Grandma and Granddad, were so much like Archie Bunker and Edith, that I was convinced that the writer of "All in the Family" knew them. They even looked like them. My Granddad was just as loud, opinionated, and prejudiced. He loved to rail against blacks and Christians, and he despised long-haired hippies.

He bragged about how he once was sitting on the porch of the old homestead. He recognized some "Bible thumpers," walking up the long driveway. He grabbed a rifle and shot the gravel at their feet. He howled with laughter, at how they danced. "They ran off, with their tails between their legs." He bragged!

Over my lifetime I heard him tell that story many, many times. Needless to say, there weren't any Christians in the family.

Family reunions were Beer fests. Many times, there would be several kegs at the reunion. When I was younger, there would be a hundred and fifty show up. Many of the adults would have a beer in one hand and a cigarette in the other. Alcohol was at every family function. As I became a teenager, all the family functions happened at my uncle's house, because he had a bar and pool table.

C. B.

Granddad loved to argue. He was just like Archie Bunker. One night in my teens, Craig my cousin, and I, got into a yelling match with Archie…. I mean Granddad. The argument started, when I lamented that the police won't even come and take a report of a stolen car. You have to go into their police station and file a report there.

Granddad mocked us. He insisted that if someone tried to steal the C.B. out of his car, the police would block off the South hill of Pendleton, just to catch the thieves. Craig and I, burst into hysterical laughter. That made Grandad angry, and we spent the next hour arguing with him. We told him he was delusional! It was absurd to think the police would even send a car out to investigate! We reasoned, "If they won't even come and take a report of a stolen car, what makes you think they would care a whit, about a C.B. radio?" On and on we screamed, back and forth at each other. Finally, we left and walked down to Craig's house, which was about five blocks away.

The next morning, we were shaken awake by my uncle, who was clearly angry. He jerked us both out of bed and demanded to know where Granddad's CB radio was. It seems that while we were arguing the night before, someone happened to be walking by, heard the screaming, and broke in and took the CB out of Granddad's car! We spent hours trying to convince the family we did not take it. No one would believe us! NO ONE!!!! The truth was we had NOT taken it. My grandfather went to his grave, convinced to his core, that we had stolen that stupid CB.

Sometimes I wonder about the true perpetrator. He must still be laughing, as he tells his grandchildren, "One night I pulled the ultimate prank! This old man and these two teenage punks were arguing, ya see….and while they were screaming at each other, there I was, just feet away, cutting the wires…."

I would love to know what truly happened to that C.B. radio.

The Heirloom

Because of our family's poverty, we hunted for our meat. Hunting season was a huge family affair. Our hunting parties were large events, of 30 to 40 people. Everyone who was legally able bought deer and elk tags. Everyone hunted including the woman and children.

My great-uncle had a cabin in the mountains. Complete with corrals for the horses. Many Arbogast families would meet there every year for hunting season.

One hunting season, with great pomp and circumstance, I received a family heirloom, that was envied by all my cousins. Granddad made a big deal of this occasion, full of speeches and celebration. I cannot overstate the event. It was a cross between a "rite of passage" and a "coronation."

There was a tradition in the Arbogast family, that had been passed down through the many generations. On the first legal hunting season, (which in Oregon was 14 years old), the first-born grandson, received a hunting rifle. I was given a 270 Winchester; one that Granddad had received in the 1920s. I took that rifle and did a full restoration over the next few months. It was one of the first things in my life, I could call my own. I added mounts and a high-end scope. It was my pride and joy. There is more about that beautiful rifle later in my story.

Getting that rifle, was a bitter pill for Marie. She detested any thought of my happiness.

Driving Test

Marie's hatred of me knew no bounds. I desperately wanted my driver's license, and Marie knew it. She was relentless in her mocking of the idea. She insisted I was too stupid to drive. One morning near my 16th birthday, while the family was sitting at the table eating breakfast, she was laughing at the idea of me driving. She told Bud "He may pass the written part, but there was no way in {#%&) he is going to pass his driving test." I argued that I had been studying hard and knew the driver's manual forwards and backward. She glared at me and in a sinister tone, then slowly intoned, "You... will... NOT... pass the driver's test the first time." Even Bud protested, "I wouldn't be so sure, I've seen him drive, and he does ok". She became enraged and screamed something at the two of us. This should have been a clue that something was up. She then got a wicked sneering grin on her face and told Bud, "I'll take him to the DMV myself and I'll guarantee he can't pass the first time!"

In Oregon, if you don't pass the first time, you have to wait 30 days to retry. So, I practiced with friends, without her knowing, and relished proving her wrong. On the big day, she told me she would meet me at the DMV after school. When I arrived, she wasn't there, so I took the written test and passed with ease. Marie came prancing into the DMV, with an evil grin on her face. Tossed the keys at me and sneered with a wry smile, "Knock yourself out!"

The driving examiner took me outside, with a clipboard in her hand, and wanted me to do a walk around the vehicle. To my horror, it was not the car I had practiced in, over the previous six months. Marie had brought a large pickup. When I jumped in, I had no idea where everything was. Everything was so different. The examiner was asking me to point out wipers, defrost, blinkers, headlights, etc. She was patient with me, as I explained to her, that I had never been in this truck before.

Then she asked me to start it. I turned the key but nothing happened. The examiner could tell what was happening.

"You have never driven a stick shift, have you?" the examiner asked.

I explained that I had only practiced in an automatic. She looked at me and said, "The test is over". She got out and walked back inside.

A few moments later Marie came walking out with an evil satisfied grin on her face. "I thought you said you were going to pass the driver's test? She burst into taunting laughter.

I seethed with rage. I was just biding my time before I killed her.

The First Accident

The next month I left nothing to chance, I didn't tell anyone I was retaking the test and had a friend meet me in his car. I got my license.

I got a job as a box boy for Safeway and soon bought my first car. One afternoon I was driving home from school, when a large Pontiac, pulled across the highway in front of me. I hit her broadside, just behind the passenger front wheel. The impact had such force, that it nearly took the front of her car off. The engine of her car was nearly ripped completely out of her vehicle. The force was so violent, that her car spun several times. It came to rest, in the middle of the highway, about 30 yards from the intersection.

My vehicle veered sharply right and struck another vehicle sitting at the intersection. That vehicle was a large Jeep, with a solid metal bumper. The Jeep was outfitted with a winch, and the side of my car was demolished by it. It just so happened; it was driven by the judge in our town. He saw everything!

I could hear children screaming from the other car. I desperately wanted to help them but my doors were jammed. So, I jumped out of the driver's side window.

I was not hurt so I began running toward their car. That's when this big guy, tackled me on the pavement…. Now I WAS hurt!

"What are you doing?" I screamed. "Get off me, we have to help them!" I pleaded.

He had mistakenly thought I was angry and was racing to attack her. What an idiot!

The impact of the accident had torn the muffler system, off her car. It was setting on the pavement, under her vehicle. The fire department and police were concerned. The muffler could potentially catch the car on fire. They were on their hands and knees looking under the car for any gas leaks. Two firemen were pulling the muffler free from the wreckage, so they could safely extricate the victims.

I didn't know it at the time, but my brother, who was on the school bus, saw the aftermath of the accident. When they went by the accident scene, the kids told Carl, my brother, that the Fire department was trying to pull a dead body out from under the car. My brother made it home, with a report that I had caused an accident that had killed innocent people. He had personally seen one of the bodies under the car.

Fortunately, no one was seriously hurt. But back at home, Bud and Marie were conjuring up the worst. They were fit to be tied! By the time I arrive at the house, they had already made up their minds.

I came into the house and was immediately confronted with a barrage of accusing questions…. "What have you done? How many did you kill? Do you know what this is going to do to our insurance rates? Are they going to arrest you for vehicular manslaughter?

It struck me later that they had not even asked me "Are you ok?" What jerks!

Bud was particularly obnoxious that night. He was insistent that every accident could be avoided. "Every accident is avoidable if you simply drive defensively." He railed.

"If you had been paying attention, you could have avoided the collision." He chided.

I kept trying to tell them, I did see her and slammed on my brakes the instant she took off. But it was too late, she came racing in front of me. But there was no talking sense to them; they had made up their minds. Talking was futile.

My driving nightmares were far from over.

The Nightmare Drive

That same year, I had decided to drive from Burns, up to Pendleton, for Christmas. I called my grandmother and told her of my plans. She was thrilled. Bud and Marie didn't celebrate Christmas, but the extended family did. My Aunt, Uncles, and cousins would all be there. I was looking forward to a normal, family Christmas.

I planned to get there on Christmas Eve and spend all Christmas day with them. So, after work, I jumped in my car and headed out. A severe winter storm came in that day! When I started the trip, the snow was already building up on the roads. I drove slowly and carefully, into the mountains. Highway 395 up to Pendleton, is a lonely road and not well populated. After leaving John Day, I didn't see any cars on the road again; Partly because of the storm, and partly because it was late at night. When I passed through the little town of Dale, I headed into a very remote canyon, called Camas Creek.

My car started to lose power, and my headlights started to dim. My battery lights came on and I knew I was in trouble. I hoped I could limp into Ukiah, the next small town ahead. But the car lost power, and I was now creeping along. I turned off the heater to save energy, and it worked. I turned off everything but the headlights, which were so dim I could hardly see.

The snow was coming down hard and building up on the road. There were no tracks in the snow, which meant there were no other cars out on the road. I was the only car leaving tracks and that concerned me. I also knew I didn't have the winter clothes to survive a freezing night.

By now the car was only able to go about 10 miles an hour. The headlights were a dull yellow, and ice was building up inside the car. I could barely see out the windshield. I was desperately thinking about how could I stay alive. I remembered an old abandoned cabin, and if I could make it there, I could at least make a fire and survive the night. Finally, the car just couldn't go anymore. I pulled off the road.

I can't explain how dark it was. I could not see my hand in front of my face. I was freezing and I knew I could die. I decided to follow the sound of the Creek and try to stay on the Highway and hike to the cabin. I was walking blind, trusting my hearing. I only had tennis shoes on, and I was shaking from the first stages of hypothermia. I was angry with myself for not preparing for this trip. But in my excitement to get to Pendleton, it never occurred to me that I would have car problems. I had never broken down before. It just never occurred to me.

I knew the Canyon fairly well and had traveled it many times growing up. I knew the cabin was only a few miles ahead. But I couldn't see. I had to tread carefully, so I wouldn't lose the highway. By this time, the Highway had about three or four inches of freshly fallen snow on it. I could hear the river when I would get near the bank. I felt my way several miles, by touch and hearing. My feet were completely numb and I feared frostbite. I also knew that the river would drift off to the right just a quarter mile from the Cabin. So, when I realized I was getting farther away from Camas Creek, I knew I was getting closer.

I have no idea what my core temperature had dropped to, but I was shaking terribly. By this time, I knew I would probably die, and I didn't care. I just wanted it to end. I had decided to walk along the side of the highway now, so I could feel the road that led to the cabin. I also knew I would be heading up a hill, and it would be just past the crest on the left. I could feel the uphill climb and it gave me hope to keep going.

Just a few minutes more, I kept telling myself. As I crested the hill, I was shocked to see lights on in the cabin. I had been by that cabin, for 16 years, and no one had ever been in that old, abandoned cabin. I began to scream for help. The door opened, and I could see the silhouette of a woman. I knew I would live! I had made it.

The shock and fear on her face told me I must have looked really bad. She quickly built up the fire and made me some hot chocolate. She asked me "Where in the world had I come from?" She couldn't hide her incredulous look. She was probably thinking what a fool I was. She was right.

She told me that her husband was a mechanic, but he was late getting home because of the storm. A mechanic? I had stumbled into an old abandoned cabin, that now housed a mechanic! Are you kidding? I was amazed at my good fortune.

I told her that my family used to live in Ukiah and I had grown up in Dale. In all that time, I had never seen anyone living in this old place. She said that they had just moved in, and were going to make it their home. "It may have saved my life," I told her.

When her husband arrived home, he took me back to my car and you could still see my footprints in the snow. He kept saying, "You walked all this way in the pitch black of night?" "You are so lucky to be alive!"

I explained what was happening to the car before it finally ran out of power. He told me because it happened so quickly it probably wasn't a bad battery. He opened the hood and said, "Your relay came unplugged on the firewall."

He plugged it in and gave me a jumpstart. The car roared to life and the headlights were as bright as ever. I asked him what I owed him, for saving my life, and getting the car back on the road. He just laughed and told me to, "Drive safe."

There is a scripture that says "Many have entertained Angels and did not know it." I have always wondered if those two were Angels. God saved my life again.

I began driving towards Pendleton. I was worried about my grandmother because she would be worried, I should have been in Pendleton hours before. But there were no cell phones in those days, and the old cabin had no landline.

I was also in a euphoric state of relief, that I was back on the road again.

I came to the town of Pilot Rock, the last small town before Pendleton. Nothing was open. Everything was closed including gas stations. So, I kept going. Just outside town, I could see something that didn't look right. As I neared the scene, I could see a car accident. I pulled up next to it and jumped out to help the people. They had nosed into the embankment and were stuck. As we were standing on the embankment, I looked up and saw headlights twisting and weaving on the highway. I thought to myself, if that car doesn't get under control, he could crash into my car…. which is exactly what he did.

My car slid forward and hit the car that was in the ditch and flattened my passenger front tire. We all ran down to help the guy who had just crashed into my car, but when he got out, it was readily apparent, he was completely drunk. He was so drunk that he could barely talk.

I ran to the nearest house and knocked on the door. It was the middle of the night. I obviously woke them up. I explained there had been two accidents, and we needed the police and a wrecker.

As I ran back to the accidents, the snow had changed to freezing rain. I began to slip and slide around. I was again freezing cold. My flimsy coat was now wet and freezing. When I got back to my car, I turned on the heat and tried to warm up. I invited the people to sit in the car and warm up as well. Only the drunk refused. He was out trying to bend the fenders away from his front tires. We ignored him.

Then to our shock, he drove away on two front flat tires. Weaving and sliding on the iced-up highway. We just started laughing, knowing he would not make it far.

It took about forty-five minutes for the police to arrive. Normally it would be less than 10. When the officer arrived, he said he would have made it sooner, but a drunk had driven off the road and into someone's house. We described the car and he looked at us, "Yes, how did you know?" We all burst out laughing again. We explained the story to him, and he filled out another accident report, for me. When he was finished, he told us he had to go to another emergency, and left.

It took a while for the wrecker to get there. My car was warm and I instinctively turned it off to save fuel. Unfortunately, I left my emergency flashers on and it drained my already weak batteries. When the wrecker got there, he positioned his truck to pull the first car out of the ditch. He hooked up the car in the freezing rain and snow. But couldn't get it out because my car was in the way. He asked me to back up. When I turned the key, the battery was dead and all it did was click, click, click.

I had to get out and run up to the driver and tell him I needed a jump. You could see the anger and frustration on his face, as he realized he would have to unhook the car, turn his truck around, and give me a jump. He was not amused.

The tow truck driver was also very cold by now, and working in these conditions was miserable. The last thing he said to me was "Whatever you do, don't turn off your car once we get it started." So, I pulled out of the way, and that is when I realized the front tire was flat. I was tired, cold, and irritated. I didn't appreciate being yelled at, by the wrecker driver. Now, I had to change a flat tire in freezing rain. In my frustration, I forgot and turned off the car to change the flat.

It took three times longer to change the tire in the dead of night, in freezing rain and snow. When I finally got it changed, I jumped in the car and realized I had turned it off. The battery was of course dead again. The only one there to give me a jump was the wrecker driver. He had gotten the car out of the ditch and was setting facing Pendleton in front of me. We were both headed in the same position.

I sheepishly knocked on his window and explained that I had turned off my car to fix the flat, and the battery was dead again. I learned some new words that night. I also heard some things about my lineage I had not considered. If he had been armed, I think he would have told the judge it was justifiable homicide and probably been set free.

So once again he had to unhook from the first car, turn his truck around to face my car, and give me a jumpstart. This time he shouted at the top of his lungs "DON'T TURN IT OFF!" and then something about my mother, I didn't hear some of it, but decided not to ask him to repeat it.

I followed him into Pendleton on sheer ice. A trip that would normally take ten or fifteen minutes, but on this night, it took nearly an hour. It was treacherous.

When I reached the road that leads to my grandmother's home, the sky was lighting up. It was morning. The city had already been out with salt and gravel trucks, so I gingerly made my way up the south hill, to my grandparent's house. I was about three blocks away when the inexplicable happened. A woman coming down the hill lost control of her car and plowed head-on into my car. I was sitting completely stopped when she finally ran into me. Twice in a matter of hours, my car was stationary when someone crashed into it.

In just one trip, God had kept me from freezing to death, sent a mechanic, and kept me safe through two accidents.

Later when I was filling out the insurance papers, it asked me to shadow in the dented parts of my car, I literally shaded in the entire car. All four sides of my car were damaged.

None of it was my fault. I do remember thinking about the ridiculous logic of Bud, and how every accident is avoidable. I wonder how he would argue that these accidents were avoidable!

My car may have been dented on all sides, but all the accidents were at fairly low speeds. So, the car was drivable. So, after getting the driver's information, I made my way up to Grandma's house. I felt bad for her. She had spent a restless night, wondering where I was. I explained that nothing had been open, and I would have called if I had had a chance. I loved my grandmother. I knew it had been a miserable night for her.

I was fairly close to both Grandad and Grandma all through my life, not so much with my immediate family.

Sherry

In an odd twist, although Sherry never went through the abuse I had to endure, she received the worst beating any of us would ever receive.

We were in High school at the time, and Sherry had angered them.

26

Marie and Bud flew into a rage and began beating her savagely. Bud was wearing heavy-duty logging boots, and when she fell to the floor, he kicked her so hard in the face, that it spun her body around. I watched in horror, as they nearly killed her. I was sick to my stomach. The hatred I had for them, only intensified.

They hid Sherry away for several months as she healed. Sherry was never the same after that. She suffered pretty severe brain trauma, from the beating, not to mention the emotional devastation. Her head and face were battered and swollen. They brutally beat her mercilessly.

When she recovered, she joined the army to escape. She eventually moved to the Midwest, where she has lived the rest of her life, far from Oregon, and far from Bud and Marie.

I was a Junior in High School at the time and determined to kill them for what they had done. I would lay there at night and play out in my head over and over, how I would slowly and carefully torture them to death.

The Breaking Point

One afternoon before I left for work. Carl, my brother, was sitting on the back porch. We were having a conversation, and I asked him, how much had the new keyboard cost which Bud and Marie had recently bought. Marie overheard my question and shouted from the other end of the trailer, "None of your &#$% business!" But Carl had already called out the price. When Marie heard him give me the answer, she ran down the hallway, grabbed him by the hair, and began slamming his head into the floor. His head began to bleed.

I was Six foot two by then, and even though she outweighed me by 50 pounds, I had reached my threshold of enduring her bulling and abuse. I stood up for the first time in my life and spoke to Marie with authority.

"Knock it off, leave him alone!" I said in an authoritative, firm manner. She snapped her head in my direction, and in a sneering guttural voice slowly asked, "What – did – you – just - say?" Pausing between each word for effect.

In the most condescending tone, I sneered back and said defiantly, "You're out of control!" At that instant, several things happened simultaneously. I felt the most exhilarating and empowering freedom of my life. Yet at the same time, she came rushing towards me like a raging bull.

As I already stated, I was an athlete by then. So, when she raised her fist and swung, I grabbed her hand, spun and twisted it behind her back and grabbed the other arm, and, lifted her off the ground. I was amazed at my strength. She then tried to kick me in the groin and bite at my hands, but it was futile. I had complete control of her. She screamed at me to put her down. I just chuckled at her and calmly said "Not until you calm down. You are out of control"

I must have held her for several minutes. She tried threatening me, I gently said "Not until you settle down." She tried every manipulative trick in the book, but I was resolute.

"I'm not letting you down until you calm down!" I told her with a defiant tone.

I had never felt the power I felt that day. Eventually, she relaxed and in a contrite submissive tone said "Your right, I'm better now, I've calmed down."

I was not stupid, I knew that as soon as she was free of me, she would run to the gun closet, grab her pistol, and come out shooting. But I also knew I would be long gone before she could retrieve the guns.

After I let her down, she turned towards me and as I stood there towering over her, I saw the faintest sign of fear in her eyes. She didn't run for her gun because she knew I would tackle her. Yet as soon as I grabbed my car keys, she took off running, and I knew she was looking for her gun.

I sprinted outside and jumped in the car. I sped down the long dirt driveway, yet kept looking over my shoulder towards the trailer. I wanted to put distance between myself and Marie. I saw her step out on the back porch and as Carl told me later, "She had the gun locked and loaded. You would be a dead man if you had stayed." Once again, an example of providential protection. Once again God watched out for my life.

I drove to work and called my grandma, Nettie Arbogast, Bud's mom. I explained the entire story and shared my fear of what Marie would tell Bud. She knew as well, that as soon as Bud came home, Marie would concoct a lie that would make Hollywood blush. I could just imagine the exaggerated lies Marie would embellish. Grandma said she would call later that night and talk to Bud. Grandma was the one person in the world, I could trust.

I kept looking over my shoulder all night at work. I feared Marie; she was mentally unstable and incredibly violent. She could very easily walk up behind me and shoot me in the back. She carried a loaded pistol in her purse.

It was 10:30 at night when I drove up the long bumpy driveway. All the lights of the trailer were off. As I drove in, I half expected to be hit by gunfire. As I neared the trailer my headlights caught a glistening in the large living room window. I could see Marie's silhouette standing with a knife in her hand. I was somewhat relieved. I was convinced she would use the pistol. When I exited the car, I could faintly hear her trying to sneak down the hallway toward the back door. Ya gotta love mobile homes.

She had planned to stab me when I opened the back door. I knew not to walk up the steps. I stood on the ground next to the steps and reached up to the doorknob, and opened the door. She was standing there with the knife held back and a puzzled look on her face. In a calm, condescending voice, I simply said "Put the knife down and go to bed." She walked back up the hallway, set the knife on the kitchen table, and continued into her bedroom. I waited till she was out of sight, before I jumped up onto the steps, and entered the trailer.

I locked my bedroom door and left the light on. All night long I lay on the floor with my feet against the door. The next morning was Saturday. I waited until I could hear everyone getting breakfast and went to bed. I assumed she wouldn't try anything with everyone around. So, I jumped into bed and fell into a restless sleep.

At noon I finally got up and came out into the kitchen. There was an eerie silence. No one was talking. No one was acknowledging me.

When I placed the plate in the sink, I heard the distinctive thump of Bud's Lazy boy recliner. He normally had his feet raised, and there is a distinctive thump when the footrest is lowered. I thought to myself, here we go! Without a word, he walked into the kitchen and motioned with his hand, to walk ahead of him down the hallway. Marie was sitting gleefully in a position she could see down the hallway. She cheerfully called out to Bud, "No need to have him suffer just put him out of his misery." I looked back to see if he had a gun, but his hand was empty.

As soon as I entered the back room and turned towards him, he sucker-punched me in the face with all his might. My head snapped back and blood started coming out of my mouth.

He shouted, "So, you think you're a big man and can beat up a woman?" He began to punch me in the chest, "Come on you think you can hit a woman? Hit me!" I deduced from what he had said, that the story she had told him, was that I hit her. I hadn't done anything except hold her arms. I never so much as swung at her, much less hit her. I could only imagine the ridiculous lie she had fabricated. I could also see that talking to him was useless. I remember not making a fist. I had no intention of fighting him. I kept telling myself "Don't make a fist."

After a few more punches and no response from me, he stood back. He said, "I want you out of my house." "Don't need to pack up your stuff, I'll bring it to you."

Then everything took on a completely unexpected twist. Bud looked at me and said one of the most shocking things I had ever heard. "It's not your fault, I've watched you try all your life to get along with her, she wants no part of you. I've called and reserved you a room at the local motel; I'll bring your stuff there."

I walked past him, grabbed my keys, and without a word, I left for the last time. I made a decision that day as I drove away. I hated them with everything in me. I never wanted to see them again in my lifetime. I made a vow to myself; I would never, **EVER** see them again. I would never attend a family event if I thought they would be there. I would never have to see Marie's disgusting face again. They were dead to me forever.

Glorious Freedom

All my life I had lived with fear. I never knew when I would be attacked. I never knew when she would explode in a rage. I had lived a life always on edge, watching my every word. I had to walk on eggshells because anything could set her off. Now I was in my own place. I was never going to have to go back.

Later that day, I went to the motel office and picked up a couple of boxes that had been left for me, and reveled in my glorious freedom.

I continued to attend school, and my grades dramatically improved. I could study in peace and quiet.

I was making great money at Safeway, and I had my own car. My friends envied me. Wow what a stark contrast, friends that wanted to be like me. All my life I had heard "I feel sorry for you; I wouldn't want to be in your shoes." Now they came over to my place and envied the freedom and adulthood I had stepped into.

If I had stayed, I'm afraid I would have killed Marie. My level of vindictive hatred for that bully was dangerously high. I detested everything about her. Both of them were an embarrassment to me.

Close! Oh, so Close!

I was ashamed of my parents! I was disgusted with the level of filth they lived in. I had always been humiliated by poverty. I found it hard to get the confidence to talk to girls. In fact, part of the reason I never had a girlfriend in High school, was that I was terrified of what she would think if she saw the dirty squalor, I lived in.

In my senior year of High School, I decided to finally ask a girl out to the Senior Prom. I fretted over how to ask her for weeks. Finally, a friend of hers told me she would accept if I asked.

I had a deep crush on this girl. All night long I rehearsed how I would ask her out. It was hard for me to talk to her; she was very pretty and popular. I was surprised and anxious that she was interested. I had determined to ask her, first thing the next day. We had a class together during the second period and I would ask her before class was out.

As the bell rang for the first period to end, I made my way to my locker. I was on the lookout for her. As I was getting my books out of my locker, her sister came up to me. Now I didn't like her sister at all. She was older and had a reputation around school. I was not attracted to her in the slightest. I assumed as she addressed me, that she had heard that I was going to ask her sister out. But to my shock, she says "Hi Perry, I was hoping you would go with me to Senior Prom!" I froze in terror. All that I could think of was how to escape!

Before I could shift my brain into gear I blurted out "I'm sorry; I have to work that night!" Then I realized what I had done. If I asked her sister out now, she would be hurt that I had lied to her. I didn't want to hurt anyone, so I decided to forgo the dance.

I didn't go to any high school dances. I never got the courage to ask another girl in high school out. Later I wondered if she had done that on purpose, as a vindictive move against her little sister. I have often wondered if God timed that, so I would not get distracted from the plans He had for my life.

Pendleton

After I graduated from High school I moved to Pendleton. I transferred with Safeway and continued to work full time. That fall I began attending college at Blue Mountain Community College, as a business major. I had always dreamed of being my own boss.

All my life, Pendleton, was the center of our family's life. Grandma and Granddad lived there. Jerry and Terry lived there, with my cousins. Not only were we cousins, but we were double cousins. What is even more remarkable is that all seven grandchildren were born in a 30-day window. It started with my birthday on February 16th and ended with Craig's birthday on March 16th. He and I were the same age, born just 30 days apart. We were the bookends and the five other grandchildren were born in between those dates. My grandmother used to say she was always broke because she had two Christmas seasons a year.

I had always loved traveling to Pendleton. Now I was working for the very Safeway store, I grew up with.

That particular Safeway store and I had a history. When I was just a little tike, I wandered off in this Safeway store. When it was discovered, I was missing, the store employees mobilized and a hunt was started. But no one could find me. I guess there was quite a hunting party sent out to look for a little missing boy. They searched up and down the block, and every room in the store, including the downstairs stock rooms and restrooms. I had just vanished.

Normally when a child is separated from their parents in a store, they find the child wailing for help. So, they assumed I had been abducted. Finally, the time came for the store employees to return to their jobs.

It was a while later when a Bakery employee let out a blood-curdling scream. I guess I had gotten tired and without being seen, I had wandered into the bakery. I had climbed down into the racks of freshly baked bread and squeezed myself in between some soft bread completely hidden.

That poor bakery lady was busy at her job when she decided to stock the shelves with bread. I guess it was only after she lifted one of the trays, she found me cuddled up, fast asleep. She is probably still in counseling!

Later in my life, I was running out of that same Safeway store. I glanced to the right and spotted a gorgeous young lady sitting in a car. She smiled at me and I promptly ran into one of the many solid steel pillars. I hit so hard, I was knocked backward to the ground, and suffered a deep gash to my head. I looked again towards the car and she was laughing hysterically. One of the many times in my life I wanted to push "rewind!"

Now I found myself working at that same store. I was bedding down in the garage of my grandparents' house untill I could get an apartment.

Why?

Living with them allowed me the opportunity to sit down with my grandparents, and asked them why the family had not stepped in to save me. Why hadn't they called the police? I told them that I didn't dare call the authorities. If they had come and just taken a report, I would have faced a horrific beating or worse when the authorities left. If I had even hinted that she was beating me, she would have killed me.

My Grandmother started crying. She told me that she felt ashamed that she never stepped in. She said that people just didn't do that in those days. "We, in the family all talked about it, but no one felt comfortable stepping in." She confessed.

She said that when I was a small boy, each time we left her house, she wondered if she would ever see me alive again. Granddad told me, that families didn't stick their noses into how others were raising their kids. It was just taboo.

At the end of that conversation, I realized that they were more comfortable with letting me be killed, rather than stepping in. I made a private vow to myself, not to let a child be abused, because I might offend someone. I would step in, and save the child.

By the grace of God, I had not been killed. I was allowed to grow up. Some children don't get that chance.

Tennis

In high school, I had become an accomplished athlete. Although I participated in Cross Country, track, and basketball, my love was Tennis.

Tennis is a strategy sport, exploring and analyzing the weakness of your opponent. Coming up with a strategy that incorporates your strengths, and exploits their weakness. It's a lot like chess, in that you must think in terms of many moves ahead. In tennis, during a point, you must be setting the opponent up, all the while not allowing them to get the advantage, or as they say, getting ahead in the point.

In chess, execution is as simple as reaching out and moving the piece on the board. In Tennis, you must not only come up with a plan, but you must execute it. In Tennis, your body must be incredibly fit. Your hand Eye coordination must be flawless. Your mind has to think fast. Thinking through every move and counter move. You must always be aware of the direction of the wind, the position of the sun, and the placement of every stroke. You must be quick at discernment. The best athlete does not determine the winner. A brilliant strategist will win the day. There is a saying in Tennis; "Wisdom and craftiness over strength and agility every time."

I was not always the best player on the court, but I could work their weakness and get them so frustrated that they would make errors. Tennis has a lot to do with psychology and temperament. In High school, I qualified for State but lost in the first round. That bitter loss motivated me in college.

In high school, your tennis coach is a teacher willing to take on the task. Most of them know nothing about tennis. It was just a way for them to make extra money. In college, I had a real Tennis coach.

In my second year at college, I improved in every area of the game. Not only did I qualify for state in doubles, but my partner and I also dominated and won the state title. That qualified us for Northwest regionals. The game plan was to make the national tournament. To do that, we needed to make the finals. The last pairing would secure a place in Nationals, which that year was in Nashville Tennessee.

At this level everyone is good. They are not just good, they are all superior players. Everything moves faster. Every player is honed and skilled. The ball is hit with a lot more authority. There is no one left that hits tentatively. You can't hope for free points. You have to earn each and every point. A tentative serve will be crushed down your throat. These are the players who have sacrificed everything for the game. Every win is monumental. You have to trust your game and go all out with every shot. This is high-level tennis. At this level, you have to scout out your opponents and trust your coach.

I was playing the best tennis in my life. My Tennis partner and I kept winning and creeping up the bracket. The sweet 16, the quarterfinals, the semifinals, and then we had done it. We had made the finals and qualified for Nationals. In a twist of fate, we would be facing the same doubles team we had beaten in the state finals. We split the first two sets but lost the third set. Yet I was ecstatic. We had qualified for Nationals.

Little did I know, but later that same day, my life would change forever. I shattered my ankle. More on this later. A number of other things were happening in my life at the same time, and they all converge at this time in my life. The first was a relationship.

My First True Love

I walked into the department store, and as I walked past the perfume stand, I saw one of the most beautiful women I had ever seen. She was drop-dead gorgeous. I was awkward and extremely shy around women, in fact in high school I had never really dated or had a "Girlfriend."

I determined that now that I was in college, I would be bold. I walked up and started chatting with Kelly. To my surprise, she was cheerful and showed that she was also interested in me. I asked her to dinner and she accepted. We went on several dates, and since we were both in college, we saw each other on campus.

Eventually, she asked me if I would be interested in attending church with her on Sunday, and lunch after service, with her family. Now I had never really been to church. But I was interested in her, so I accepted.

I had not met her family yet. I knew that this was Kelly's way, of making me look good. If I attended church with her family, it would give her parents a favorable impression.

When Sunday arrived, I was as uncomfortable as I had ever felt. I didn't know what to wear. I didn't know what to expect. I was completely out of my comfort zone. I was sick to my stomach. I was worried about how to greet her dad. Did I call him "sir?" Mr. Falgren? George? How do you meet the mom? Shake her hand? Give her a hug? Wave? What kind of Church do they attend? Did I need money for church dues? Was I supposed to have a suit? What about a tie? I didn't even have dress shoes. I had no idea what I was doing.

They come by my place, to pick me up. They were driving a beautiful and expensive car. FAR AND AWAY above my pay scale. Turns out he is an attorney and she is a Registered Nurse. I was way, way out of my element. These are upscale people and I had grown up in a scummy trailer court. They were dressed to the hilt. I was in tennis shoes.

We drive up to a Catholic Cathedral. It was ostentatious in appearance. It was also imposing and intimidating. We walked in and I felt overwhelmed. It was beautifully adorned with stained glass windows. The wooden benches were ornately carved. The organ was playing and everyone was dressed in expensive clothes. I was desperate to find a seat quickly and sink into obscurity. I just wanted it to be over.

When the service started, they were standing, then kneeling, then standing again, quoting something in Latin, up and down…. I was trying to follow, but I was utterly lost. Then to my horror, some priest-looking guy taps me on the shoulder and handed me this long pole. He asked me to help take an offering. I looked at Kelly with terror in my eyes. She could tell that I was petrified, and gently let the guy know, "He is a guest."

When the services were over, we headed to their house for Sunday dinner. Of course, it is one of the nicest houses I had ever been in. It was spotless and perfectly clean. I cannot overstate the contrast to what I had grown up in. I had very rarely been in such elegance. The table was absolutely stunning. China dishes, not the plastic Melmac I had grown up with.   The disgustingly filthy mobile home I had grown up in, was not unlike the ones you see on the television show "HOARDERS."

Kelly had mononucleosis, so we were not able to hold hands or even get very close to one another.   Her Father, the Attorney, stated emphatically at the dinner table, "Kelly it is imperative you do not touch any of the dishes being passed around the table, simply have someone else dish your plate."

Kelly quipped back, "I feel like a germ".

In my nervousness, I have always turned to humor to ease the tension. So, I snapped off a quick comeback to her.

"Your no ordinary Germ, you're a wonderful.... And I was going to say "Organism" but that is not the word that came out.   Everyone became completely silent and I thought I heard crickets....!

That relationship ended quickly.   Yet it played an integral part in my life. I had gone to church for the first time in my life and I wondered about the existence of a God.   At the same time, I had another important relationship that would impact my life.

My Roommate

Working for Safeway in Pendleton, I became friends with a fellow employee, Kent Couch. Kent and I were both courtesy clerks, and both of us were wanting to become a manager of our own store. We both were the same age and had both just graduated high school. We became friends and decided to become roommates to save money.

Kent and I became lifelong friends. Our friendship greatly impacted the direction of both of our lives.

The only other high school friend that had also attended Blue Mountain Community College (BMCC) was Candy. I eventually introduced Kent to Candy, who would later become his wife and the mother of their kids. Candy and I knew each other through Jr. High and High School in Burns Oregon. We were in the same class and graduated together. Now we were attending the same college together as well. Candy and I ran in the same small group all through high school. We were just great friends, but never an item.

Not long after Kent and I became roommates, Kent and Candy, (both Christians) began praying for me.

Kent and I lived in an apartment complex just across the parking lot from the church he and Candy attended. Even though Kent was a Christian, we got along well. Kent and I had some amazing adventures together.

The Race

One of the first adventures started when we found out that Safeway was building a brand-new store in Pendleton. The old store had been there my whole life. I had a lot of memories there.

When the new store opened, Kent and I were selected by the manager to head a transition team. We were tasked with boxing up everything in the old store, and putting everything on pallets. We would then load the trucks, and they would transport them to the new store.

Every morning we reported to work at the new store and drove over to the old store. On this particular morning, we both jumped in our separate cars and were making our way to the old store.

Pendleton was a town with a population of around ten thousand back then. The streets were two lanes, but the city had made the four main streets one way. Two going north and two coming back south. These streets are straight and you can see nearly a mile into downtown. Right in the middle of town are railroad tracks with crossing arms that cross perpendicular to these four streets. The tracks are somewhat elevated. So even though you can see over them when driving, you still rise up, go across the tracks, and back down the other side.

This particular morning, since Pendleton was still asleep, and there was no traffic, Kent and I decided to race. We lined up side by side and counted down 3,2,1 GO! We took off squealing our tires. We were still side by side at the railroad tracks and both became airborne together. Just then I noticed a policeman sitting in his car, watching the whole thing. He hit his lights, and I honestly think my heart stopped beating. I glanced down at the speedometer and we were above 90 miles an hour.

Kent saw him at the same time, and we both slammed on our breaks. Unfortunately, it took a block or so to get our cars stopped. We were at the old Safeway store before we could pull over. We pulled into the parking lot and waited.

The policeman must have had his engine off. We were already out of our cars and standing at the back of them before the cop came pulling into the parking lot. He had his lights and siren going when he pulled into the parking lot.

There we were, two young men still in our green Safeway smocks. I saw my life flashing before my eyes. I had never had a run-in with the law. I knew that going that fast, in a 25-mph zone, was more than a speeding ticket. This was an arrestable offense. I would lose my license and probably my job. I wondered if they would impound our cars. I also knew I deserved it.

He turned off his siren but left the lights blinking. Kent turned to me and said, "We are in such big trouble." I just nodded. I was so mad at myself.

We watched as the officer sat talking on his radio. Probably calling for backup, I thought. Suddenly the siren came blaring on again and I literally jumped. The police car went speeding out of the parking lot and raced off, leaving Kent and I standing alone, in the quiet of the early morning. All day long we kept looking over our shoulders, waiting for the officer to return and arrest us. He obviously knew we worked for Safeway; we were in our green smocks, and he knew where to find us.

By the end of the day, we still hadn't seen another policeman and realized we had been given a free pass.

I have often wondered what God allowed to happen, that would have trumped an open and shut case for our arrest. Another divine interception.

Another exciting adventure involved an expensive accident.

Wesson Oil

When Kent and I were dismantling the shelving at the old store, I was stunned to find a layer of Wesson oil under the bottom shelving of the Isles. Kent and I had a good laugh. We both knew, who was responsible for that mess.

One of my favorite jobs at Safeway was building end caps. When there was a sale item, we would build a large End base of those items. This particular night, I was building an end base of gallon-size Wesson oil glass bottles.

To do this correctly, we take and cut the top of the box off with a box knife. This leaves a small tray, to sit the bottles on. We then stack these on a pallet about six to seven feet high. I am 6' 2. so, I could stack it extra high and save trips. We use a pallet jack to transport the pallet of "trayed" oil.

As I was headed up to the front of the store with the Wesson oil, the wheel of the pallet jack hit a piece of glass, and instantly jerked to a stop. The entire load continued forward and crashed to the floor. Glass exploded and oil spread over the floor. One gallon would make a horrible mess, but this was an entire pallet full. The mess was astounding. It was flowing from aisle to aisle under the shelving. You could not walk on it. It was incredibly slick, especially on that old fashion tile. The oil lake just kept growing, spreading out over most of the store.

We began the monumental task of cleanup. This would prove to be much harder than we could have imagined. The glass shards were floating in the oil and spread out across the store. It made cleanup dangerous. It was so slick, you couldn't walk in it, and if you fell, you would be cut up by the glass.

At first, we used cat litter, which would soak up the oil. But we soon used all the bags we had at the store. I sent other workers out, to all the other stores in town. They bought every bag of cat litter in Pendleton. Even though the other grocery stores were closed, they also had night crews, that were willing to help us out. But even though we used every bag of cat litter in Pendleton it was not enough. It took hours to clean up the mess. We found that dog food would also soak up the oil. The oil kept seeping out from under the shelving, up and down every aisle.

Once again, I wanted to push the "rewind" button of life.

Needless to say, we were still working on this horrific mess all night. The next morning when the manager came to work. Nothing had been accomplished that night, except cleaning up the mess. Of course, you can imagine how this endeared me to the manager. We were buddies.... NOT!

So, now it is a year or so later and Kent and I are tearing the old store down and we find Wesson oil under the store shelves. Sometimes in life, the evidence of your mistakes will be there years later. Thankfully, God says that all our failures, sins, mistakes, and shortcomings are washed away as if they never happened.

He tells us that He throws them into the sea of forgetfulness, and remembers them no more. Imagine what that must have sounded like two thousand years ago. Whenever they were in the ocean or a lake or even a river, when you drop something in the water....it was Gone! Never to be seen again. They had no snorkeling equipment, no submarines, and no diving equipment. When it fell overboard it was lost forever.

He also says He tosses them as far as the east is from the west. The humor is that if you go east, you will never come to the west. His point is that He eternally forgets them. Whether it is a mistake or blunder, or even deliberate sin, God is dying to forgive you.... literally.

Rookie Mistake

As bad as my accident had been, it was not the worst accident I witnessed at Safeway. I was working the register, on an extra busy day, when I noticed a new stock boy, working on a large end base display. Normally when someone new begins working, we have someone working alongside them, to teach them the dos and don'ts. On this particular day, everyone was busy working the long lines of customers, so no one noticed the impending doom.

Let me set the scene. Often when setting up an end base, you match sale items on the same end base. For example, Cheese and crackers, Pop and chips, or in our case, Cake mix and Evaporated milk. The evaporated milk was in cans and very heavy. Cake mix is also very, very heavy, especially a case of cake mix.

So, our new stock boy "trayed" the evaporated milk. There were around 300 cans on the display. He spent the next hour stacking "trayed" Cake mix on the other half of the display. He stacked it nearly nine feet high with the help of a step ladder. The cake mixes far outweighed the evaporated milk...Suddenly the table flipped. Launching the 300 cans to the ceiling and shattering the lights. Then the broken glass, and cans of milk, came raining down on everyone. Not to mention the tower of cake mix that tipped over on customers. There were people that got hurt, but no one seriously. Mistakes happen to everyone including corporate executives.

Ping Pong Balls

When Safeway was planning their grand opening of the new store in Pendleton, they were looking for a novel way to draw in the crowds. They wanted publicity. Someone in Corporate came up with the idea of giving away money. The idea was to buy ping pong balls. Tens of thousands of them. On selected balls, was written a dollar amount, $1, $5, $10, $100, and one with $5,000 dollars. The idea was to drop them from a helicopter down onto the crowd. So, they rented a helicopter with a firefighting bucket. The pilot flew over the crowd assembled in the parking lot and hovering at several hundred feet, released the catch on the bag, and out came tens of thousands of ping pong balls.

It was thought that they would be caught in the wind and rotor wash would scatter the balls in a wide area. What no one could have imagined was what was about to happen. The bucket of balls fell in one giant globule and flattened many in the crowd. They were crushed to the ground and some suffered injuries. Evidently, the static held the balls together.

The weight of one ball is insignificant. But multiplied by thousands, and traveling at a high rate of speed, fell like an anvil. I can only imagine what happened to the corporate executive, that came up with that idea…, he was probably digging ditches the following week. On the bright side, they did get publicity, and they did give away a lot of money….in lawsuits.

Say What?

There are very clear guidelines for using the intercom system at Safeway. During the training process we are all taught, never to ask for a price check on an item that might make customers uncomfortable. We are also taught the protocols and etiquette of customer service. One of the big no-no's, NEVER, EVER, YELL ACROSS THE STORE. We were all taught, to run up to the register, and give the price personally.

It was a summer day and we were running all available registers. There was a loud buzz of chatter as the lines at the check stands were somewhat long. Suddenly over the intercom, we all heard, "Price check on Tampax twelve-count size." The place went quiet as everyone asked themselves, "Did she just ask what I think she asked?"

You could hear some people snickering. I looked at the young girl buying the item. She was standing at the register, frozen in terror, glaring at the Cashier.

Just then, a box boy, stepped out from one of the Isles, and yelled across the store, "HEY, IS THAT THE KIND YOU PUSH IN WITH A FINGER OR HAMMER IN WITH A HAMMER?" He thought she said, "Thumb tacks". A roar of laughter filled the store. I believe the young lady ran out of the store.

These are just some of the adventures and experiences I shared with Kent at Safeway. But we also shared an apartment and mutual friends. Yet we were about to share something even more important together.

Painting the Cross

Kent and I started as box boys, and worked our way up the ladder within Safeway; both of us aspiring to become Managers of our own store. Kent would eventually become a manager, but my life took an unexpected turn because of Kent.

One Saturday morning, Kent asked me if I would be willing to help out at his church. The Church had a wooden cross that could be seen from the freeway half a mile away. It was extremely tall, and no one was willing to paint it. They had painted the rest of the building, but the cross had been left, with no one willing to risk their lives. I was not afraid of heights and even got a thrill out of the danger. I agreed and, on a Saturday, I walked down to the church Kent and Candi attended.

They strapped me into a rope, and up the cross, I went. While I was up sitting on the crossbeam, the pastor saw his opportunity for a captive audience. Pastor Jerry May began asking me questions about God. I do not remember the exact conversation, but I do remember Pastor Jerry's frankness and no-nonsense approach. I appreciated his boldness. I had always assumed that Christians were "sissified".

When the cross was painted and I had come down, pastor Jerry and Kent invited me to church that Sunday.

The next morning Kent and I walked down across the parking lot, from our apartment, and into his Church. Pastor Jerry greeted me with a hearty "Hello!", and introduced me to others my own age.

I still remember Pastor Jerry's message. God taught His people, the Israelites, to "Consecrate to me every firstborn male. God had informed the Israelites that *"The firstborn males of every womb belong to Me, including the firstborn males of your livestock."*

A knowing sense within me, said "You are My firstborn." I was startled because up to that time, I had never heard God's prompting. I was overwhelmed by the Presence of another living being around me. I couldn't see Him, but I felt His presence.

Then Pastor Jerry began talking about how God had chosen the Levite tribe, to be set apart for the priesthood. In lieu of the firstborn, God told Israel that he would take the Levite tribe in trade for the firstborn. The Levite tribe was dedicated solely to being God's ministers. Then, suddenly, it happened again. I heard very clearly...." I have chosen you and set you apart as the firstborn, in the footsteps of Aaron the first priest and the Levites"

I have spoken of three spokes of the wheel that converged in my life simultaneously. My shattered tennis career. The relationship with Kelly and the fascination with the possibility of a God. The friendship with Kent and Candi, both Christians. Now at the same time, there was a fourth spoke.

The Fourth Spoke

At that time in my life and Safeway career, I had become very disillusioned. I had been asking myself, what's the point? For years now, I had filled the shelves one day, only to return and fill the shelves the next, and the next, and the next. It was redundant futility. It seemed as useless as a hamster running in a wheel. A lot of work, but it's in the same place when it jumps off. That poor critter goes nowhere, which is exactly how I felt.

As I was sitting there that voice inside me said, "From this day forward, you will not find satisfaction, in the futility of work that only has temporary results. From now on, everything you do in My service will have eternal consequences. It will have eternal value!" God was speaking to me as if He were standing next to me. It was in my head, but I was not in control of the conversation.

At the end of the service, pastor Jerry asked if anyone wanted to surrender their lives to God, and be saved from their sins. If they felt the need, to come and kneel at the altar. A bold challenge! Straight forward! No wishy-washy tinkering, but wholesale commitment! I bolted up and walked down. God had just spoken to me, so forcefully, that I didn't even question it.

When I was down at the altar, all by myself, the conversation continued with God. He asked me to put my life on the altar. He asked me to put my future on the altar. He told me that from that day forward, He would determine my path. He asked me to trust Him, and that He had a wife, already chosen for me. He then asked me to put my wallet on the altar, and I did, He said, "From this time forward, I will take care of your financial needs."

I look back on that encounter with amazement. But at the time I thought it was normal. I thought all Christians must have had that experience. I thought everyone that became Christian were ALL IN. I have always been an "all or nothing" person. If it was worth doing, it was worth doing 100%. I don't suffer futility well. I believe that may be why I had always been successful in Academics, Sports, and advancement in Safeway. I was ALL IN! So that day, in becoming a Christian, it seemed to me a natural step to surrender everything to Him.

I didn't have to question if there was a God. I had just spent the better part of an hour having Him talk to me. I know now, that what I experienced was unique. But at the time, I assumed that God spoke to everyone that way. I had heard people mention that God spoke to them, now it was my turn. That is how I looked at it at the time. I started my walk with God with utter faith!

I was still at the altar just conversing with God, oblivious to what was going on around me. In the wheel of life, I was utterly surrendering every spoke of my life one by one. God was asking me to put things on the altar, and leave them there. He told me that from that day forward, He would be my Father, and I would be His child. I knew absolutely nothing of the Bible, Christianity, Religion, or what lay ahead. All I knew was God called me personally. No man had coerced me. I didn't fall for some cheesy sales pitch. This was between me and God. A God I didn't even believe in when I entered the church that day.

I saw my life as a Castle. I not only lowered the drawbridge, and invited God into my life, I gave Him the Title to the property! My life was His. I also stepped down from the Throne and crowned Him King. I just assumed that was what every new Christian did. Later of course, I learned that many people lower the drawbridge and invite God in, but hold onto the Title and refuse to abdicate the throne. They see God as an adviser, He is there to rubberstamp their agendas.

What utter futility. How utterly ridiculous to call him Father, and in the same breath say, "You're not the boss of me!" God **IS** King! Anything less and He is not really your King.

When I left the church that day, I began an adventure with God. Part of that adventure was allowing God to reparent me. What I mean by this, is allowing God to break my destructive thought processes, and replace them with wise and intelligent ways to think. God had to eliminate my "stink'n think'n" and replace it with Holy and Pure thoughts. Remove the destructive behaviors and build constructive behaviors. Break the harmful cycles passed down through the generations and teach me how to handle life correctly. I was brought up in a completely dysfunctional family paradigm. I needed God to teach me what a healthy family looked like. Natural tendencies are not always the best ways to handle life. Just because it feels right, doesn't always translate into correct or effective action. The art of becoming more Christlike, for me, was allowing God to reparent me.

U-Turn

Remember the tennis match? I had just qualified for Nationals. I had also just become a Christian; God was in the process of reprioritizing my life. I was wrestling with the high degree of commitment, that tennis at this level, required. I knew that I would be transferring to a larger college that offered a Theological Education. That college also had a tennis team. My problem was, how was I going to marry the two worlds?

The night I qualified for nationals; we were celebrating at our hotel. I had just run up to my room, on the second story, and was returning to the parking lot. I was in a hurry and decided to jump a few feet, instead of walking the full length of the building. My impetuousness cost me, for when I jumped, I accidentally caught my foot on the edge of the curb and shattered my ankle. I never made it to Nationals. Unfortunatly, I was never able to reach that level of tennis again. From that time forward I devoted all my energy to God. The problem had been solved. My U-turn was complete!

Some have suggested that perhaps God broke my ankle, to keep me from dividing my loyalties. That's absurd! My heavenly Father is not some kind of a cruel prankster. He gives us free will. We are free to make decisions. He allowed me to make a poor decision. I was completely to blame for the broken ankle.

Sometimes God allows what He does not desire. Just like parents who let their children learn to drive or play in the ocean. There are risks and dangers with driving. We teach them the rules of the road and hope they listen. We allow them the freedom to drive, knowing full well that they could be killed. We certainly don't desire them to be involved in an accident. Playing in the ocean comes with all sorts of dangers, rip tides, sharks, and rogue waves. A parent has no desire to see their child hurt, but allows them the freedom to play in the ocean.

God had no desire to see me get hurt but gave me free will to make choices. My own impatience caused my broken bones. As it would turn out, that break was one of the best things that could have happened to me. It forced me to evaluate life's priorities. Compared to God and Eternity, the temporary fame of a tennis match seemed empty. Compared to the lives that need help and direction, hitting a green ball around on the ground, seemed like a waste of time. The most valuable thing on earth is a human being. Not a trophy, which no one will remember four years from now.

I still loved to play tennis, but it wasn't the center of my universe anymore. I still loved competition and staying in shape, and those things are important, but I wasn't letting the important things in life, crowd out the invaluable ones.

God gave me an acronym, JOY! It became the priority list in my life. Jesus, Others, Yourself. God first, then others. There is an encouraging teaching in which God says Honor one another above yourselves. Consider others as more important than yourself. Imagine if the whole world lived by just that teaching! Romans 12:10

Tennis or Others? Temporary or Eternal? The choice was easy. That broken ankle turned out to be one of the most beautifully ironic things to happen in my life. In the eyes of man, a broken ankle seems tragic, but in the light of all the people who were saved from eternal hell, it was perfect. How many thousands of people will come up to us in heaven, after only one year, and thank us, for our priorities, that saved them from millions, and trillions of years of lostness?

Sometimes, I believe the only way God could get me to slow down, was by allowing an injury. It was in those long quiet hours of healing that I truly considered my life.

My First Motorcycle

After I had healed from the broken ankle, I decided to buy my first dirt bike. Friends had loaned me their bikes in the past and I had always had fun riding. Now, I decided to buy my own.

I went out riding one day by myself. I was only a few miles from town, riding on dirt trails. I was racing along fairly quickly when I hit a rock. The rock threw the front tire violently to the left, and the bike came out from under me. My right shoulder hit first. I was traveling so fast that I flipped like a rag doll. When I came to rest, I tried to sit up and the pain was excruciating. I looked toward where my right shoulder should have been, and it simply wasn't there. I had hit the ground so hard that my collarbone snapped. My hand was down near my knee. I had separated my shoulder as well.

I tried to stand, but my leg gave out and I could see I had rebroken my ankle. I had also done something serious to my pelvic region. I became sick to my stomach. I was also dehydrated. I don't know if the nausea was because of the shock, or dehydration. I was down in a ravine and contemplating what to do next. I couldn't walk with a broken ankle. I couldn't hop with a shattered shoulder. The bike was trashed. Yet I knew I had to get to the hospital, and at the time I wondered if I was bleeding internally. I once again wondered if I was going to die.

What I **could** do, was push with my good leg and scoot on my backside. The pain in my shoulder was raw, but I knew it was up to me, to survive. There was a trailer court a mile or so from me. I knew if I could get close enough, I could scream for help. So, I started the long crawling journey out of the ravine, towards that trailer court.

Early on I was using adrenaline, and perhaps I was in shock. The pain was horrible but I feared this torturous death, so I pushed on. As the day wore on though, the pain became more intense. I was also extremely fatigued. My breathing became labored and again I was worried that I had burst something internally. The will to live is powerful, and I pushed through the agonizing pain.

By late afternoon, I could see the trailers. I would crawl for a while and begin screaming for help. Even yelling was excruciatingly painful. I would have to talk myself into crawling again, every move racked my body with pain. But no one could hear me. I had to get closer.

It took several more hours to get close enough to the trailer court for someone to finally hear me. A man came out on his porch and listened. He said later he thought he heard something so he would listen, but it would be silent, so he would go back to what he was doing. I told him I only had enough energy to yell once then I would be exhausted. It would be a while before I could muster the will to move closer.

Eventually, he came out and yelled from his porch, and I yelled back. He came out into the sagebrush to find me. At first, he had no idea which direction the scream was coming from and encouraged me to keep yelling. Every once in a while, I would give a small yelp. He would call back "keep yelling!" But I was totally spent, and knowing someone was looking for me, I relaxed. By the time he found me, my yelps were barely audible. I was drifting near unconsciousness.

When he finally found me, he realized he could not carry me and he ran back to his trailer and grabbed his International Scout. (May I just say right here, whoever designed the International Scout, you should be shot!! Tanks have better suspensions!!! I have laid on marble slabs that were softer than those plastic seats!! Anyone who has ever owned one knows exactly what I mean! But I digress…)

He put me in the Scout and took off across the brush like a madman. I was screaming for him to slow down. Every bump felt like it was breaking bones. He kept apologizing but told me he had to get me to the hospital. When we were racing through town, I heard a siren and he let out an expletive. He pulled over and jumped out and ran back to the police car that had stopped us. Just as quickly he returned. The police car was leading the way with lights and siren.

It was then I learned he was an off-duty police officer, and he had asked his buddy, to escort us to the emergency room.

I had another pleasant surprise when I got to the emergency room. Kate Reynolds was the admitting nurse. Her Husband was a Fireman, and I had just recently met them at the church. They were the couple who had taken me under their wings when I began to attend. They taught the Sunday school class I had been attending. Todd and Kate have since become lifelong friends.

Kate could see the seriousness of my situation and called the church to pray.

I do remember her chastising me for not wearing a helmet, and I told her I was wearing a helmet, but that it had been ripped off in the accident. When my helmet was retrieved there was a large gash where a sharp rock had penetrated the shell, like a claw hammer. The rock had penetrated the helmet, ripping it off my head.

The policeman who found me returned to recover the bike and my gear. He brought the helmet into the hospital, and the emergency room marveled at my good fortune.

Kate told me, that if I had not been wearing a helmet, I would be dead. She showed me the helmet and explained, that had this been my skull, they would be attending my funeral. Again, God had put a protective hand over me. I could see the tangible evidence of God working in my day-to-day life. Even my prayers were being answered on a daily basis.

Two Keys

Kent Couch, my roommate, bought a hang glider. (Later in life he would become known in the northwest as the lawn chair flyer. He would air up helium balloons, connect them to a Lawn Chair and fly across Oregon). We both loved to fly and he invited me to hang glide that day.

We drove my car up to the top of the Blue Mountains, on the old highway. We set up the kite, and Kent took the first flight. We took turns flying it out over the valley below. At the end of the day, we packed up the kite, and I reached into my pants pockets for the car keys. To my horror, I had a hole in my blue jeans and the keys had fallen out. Somewhere, while I had been flying that day, the keys had dropped out and fallen to the ground.

I only had two keys in my life at the time. One for the car, and one for the apartment. They were dull brown in color and attached to a single ring.

I turned to Kent and gave him the bad news. I could tell he was utterly disgusted, and he suggested we get started on the long 15-mile walk back to town. This was long before cell phones. We were in a bind! It gets very cold at night, and neither of us was dressed for it.

I was such a young Christian at the time, but I knew God was aware of my situation. He also knew where my keys were. So, I turned to Kent and said "Let's pray and have God show us where the keys are!" Kent became agitated and insisted we not delay even a moment. He reminded me, that the sun would soon be going down, and we needed to expedite our departure.

I had just heard a message about believing and not doubting in prayer, so I simply asked God, "Please guide me to my keys!"

I took off over the hill and headed down the canyon we had been flying over. Kent was understandably furious with my decision. He went to the car and sat sulking in the front seat. Patiently waiting for me to give up.

I know finding two small keys in a house is difficult. What are the mathematical odds of finding two keys in the wilderness with mountains and valleys. These weren't even shiny keys, they were dull. It was evening and the sun was going down. I just kept walking and asking God to lead me to the keys.

I had been walking in no particular direction, just wandering in the brush when I looked over and there were my keys. I had faith, but when I saw those keys, I was dumbfounded. A chill ran up my spine. I felt that God was standing there and I was on Holy ground. I stood there in a state of utter shock. THOSE were MY keys!

God must have known, I would need that kind of childlike faith later in life, so He answered my prayer, with a miracle. How many square miles had I covered that day? How many places could they have dropped and hidden those keys permanently? What were the odds, of finding keys without a metal detector? No search parties! Keys so tiny, that if you were to lay them on the mountain, it might take years to find them. Yet God leads me straight to them.

When I had hiked back up to the car, I could see Kent was sitting glaring out the windshield. He was seething with anger. I called out "Hey I found them!" He opened the door and looked at me with a disgusted look, "No Way!" he said angrily. "You had them in your pocket the whole time, didn't you?"

I spent the trip back to town trying to convince him, God had walked me straight to them. God was working with me, encouraging me to continue in my faith. He was proving that He existed and that if I trusted Him, He would show Himself to me every day.

God had been guiding my life all along. I just wasn't aware of it at the time. He led me to Kelly who took me to church. He led me to Kent and Candy, so I would hear the message of salvation. He led me to others that would have a powerful impact on my new Christian life.

Mrs. Holmes

I was a young college man when I walked into the Pendleton church for the first time. I met some amazing people in those first few years. One of the most fascinating was Mrs. Meem Holmes. She was old, I mean ancient of days, she may have known Moses. She was a no-nonsense, straight-shooting, in-your-face type of person and I loved her for it. She cared for all of us young people. She would invite us over to her home, but before you could cross the threshold of her front door, she would take your hands, both of them, and she would look you straight in the face and begin praying for you...." *"God, Perry's about to enter this house of yours and I'm asking you to fill him with your Spirit, and guide our conversation. Watch over his mouth and keep it from gossip, vulgarity, exaggeration, or unkind words. May our conversation be pleasing to your ears Father. Mold this young man into the man of integrity you have always wanted him to be."* Then she would let you into her home. You felt as if she was God's mom. She spoke of God, as if he were in the room, in person.

She wouldn't allow any talking over someone else. If someone was speaking, then you were to listen and give them your full attention. She taught us to honor one another. We were never allowed to speak ill of anyone, but to encourage one another. She did this for anyone who entered the house.

Leaving was the same ritual. She would stand at the door and before you could cross that threshold, you had to be prayed over. BOTH hands in hers and she would begin.... *"God Perry is about to enter the world; he will need wisdom and discernment; in all the decisions he will be faced with. Keep his mind clear, and guide his thoughts. May his life be pure and uncontaminated by the world. May his life be a Christ-like example, to all that he comes in contact with. May lost souls be drawn into a relationship with you Father, because of Perry's lifestyle and Your presence in him."* Only then, could you leave.

Mrs. Holmes wouldn't even allow the Pastor into the house, without that meeting at the doorway. If we ordered pizza delivered, the delivery person was no exception. She would not allow anyone into her house without the covering of prayer over them. She was amazing. At the time I thought she was just a normal Christian. I thought all Christians kept their house pure and protected. What a gem Mrs. Meem Holmes was! What an influence in those early years of my Christian walk.

Family Heirloom Part 2

What a contrast to my grandfather. When I became a Christian, he disowned me. He mocked me and increased his rhetoric against anything religious. He especially tried to embarrass me, whenever someone else was around. Pointing out what an utter fool I had become. The ultimate division was when he found out I was going into the ministry.

God worked it out for me to attend a Christian College in Nampa Idaho, Northwest Nazarene College. I would be living in the dorms and so I wasn't able to take my prized heirloom rifle, on campus. I asked my grandmother if I could store it at her house.

When I returned, after the first year away at college, I went to look for my rifle. It was nowhere to be found, so I asked my grandmother. She took me aside and out of earshot of my grandfather.

She explained what had happened. "Your Grandfather was so angry, that you became a Christian that he decided to take your rifle back and gave it to your cousin. "

Listen" she pleaded, "I beg you not to say a word, or acknowledge you even miss your rifle. Can you imagine the scene it would cause? I don't need that kind of drama. Don't say a word, not to your cousin or especially your grandfather. When you graduate, I will personally buy you any rifle you choose including any scope of your choice. Just don't mention it to anyone; this is just between you and I."

I never mentioned the gun again, and never took advantage of Grandma's offer either. I felt as if God wanted me to be a peacemaker, and absorb the insult. It became a part of my walk with God, to overlook personal injustices.

God showed me, that not responding in anger, had a powerful impact on the offender. The offender deliberately pushes your buttons. They fully expect you to retaliate. They want to show everyone you're a hypocrite. They want to mock all your claims.

The offender knows that you are a professing Christian. You claim that God has made a difference in your life. You say that you are filled with love. You even profess to love your enemies. You profess that you are filled with the spirit of God. You claim that God has made all the difference in your life.

The offender gets a perverted delight in gaslighting you, so you lose your temper. Then they can mock the idea that you have changed at all. They want to show everyone that you're no different from anyone else. Ultimately, it's their way of showing that there is no God. Or at minimum, that God makes no difference.

When you bump into a cup, whatever is in the cup, spills out. God showed me that, when gentleness spills out, it completely confounds the offender. It gets their attention. Now they are confused. Now they have to consider that perhaps there is a small possibility that there is a God and that He does make a difference. You become an anomaly to them.

God showed me that one of the greatest shows of strength is *not* to respond in anger. It takes great character and control, not to retaliate. It gets attention. Real strength, is showing mercy to someone who deserves otherwise.

In the Bible, God shares what happened to Jesus. They blindfolded Jesus and when they were sure he couldn't see, they punched him in the face. Then they asked Jesus, "If you're really the son of God, you should be able to tell us who hit you." Jesus had the power to stop their heartbeats. To kill them on the spot. He could have blinded them in an instant. Jesus could have done a hundred different things to prove He was God. He chose to remain silent.

I can tell you now…. that took strength. That took real character. What a show of self-control. He had the God-like power NOT to respond or be provoked to anger. This is one of the indicators that helps prove that indeed He truly was God. What came out of the cup? It was the very love He had proclaimed all His life. Authenticity is written all over that story. "Forgive them Lord, for they don't know what they're doing"

How can God prove to a none believer that He is real? He can allow one of His servants to be bumped! And when Love, kindness, gentleness, encouragement, and mercy spill out, the offender has to consider what makes this person different. When the offender doesn't get the response, he is expecting, he considers perhaps God is real.

People are looking for hope. Most people are looking for something that will make their life better. Logic dictates that "If" there is a God, He would make life better. But when nothing seems to change in a professing christian's life, the natural conclusion is that God makes no difference. Yet when they see it working in a believer's life, they wonder, perhaps it could work for me as well?

Have you ever wondered why the scripture says…" Consider it pure joy whenever you face trials of many kinds?" For a believer, it means that God trusts you, and He believes in you, to do the right thing when bumped. The God of the universe finds you trustworthy. He can rely on you. You become a useful servant in bringing eternal life to others.

The lost world Is watching, looking, seeking to find a thread of hope that there is something out there bigger than they are. They want to believe there is a Loving God. But when it doesn't seem that God makes any difference in the lives of Christians, they become cynical, and rightfully so. This is one reason they detest Hypocrites so intensely.

Getting to Meet Famous People

Once I became a Christian, God began to work in my life in amazing ways. I became a part of a group called "God's Kids." These were college age kids from all denominations.

One of the fun things we did was put on Concerts. So, I got to meet a lot of acts. Leon Patillo, Roy Orbison, Pat Boone, and others.

During the week of the Pendleton Roundup in Pendleton Oregon, we used the Roundup stadium to host some of the biggest names in Christian music. This particular year we had Reba Rambo, a famous country western and southern gospel singer. I joined the rest of the "God's kids" as staff, working wherever they needed me.

As it turned out, during the Reba Rambo concert, I was running the sound equipment and it was located just off stage. I was singing to myself during the concert.

All through high school, I was in Choir. I loved to sing. During the concert, I was singing some harmony to one of the songs Reba was singing on stage. I had no idea she could hear me; I was just singing along, but evidently, she heard me.

To my amazement she stopped the concert, and told the audience that she had just heard some wonderful harmony off stage. It sounded wonderful, she wanted whomever was singing to come on stage. At first, I thought I was in big trouble. Yet she kept asking me to come on stage and sing a duet. I was terrified. She was so insistent, that I eventually come out.

So, I hesitantly walked out on stage, in front of the largest crowd I had ever been in. She encouraged me to sing the harmony that she had just heard. They started the song again and I found myself singing a duet with Reba Rambo. When we finished, the crowd went wild. she thanked me and gave me a big hug. I was still in a state of shock, as I made my way back to the soundboard. It was my short claim to fame.

My Grandmother, who was in the stands that day, took a picture of the duet. She showed that picture to anyone she was telling the story to. She was a proud grandmother! Even though my grandfather hated Christians, my grandmother never stopped loving me.

Air Shocks

God was showing me in a hundred different ways, that He was with me and directing my life. He showed me many small miracles. Things that were not just coincidental.

I drove a really nice car by this time. An Oldsmobile Omega. The body was identical to a Chevy Nova. I had hopped it up with air shocks. Just before I left for College in Nampa ID, I went out to the car and the Air shocks had failed. The car frame was sitting on the Tires. I drove it several blocks to the service station to air them up. The tires rubbed so bad that they were smoking and it cutting grooves in the tires. The noise inside the car was deafening. I drove it to work, (which incidentally was my last day at Safeway). The next morning, I was leaving for Nampa to attend College. When I got off work the Air shocks were back down again. Again, I drove to the nearest service station and aired them up.

The next morning was Sunday. My game plan was to go to church for the last time in Pendleton, and after church, go see Mrs. Holmes to say goodbye. But that morning the car was sitting on the tires again. I didn't have time to fix it before church, so I endured the embarrassing drive to the station! Again!

After Church, my car was sitting on tires and the Shocks were down again. The leak had gotten even worse. They were not even holding for an hour.

I had promised Mrs. Holmes that I would join her for lunch before I left for college. I had no choice but to drive to the station and air them up yet again. I was destroying the tires, but no businesses were open to fix the problem.

I was anxious because I desperately needed to get to college. So, I pushed on and got to Mrs. Holme's home. After a wonderful lunch, I came outside and was devastated to see that the air shocks had failed. It obviously had a leak in the line somewhere. I sat there in desperation, and I prayed.

"Father, you know I don't have time for this. You have been challenging me to pray and trust. So, I'm going to step out on faith and fill them up one more time, then take off to Nampa."

I drove to the nearest gas station and I aired them up again.

Once you leave Pendleton the next town is LaGrande, 58 miles away. I entered the freeway and off I went with full confidence.... well, I did keep praying, Father please keep these air shocks up.

I had one more errand to do before I showed up on a Christian Campus. There was a town just before La Grande that was named Perry. I had stolen the sign from that town and hung it in my apartment for several years.... Now it was time to put it back on the post I had stolen it from. I arrived at the town limits and waited till no one was driving by and quickly replaced the sign back on its original post.

I have often wondered how many noticed the sign was missing. The county highway department had never replaced that sign. I bet they were scratching their heads when it suddenly reappeared.

I checked my air brakes and to my wonderment, they were still up.

I made it to La Grande and kept going. Baker, Ontario, and ultimately into Nampa Idaho four hours later. I pulled up to the dorm and marveled that God had kept them up. I went in and checked in at the dorm. When I came back out a minute later it was down. God had kept the air shocks up just long enough to get me to school. My faith was greatly strengthened. God was re-parenting me. He was showing me that if I trusted Him, He would be faithful.

Freshman Again

I was now at Northwest Nazarene College. (NNC) It was my third year in college, but it was like starting over.

When I started Blue Mountain Community College back in 1978, I was obviously a freshman. I was forced to endure the indignity of being a freshman. This includes having to wait in long lines. At the end of that first year in college, I didn't have enough credits to become a sophomore. I started my second year at BMCC still in the freshman class. I was just short of enough credits to skip this frustration. For two years in a row, I was forced to endure the long lines of the freshman class.

When I entered NNC, a four-year institution, I found that they would not accept any of my college credits from BMCC, a Community College. So once again I found myself in the freshman line, for the third straight year. I had to start all over as an incoming freshman.

NNC was extremely costly, and the workload more challenging, so I only took enough credit hours to be considered full-time. At the end of that first year at NNC, I found myself several credits short. I didn't have quite enough credits to be considered a sophomore. At the beginning of the next year, for the fourth straight year, I found myself in the freshman lines. It was not until my fifth year in college, that I finally got to stand in the sophomore line. I had to endure numerous indignities in college. Most of them were self-imposed.

Phone

Case in point; As everyone knows, it takes courage to ask someone out on a date. You have to put yourself out there, and become vulnerable to rejection. I met a young lady in one of my classes. I visited with her and we became fairly well acquainted. I wanted to ask her out but was a little intimidated. I was building up the courage to ask her out. She wasn't the only one I was interested in though.

In another class, I met another young lady, and we also hit it off. This went on for several months, as I worked up the nerve to finally ask one of them out! Finally, I decided one Friday night that I would ask the first woman to a basketball game. I called her on the phone and asked her if she would like to join me for the ball game. I got a rather abrupt "NO" when I asked her out. I was really taken aback at the rejection. She was almost rude.

Not to be deterred that night, I decided to call the other girl I had been talking with over the past several months and ask her out. When she answered her phone, I explained that I had a couple of tickets to the game and wondered if she would like to join me. She almost shouted at me, "I don't play second fiddle to anyone," and hung up on me. I was stunned. How could she have known? I quickly checked the student directory and there I found the answer…roommates! Several thousand students, a number of dorms, and I picked roommates! Awkward!

Karen

One of the influential people to help me get into NNC, was a dear friend, Karen Bozarth. She had come to Pendleton as a youth intern from NNC. She took a special interest in helping me. She knew a number of the admissions staff and personally introduced me to the right people.

She introduced me to a friend of hers, who had a photographic memory. Studying with him was incredibly humbling. I would ask a question, and he would say, look on page 237, the second paragraph, it starts…"In the midst of Gnosticism…"

"How do you do that" I would ask. He would say "I just see it on the page". I had to study like a dog, and there were people like him in the world. In College, most classes are graded on the curve, and I was competing for grades with humans like this. I used to kid him, "You owe me, I made your grade possible by lowering the curve".

One afternoon I was grabbing my mail in the student union building, when he came up beside me, and asked to talk. I said, "Sure, just give me a second to open the combination to my mailbox and I will be right with you." I turned and continued fighting with the combination, and he said "Meet me upstairs." He turned and disappeared up the stairs.

It took perhaps 30 seconds to get my mail, I turned and was walking towards the stairs when I heard a gunshot. Within several seconds the dean, Jerry Hull, came running down the stairs and yelled for someone to call an ambulance. He spotted me and said, "Go get Karen!"

I was stunned. I began to run towards her dorm, wondering how I was going to break it to her. In NNC the girls' dorms do not allow boys past the lobby, so I asked the girl on duty, to call Karen, and have her meet me in the lobby. "Tell her it's an emergency."

When Karen appeared, I could see the deep concern on her face. All I could think to say was "Come with me, I'll explain on the way". She complied, but of course, she demanded to know what was going on. I just couldn't find the words to tell her our friend had shot himself.

We jumped into my car and drove quickly over to the hospital. In the back of my mind, I was grieving that I had not given Steve my full attention when he had come up to me. I was fighting with the combination, and it didn't occur to me the gravity of what he was asking me. What if I had simply said "Sure buddy, let's talk", and turned away from that stupid mailbox? Perhaps I could have prevented Steve from shooting himself. I will never know. What I do know is that I was preoccupied with getting my mail. What I took away from that experience, was that people are immensely more important than any agenda.

Thankfully our friend lived, and I learned an important life lesson. People are the single most important thing on this planet. There is a song that has an incredibly powerful verse. It goes like this. *"It is better to love people and use things, rather than love things and use people!"*

I incorporated this into my life. Whenever someone wants to talk, I put down my phone! I turn off the television! I stop what I'm doing! I honor them by giving them my full attention. I honor people by getting up and answering the door, rather than yelling "come in". I dress well if we have guests or friends coming over to the house, to show they are highly valued. I wouldn't dress sloppily if the president was coming over. I want people to know they are a VIP and cherished.

God teaches us to consider others more important than ourselves. I strived to make that a part of my life. Sometimes though I would snap.

Snapped

I was fairly well-known on campus. NNC is a small college, where most of the students live on campus. I had been there for several years and was very active in campus life. I was also a Resident assistant in one of the upperclassman dorms. In addition to this, I worked security at night, patrolling the college grounds. I was also known as a theological student studying for the ministry. There weren't a lot of students in this field. So, the few of us were fairly well known.

You might think that in a Christian college, all the students were Christians. Not at all! Many of the student-athletes are there on scholarships, and God was an afterthought. My point is that not everyone there was Christian. In fact, some students were actually hostile to the idea of there being a God. Many students hated the somewhat restrictive rules at the school.

At the beginning of the term, I was on duty and caught some pranksters who had stolen the McDonald's Clown from one of the nearby McDonald's. That incident caused one student "Sprocket" (I will change his name), to take a special disliking for me. He took it upon himself to make my life a living nightmare.

Here are some of the more memorable run-ins, I had with Sprocket. I drove a bus for the church, and every Sunday I would drive students from campus to church. Sprocket, saw me park the bus one Saturday night, and broke out windows on the bus. One time he broke into my car and smeared human feces all over the upholstery. One time he broke into our dorm room, and he and some other baseball players ate a birthday cake, we had bought for a special friend. Sprocket bragged to his buddies about these and other pranks, knowing full well I could never prove it.

Sprocket was there on a baseball scholarship. The baseball team was made up of a large number of Athletes, that had no interest in the religious side of campus life. Sprocket was a leader of the baseball team. He and his cronies were notorious for their not-so-funny pranks.

One evening at the cafeteria, I was sitting with a number of friends including my girlfriend, and the baseball team entered the cafeteria.

As they waited in line to get their meal pass punched, a fellow student with cerebral palsy happened to come in behind them. He had to use two specially designed crutches to walk. With great effort, he made his way toward the team. When he reached them, they began shoving him around like a pinball.

Something deep within me snapped. All the anger I had for bullies exploded in an instant, I jumped up on the table and leaped into the group screaming at the top of my lungs. I grabbed players and tossed them like rag dolls. I had strength that allowed me to physically pick them up and I was genuinely hurting them. I remember grabbing one guy by the hair and throwing him. When they were all scattered, I was still screaming "COME ON, COME ON, I DARE YOU!" In the fracas, I had knocked over the stack of meal trays and they went flying across the floor adding to the roar of my tirade.

The entire cafeteria was on their feet in total silence watching, wondering what was happening. Nobody on the ground dared move, fearing that I had lost my mind. They were probably in a state of shock, as to what had just happened. There was genuine fear in their eyes, as it probably seemed that I had lost my sanity. I am a big athlete at 6-foot 2inches and I was in great shape. The ease at how I had dismantled the group was astounding to me, but doubly for them. It took place in less than thirty seconds. I stood over them and if they so much as moved I would rush at them. So, they were frozen.

Finally, I stopped screaming and stood glaring at them. I began to shake, and the entire place was eerily quiet. All you could hear was the moaning of those I had genuinely hurt. Then in absolute silence, I walked out.

It was only as I was walking out of the building that I realized what I had just done. I had no idea that was in me. Where had that level of rage come from? I had just sealed my fate. I wondered if they would arrest me. Was I going to jail? What would I be charged with, attempted murder? Would I have to pay all their medical bills?

At a minimum, I would certainly be expelled. Pastoring would be out of the question. As I walked across the campus to my room, I also knew I had lost my girlfriend. Who would want to date a madman? My professors would be ashamed of me. I had let down so many people who had supported me. What would I do with my life now?

I was also genuinely afraid of what I was capable of. I had no idea that kind of rage was in me. I could have killed someone, or had I killed someone already? I was listening for sirens, police, ambulances, or fire! What had I done to my life?

I was not a violent man! I never got in fights. The last fight I had been in was in seventh grade with Kathy Hannaford. She beat the tar out of me. I knew then that the fighting game was not for me. I was a skinny, awkward weakling back then. I had never gotten into another fight after that embarrassment. Now years later I had just pummeled a group of college men.

I sat on the edge of my bed wondering what had just happened. One minute I'm eating and visiting the next I am violently tossing humans around. Where had that strength come from?

It was later in the evening when my roommate came in. He had not been there, but the entire campus was abuzz about the incident. Evidently, others who had witnessed the team's behavior had told the authorities that I had come to the rescue. The baseball players themselves were all too eager to downplay their humiliation. Even though I had hurt a number of them, none of them sustained broken bones.

My girlfriend later told me: "I was so proud of you Perry, you were amazing".

People I didn't even know, would come up to me later and say "thank you!" I was astonished! All of them told me, they had seen the bullying but were intimidated to do anything. They were thrilled when I responded.

I was never called into the Deans office. The dean of students, Jerry Hull, never mentioned it, even though he knew all about it.

In the scripture, we are encouraged to defend those who can't defend themselves. We are to rescue the weak, and care for the poor and orphaned. We are taught to protect the defenseless. God says to watch out for the widows and children. I have learned that righteous anger has its place.

Jesus overturned the tables of the crooks and scammers that were robbing the people at the temple. We should become angry over injustices such as child molesters. There are things in life that should deeply offend us. Somehow this principle has been lost, in our effort to be nice. We tend to capitulate to terrorism, instead of standing firm with integrity. A wise man knows where to strike the balance.

Our culture likes to paint Jesus as a pacifist and somewhat of a coward. The scriptures show us the truth. He stands firm against the oppressive men of His day. He calls them "Broods of snakes," "White washed walls," "Hypocrites" "Sons of Satan," and "Liars." Jesus was no sissy.

Nothing is more pathetic than good men who do nothing, in the face of evil men.

I have always tried to err on the side of mercy, but there is a time to protect, defend, and rescue.

Enumclaw

Dr. Erving Laird, a beloved professor, encouraged me to enter the same youth intern program that Karen Bozarth had been in when she met me. It was called the "Response" program. I ended up being accepted to Enumclaw church of the Nazarene. I worked as a youth intern for the summer. I worked with a team of young adult youth leaders at the church to build a strong youth ministry. One young man, in particular, was a great delight to work with. He was humble and had a servant's heart. He and his young wife were a great help.

One Sunday morning the pastor taught about fasting. He challenged the congregation to fast from something, and whenever we thought about it, to pray. It is a lot like lent, where you give up something and when the desire for it comes, you pray. The thought behind it is that we would be reminded to pray more often.

Without telling his young wife, this young man, on the adult team I worked with, decided to fast from one of the medications he was taking. This is not at all what the pastor was talking about. The pastor specifically spoke about such things as Chocolate, Ice Cream, or Soda, not at all meaning something we NEED! Like medications.

Unbeknownst to us, this gentleman was on medication, for dramatic mood swings and depression. He stopped taking his meds and went into a euphoric upswing.

While in this euphoric mental state he picked up a young woman hitchhiker. She later testified to the following:

When she jumped into the car, she could tell, almost immediately, that he was acting abnormally. He told her that God had given him the ability to walk through walls like Jesus. He had the ability to become spirit, or none-physical. He could become non-matter.

She became frightened and asked him to let her out of the car. He became frustrated that she did not seem to believe him. So, in an effort to prove to her that he could do this, he said, "Watch this, I will drive right through this oncoming car." He pulled into the oncoming lane and drove head-on into the oncoming car. Without the proper medications, this otherwise wonderful man became mentally deranged.

Luckily there were no fatalities, but there were injuries. He was arrested and put in jail.

I learned a powerful lesson through this experience.

What I learned, is that many times, when a person is euphoric and is feeling well, they convince themselves, they are fine and go off the medication. This can be one of the most disastrous decisions of their lives. The chemical balance in the brain is incredibly complex, and sometimes it gets out of balance. Medications are designed to regain that perfect balance once again. Medications are a wonderful tool if used properly.

Many years after this horrific experience, I found out that Marie was also diagnosed with the same mental condition. She had also been prescribed the same medication as this young man. I sometimes wonder how my childhood would have been different if the doctors would have diagnosed her earlier, and she had taken her medican.

Mt. Rainier

That summer in Enumclaw was full of learning experiences. Some were so powerful, that I took the lessons I learned that summer, and I carried them into the rest of my life. Here are several examples.

Three of the young men in the youth group were Steve Rashick, Kurt Petelon, and Jeff French. The four of us decided to go climbing near Mt. Rainier, the tallest volcano in Washington State.

As is often the case in the northwest, it was raining. We consoled ourselves, that if we only went outdoors in good weather, we would be mostly homebound year-round. One in a long line of utterly stupid decisions we made that day.

58

The rain made the going more difficult with mud and cold. We had to traverse some rather rugged bluffs. We were all novices at mountain climbing and were not at all properly prepared. We had no ropes. We were not dressed in rain gear.

We began to get cold and decided to make camp on the next ridge. While we were making our way up the ridge, the trail began to become less distinguishable and we accidentally left it. We weren't lost, we just lost the trail. So, we began climbing up the bluff to the ridge we could see above us. We knew that we would reconnect with the trail up there. That decision almost cost us our lives.

In mountain climbing, there is a cardinal rule that we ignored. Never leap, jump, or climb something you can't come back down. Because once you've made the leap, if you run into the preverbal rock wall, and have to retrace your steps, you will find yourself stuck on a ledge. That is exactly what happened. We could not go forward, nor go back.

We were probably only a few minutes from the top, but we came to a sheer rock wall that was too formidable to climb.

We had been climbing, hand over hand, up the cliff wall. We put our bodies up against the rock face to stay out of the wind and to protect ourselves from falling to our deaths. It was hard to look down. Any slip or misstep would be a drop of several hundred feet straight down. We had no mountain climbing gear. When we came to the wall, I knew we were all in big trouble.

I was beginning to shake with cold. I was soaked clear through. I was angry at myself for pushing on up, knowing that we could never get back down. I had been foolishly hoping we would find the path to the top. I knew the horrible plight we were in. We were standing on the ledge not able to go forward or backward. The ledge was too thin to turn around on, much less to sit on, so we just stood there. I was more terrified, at that moment than at any other time in my life. I honestly believed this was going to cost all four of us our lives. We stood there scolding ourselves for a long time, trying to think of a way to save ourselves. My legs were giving out and I knew I was about to collapse and fall. The human body can only hold on for so long, and we were all holding on for dear life.

I kept berating myself, and just kept thinking STUPID! STUPID! STUPID! How could I have been so stupid? I knew better. I did this to myself, with my eyes wide open. I knew better. Why, why, why had I kept going? With every step, I knew I was getting deeper in trouble, but I just kept belligerently pressing on. I became extremely angry with myself. I had always mocked idiots who get in trouble, because of their own poor decisions. Now, I was here on the cliff face, regretting the number of idiotic decisions that had led us to our deaths. I had never been afraid of heights, but I began to panic as I visualized falling to my death. When I say panic, I mean real panic that you have to talk yourself out of. I began to become irrational. I even accepted that I was going to die.

After a long time, we decided that if we were going to die, it would be better to die trying, than to one by one, drop to our deaths. We inched our way back and came to one of many places we had been able to climb but was nearly impossible to climb back down. We decided to hold onto the first person in line and using a coat or belt or whatever we had we could lower him to a ledge: if he made it, he could help the second person find a foothold and make their way down.

I have no idea the mathematical odds, but it had to be less than one in a thousand. Of all the times God saved this utterly stupid human, getting off that cliff was utterly miraculous. Time after time we defied certain death but jumped anyway. When we made it back down, we stood looking at where we had been and could not fathom how we had done it.

Even writing this, I am amazed that God got us out of that situation. I should be dead many times over, yet God must have decided at creation, He was going to save four idiots from themselves.

That incident branded deep in my soul the fear of regret. I never wanted to feel the agony of regret. I never wanted to feel what I felt on that cliff face, ever again. The terror of regret, because of a self-inflicted decision, was something I avoided for the rest of my life.

Clear Lake

After we set up camp and had the fire going, it became dark and we were all physically exhausted. The rain had been relentless and we had been in clouds all day. It was miserable. We got in our tents and fell fast asleep. In the night it stopped raining and when the morning light came it was actually sunlight. Warm streaks of light through the trees woke me up. I got up and made my way out to start the fire. Everyone else was still asleep.

I went to find firewood and discovered something that was so beautiful, that unless you have experienced it you won't fully appreciate it. I found myself looking over a cliff. About four or five hundred feet below me were the clouds. They were brilliant white and looked so solid it felt like I could simply step out and walk on them. They stretched out to the horizon. The only thing above the clouds was the majestic Mt. Rainier. Its mass is jaw-dropping. It makes you feel as though you are insignificantly tiny. I just stood there in utter quiet. No sound at all. Not a breath of wind. I was by myself.

It was as though God was saying "Good morning, Perry, I made this just for you this morning". "No other human eyes are seeing what you are seeing right now." I stood there for a long time not wanting to make a sound. Even the thought of speaking would have tarnished the holy presence and purity of that moment. I had never experienced such private tranquility. I felt the presence of Him with me.

I turned around and was stunned to see an alpine lake just behind me. The water was so still it acted like a mirror. I could see the reflection of the trees as clear as if it had been glass. God taught me that morning a lesson I have used all my life.

It was as if He asked me "What do you see in the lake?" "I see trees," I answered. Then God spoke to my heart, what you see is only the reflection of the environment around the lake. That is not the lake; the lake is thousands of cubic feet of water below the surface. All the life in this lake is below the surface. All the fish, plants, and nutrients are found below the reflection. The reflection is on top. It has no depth. In fact, it is not the lake at all, just the mirror of its surroundings. The only way to discover the hidden treasures of a lake is to dive below the surface. Then God gave me insight into what he was teaching me.

He taught me that people are a lot like that lake. They are simply a reflection of the environment around them. If you look at the outward appearance, which is only the surface, you will miss the person entirely. The real person is deep below the façade.

You may see their stormy waves, and let them intimidate you. But if you take the time to dive in, you will find the real person. Their dreams, hopes, fears, and loves. You can never get to know someone unless you are willing to go deeper and dive in.

He taught me something else. A lake can form ice on the surface. A cold arctic blast across the surface can produce a thin layer of ice. Over time the ice can thicken. People are the same.

Criticism is like an arctic blast to people. They will begin to harden. A protective layer of ice begins to form. With years of abuse and criticism, sometimes the ice becomes extremely thick. You will come across people like this in life. They may have been hurt so many times, that to protect themselves, they may come across as cold and harsh. The only way to melt ice is through time and warmth.

God taught me a lot about people as I stood there by that alpine lake. He was teaching me to be genuine, warm, and gentle.

The Slough

On one of the outings with the teen group, we came across an old slough. A slough is a manmade waterway. Also known as a water channel. It had a small amount of water running through it. I was in an adventurous mood, so I climbed in. The bottom was covered in a moss-like substance. It was extremely slick and I immediately slipped and fell. I was laughing, and it looked fun, so the rest of the kids jumped in, and we were all slipping and sliding and having a ball.

We were having so much fun that we hadn't noticed that we were actually slipping and sliding quite a way down the slough.

Then it occurred to us.... it was impossible to get out! The sides were now some ten feet high. In addition, going back up the slough was out of the question, it was far too slick. A small twinge of panic began in my mind. How were we going to get out? I'm not sure any of the teens were aware of what was becoming painfully obvious to me. We were in a potentially dangerous situation.

We continued to slide further and further down the slough. I was now almost desperate to get to my feet, but it was impossible. We were beginning to pick up speed. Now everyone was on the seat of their pants and we were sliding faster and faster. We were utterly at the mercy of the slough. It became quiet as it began to sink in. We were helpless. The further we traveled the more speed we picked up.

The slough turned back and forth, so you couldn't see what was coming. Then to everyone's horror, we came around a bend and you could see the slough ended. We could see nothing but the sky. We were going over. My mind raced! How large is the drop? Could we survive? What was on the bottom? I could picture boulders. I knew we were all going to be seriously injured, perhaps even killed. There wasn't a thing we could do but shoot out the end. The girls started screaming and we braced for our fate.

They started to fly out the end, one by one, and then my turn came and I too became airborne. The drop was about 50 to 60 feet, but thanks be to God, it was into a lake. Again, God had saved my life. Once again, I should have been killed or crippled for life, and yet we were all ok. I used that as a life lesson.

Life offers lots of things that at first are a blast and fun. Drinking, Drugs, Sex, Gambling, Porn.... you name it. For a brief season, it's fun, then before you realize it, you're hooked. You find your life is racing out of control. Unfortunately for many the end of the Slew is an overdose, car accident, Aids, or jail. Satan is real and he knows how to make it look fun, but in the end, sin always leads to disaster.

The Fence

After returning that fall to NNC, Rob McCaully, one of the young men from the Enumclaw youth group called. The phone call blew my mind. He told me the following story.

The Enumclaw High School was having its regular election speeches, at assembly, for class officers. A popular young man who was running for school president stepped up to the microphone.

He said something to this effect; "This summer someone I never met, taught me something, that not only changed my life but my eternity. One afternoon I was sitting behind our backyard fence. A youth pastor brought his youth group to the park and they all gathered near my backyard. They couldn't see me but I could hear them.

The youth pastor was telling them about the dash! What is the Dash? On a tombstone is the date you are born and the date you die, and in between is a dash. That dash represents our entire lives on earth. He said, for most humans, that will be the only memory of their existence. Yet the God of the universe never intended for us, to be a simple dash.

He went on to tell them, how God set in motion, a plan to turn our dash into an eternal line. I was fascinated by what he was saying, so I stayed hidden behind our backyard fence and listened. Life is a quest, and the quest is to discover how to transform that dash into an eternal line. No other accomplishment, no other purpose in life, no matter how noble or spectacular, is as vital as discovering the answer to that quest.

Some people complain that life is meaningless. They ask: What's the point? There has got to be more! Is life just existing, and then you die? There has got to be more!

God set up life as a great treasure hunt. Instead of a hidden map, he gave the answers to the quest in the Bible. He talked about how we are born sinners, utterly imperfect. All creation knows we are sinners, the last to come to the party is us. That's a problem, because the only way into eternity, is absolute perfection.

So, the quest is to discover how to become absolutely perfect in God's sight! The answer to the quest is amazingly simple. Someone absolutely perfect must die in our place. Jesus, God's son was that perfect someone. We, humans, have no chance whatsoever of being good enough. No matter how good we are, we can never attain perfection! At the time of their death, if anyone is trusting in their own goodness, they lose. They will discover that they weren't good enough.

Yet when we come to realize that fact, God already has the answer. He **came** as the answer! He completed the remedy. God died in our place. He paid the price for our imperfection. That's the answer to the quest…because Jesus Christ was perfect, and without sin. All we need to do is accept His Gift of death on the cross in our place.

That entire story is told in the bible. That Youth pastor, challenged them to read the book and ask the hard questions. That caught my attention. Instead of expecting them to blindly accept his story, this youth pastor was actually encouraging them to challenge everything he was saying.

I always thought churches didn't want you to ask questions, and to buy everything they were selling. Yet this youth pastor was not only giving them permission but challenging them to ask the hard questions.

Then the youth pastor ended his challenge by making this statement. "Nowhere in the Bible is Heaven or eternal life ever called a reward! It is ALWAYS called a GIFT!"

So that day I went into the house and actually read the New Testament. Sure enough, it's as simple as he explained. The Bible says 'it is by grace you have been saved, through faith, not by good works, so that no one can boast; it is a gift of God.' All on my own I accepted Jesus' gift. I became a Christian and changed my dash into an eternal line. I became an eternal being. I no longer feared death. Death is simply a doorway into a different existence."

Rob McCaully said: Perry, that youth pastor was you! Remember when you took us to the park and told us about the Quest and the Dash?

That phone call made my day. Here is another example of a Divine appointment in my life. Proverbs says. "In his heart, a man plans his course, but the Lord determines his footsteps." God put me in the right place, at the right time, to save a soul, I would never meet…., at least not on this side of life's doorway.

I loved working with young people. The teen years are full of discovery. I wanted to work in youth ministry, so when I returned to NNC that fall, I began applying for youth pastor positions.

Falling Asleep

I got a youth pastor position at Deer Flat Free Methodist church. I had some of the most challenging experiences in life in that church.

At the end of the fall term, I was exhausted. I had spent weeks leading up to Finals, studying into the early hours of the morning. The last Sunday before Finals I was sitting up front at church. I normally read scripture or made announcements, so I sat up on the platform looking out at the congregation.

We didn't sit on chairs; they were more like benches. I would sit on one bench and the assistant pastor sat on the other. The pastor would preach from the pulpit which was in the middle. He would be facing the congregation and could not see what was going on behind him.

On this particular Sunday, the pastor was going long, and I was struggling to keep my eyes open. I closed my eyes and must have fallen asleep. I started to tip, fell onto the bench, and instantly bounced back up eyes wide open. The congregation roared with laughter. The pastor glanced back at me, but I was already sitting there with an innocent look on my face. This caused the congregation to laugh even harder.

With a puzzled look on his face, the pastor tried to continue, but as he turned around to face the congregation, I looked out and gave the crowd a mischievous grin and that set them off. I knew I had them in the palm of my hand. I looked back toward the pastor and started shaking my head in agreement as if I was following his every word. This set them off into another frenzied roar of laughter. The pastor knew something was up behind his back, but every time he turned around; I had an innocent

"What?" look on my face. The pastor glanced over to the assistant pastor and he just shrugged his shoulder as if to say "Don't look at me, I have no clue what's going on!"

After the service that morning, people came up to me and said they had been watching me for quite a while, nodding my head and were guessing with others how long before I fell asleep.

Shotgun Shooting

One of the challenges of youth ministry is dealing with a level of stupidity that is sometimes hard to fathom. Teenagers are without a doubt, some of the most dangerous creatures on the planet. Case in point:

I get a call late one night. One of our teens has been shot and several other teens in our youth group are missing. The next morning the rest of the story comes out. All three of the kids involved were part of our youth group, and their parents were also actively a part of the church.

We had a pair of brothers, that were a real challenge. Even though they attended, they were not at all interested in the Christian way of life. I was not surprised when I found out the whole story.

The night before, the brothers were home with their good friend. It was just the three boys left alone at the house, while both sets of parents went out to dinner. The two brothers decide to scare their friend with a shotgun. They took the shotgun shell and emptied it of pellets. They filled the shell with ketchup and hatched a plan to scare their buddy.

They planned to goad their friend into a fake argument, then act so angry that they would shoot him with the ketchup-filled bullet. He would think he was actually shot and they would have their laugh at his expense.

They get into an argument and one of the brothers grabs the shotgun and the other kid takes off running down the hall when "BOOM" the shotgun goes off. He falls to the floor screaming in agony. The two brothers are laughing in hysterics, while the kid on the floor is screaming that they shot his leg off.

What the brothers didn't know, was that in a shotgun shell, there is a piece of hardened plastic or compressed paper, called a wad. That piece of wad is solid like a bullet. Especially at point-blank range. They had shot him square in the buttocks. It had blown off his buttock's cheek. Luckily, they did not shoot him in the back or they could have killed him.

The kid was writhing in genuine pain. The "Wad" had totally torn through his blue jeans and he was bleeding all over the hallway floor. The brothers meanwhile, are unaware of what they had done and are in the living room mocking him, telling him it's only ketchup.

After a few minutes, they finally come down the hallway and see the pool of actual blood. They panic and run out of the house, thinking they may have killed their friend.

The young victim crawls to a phone and calls for help. When the emergency personnel arrived, they find a bloody mess. The victim is taken to the emergency room and the police wait at the house for the parents to return.

The parents don't find out about this till they drive into their home and see the police, and fire truck lights. The other two boys are nowhere to be found. The parents were understandably confused as to why the brothers, would shoot their best friend. I can only imagine the strained conversation between the parents that night.

It isn't until the next morning, that the two boys finally come home on their own.

It all came to light when the brothers confessed their ill-conceived plan. They had spent a sleepless night hiding in the branches of a tree out in a nearby orchard.

The following Sunday all three of them were in our youth group class. They were all standing throughout the morning. The young victim stood because the wound would not allow him to sit. The two brothers found it hard to sit, for other reasons.

Knifed

Deer flat is a church set in a rural area outside Caldwell Idaho. During the summer the youth group looked forward to camp. This particular year I had an opportunity to take them to a camp in a more urban setting near Portland Oregon.

Some parents were a bit concerned that there might be some gang-related inner-city kids at the camp, which could be a recipe for trouble. Our kids were mostly from the farming community. I assured them that Christian camps were perfectly safe, and tried to assuage their fears, by personally guaranteeing, that I would keep an eye on things.

We arrived in Portland after a nearly eight-hour trip. We were still unloading the vans when one of our kids came running up to us and screamed that one of our boys "just" gotten stabbed. My first reaction was inner panic. As I was running to the scene, I felt sick to my stomach. I had guaranteed their safety and within ten minutes of arriving, one of the teens had been stabbed.

I ran into the cabin and blood was all over the floor. The young man was holding his arm and blood was running through his fingers. I grabbed a towel and wrapped the wound tightly. I was holding his arm above his head as other adults arrived. I was afraid he would bleed out, so I shouted for someone to "take us to the nearest hospital", we "didn't have time to wait for an ambulance."

We were rushed off to the emergency room. On the way, we asked what happened. Who had stabbed him? When he said, "John" (not his real name, so as to protect the idiot). I said John who? Your best friend? Why in the world would he stab you? I was incredulous.

He then told me what had happened. He had arrived without a short sleeve shirt. So, he asked "John" to take his knife and while he held the sleeve up, cut the sleeve off. So, our victim held the sleeve up in front of his own face and John started sawing back and forth towards him. When the knife burst through, it thrust into our victim. Luckily the knife sliced the arm and not directly into the chest.

I just sat there shaking my head. How do you explain to parents this level of stupidity? "Don't let them reproduce!"

David Sunquist

I was not only working as a full-time youth pastor, but I was also still attending college. God was still rebuilding me from the inside out. He was reparenting me constantly.

Every year, the college would have a special speaker at chapel. This particular year they brought in a guy I had never heard of, David Sunquist. I felt that God had sent him specifically to speak to me personally.

David hated his father as much as I loathed and despised Marie. He told of how God had miraculously come into his life and that after several years, God confronted him, on the hatred he harbored against his father. What deeply spoke to me, was the story of his alcoholic father.

His father abandoned the family and lived in a studio apartment on skid row. David spoke of how God had asked him to go down to the ghettos and retrieve his dad. When David finally went, it was worse than he had expected. He found his dad, passed out in filth and squaller, surrounded by empty bottles. David cleaned his father up and over time, helped his father sober up.

David explained that the hatred he harbored for his father had stunted his growth with God. Yet when he obeyed God and humbled himself, the blackness in his soul had been healed.

After Chapel, I waited to talk with David. I was just one of the many students to talk with him that day. I shared that I had been beaten, bones broken, and bullied all my life by my mother, and that I carried a level of hatred for her that was justified. I explained that forgiving her would be one of the largest miscarriages of justice of all time. I had sworn I would never see them again, and for four years I had stayed the course.

The idea of humbling myself, and telling her I forgave her, was more than I could stomach. I could just see the smug look on her face, and I could only imagine the caustic mocking, she would inflict back. She didn't deserve it, and I refused to do it. David listened and encouraged me to work on forgiveness.

All through that next school year, I just couldn't seem to grow in my love for God. I felt that I was at a roadblock, in my Christian walk. My prayers seemed dry. I knew why, it was because I wouldn't even consider forgiving Marie. I was being disobedient. Yet, this was one time, God Himself, was being utterly unreasonable, period!

I was unwavering in my hatred! Forgive this witch? She didn't even want to acknowledge that I was her son! This is Ridiculous! The idea was absurd! I was NOT going to forgive her, not a vile woman who hated me. I reminded God as if he had forgotten; Don't you remember, she tried to kill me! No! No! A thousand times No! Absolutely NOT! I reasoned with myself, that God would just have to understand!

By the way, did I tell you I am strong-willed? Type A? Especially when I know I'm right!

A year later David Sunquist was back on campus and he walked up to me and called me by name. "Perry, have you forgiven your mom?"

I was shocked on several levels. First of all, how had he remembered my name? I had only spoken to him for a few minutes. Secondly, how had he remembered my story? There had been a whole line of students waiting to talk with him the year before. How had he recognized me?

I told him I had not and had no intention of doing so! He just smiled and told me "Perry the blackness in your soul, will rot you from the inside. Holding onto unforgiveness is like drinking poison yourself, and expecting the other person to die!"

As I lay on my bed that night, arguing with God for the umpteenth time about this issue, God seemed to ask me *"What is it you want me to do to Marie?"*

My mind started racing…. I'll tell you what I want you to do, KILL her? Better yet, torture her! Crush her to death and let her die slowly, and then rot in hell for eternity. My mind went places I'm ashamed to admit. Yet after I had exhausted myself in extracurricular imagination, God said *"Remember though…. Whatever I do to her, whatever measure you use against her, I will do to you as well."*

Suddenly God brought to my mind something Jesus taught; "…in the same way you judge others, you will be judged, and with the measure you use, it will be measured to you." (Matthew 7:1)

God asked me again, *"What do you really want Me to do to her? Just remember I'll do the same to you."*

Then God seemed to give me a number of insights. I pictured myself sitting on the throne of my own castle. God reminded me that I had lowered the drawbridge, and invited Him into my life. I had invited the wisdom of the universe into my castle but had relegated Him to an advisory role.

God seemed to ask me: *"Would you invite the greatest artists Michelangelo or Vincent Van Gogh into your house to show them how you can paint by numbers? Would you invite the master composers Beethoven or Mozart into your home to show them how to play Chop Stix? Would you invite the Surgeon General of the United States Into your home to show him how you can put on a Band-Aid? How insulting?! Why then, would you invite the all-knowing God into your presence and relegate Him, to sitting in the corner?*

I had invited Him to be my King but was treating Him as an advisor. He had asked me to forgive Marie, as he had forgiven me, but I wouldn't obey Him. In God's hand was a large key ring, with many keys. Each key opened a room in my life. He handed me a key and told me to; *"Go down and unlock the dungeon. Let the prisoners go, this is my house now and I don't have prisoners. In My home, we don't harbor unforgiveness. Go release the prisoners, and forgive them."*

My King was giving me a command. I knew that I was at a crossroads. If He were truly my King, I had to show it by obedience. I reached out and took the key of forgiveness and went down and unlocked the door that held the hatred I had for Marie. I gestured with my hand and told her she was free to go. Then in my mind, I stood and watched her walk up the stairs and out the door, and across the drawbridge. She was gone!

I turned and looked into the dungeon cell of my imagination, and suddenly where there had been ugly blackness, there was a pure clean brightness. My heart felt a level of joy, I had never felt before. It was like my heart felt so lite, that I could float.

Again, God brought a scripture to my mind. "Not everyone who says to Me, 'Lord, Lord,' (which is the word for King) will enter the Kingdom of Heaven, but only he who does my will." Then I heard God's voice, *"Now go back home and tell her personally, you have forgiven her!"*

I got in my car, after over five years, and headed to Oregon. I drove up to the house and walked to the door. My stomach was churning. I knocked on the door and waited. I had already memorized what I was going to say. My thought was, I will say it and leave. (God knew, even though I was planning on going through the motions, my heart wasn't really in it,) Finally, the door opened and Marie was standing at the door. All the gut-wrenching memories came rushing back in an instant. Just seeing her face made me tense up.

Before I could say anything, Marie calls out "Bud, it's Perry!" It was in an excited tone, almost of delight. That caught me off guard. The last time I remember seeing her was when she was encouraging Bud to put me to death, "…but be merciful and don't make him suffer."

I looked at her and said with a firm and controlled voice. As you already know I have become a Christian. I wanted you to know, I am not here to condone anything you have done to me, but I AM here to tell you, I forgive you completely.

I braced myself for the caustic mocking, but instead, she began to tear up. In a broken voice, she asked me to come in, and Bud was hollering from the EZ chair, "Invite him in!" I was not prepared for this. This was awkward and intensely unnerving, but I found myself walking into the house.

I felt that my Heavenly Father was asking: *"Now share all the love and healing I have brought into your life."* Over the next few hours, I shared with them how God had reparented me. I admitted my struggle with hatred for all the cruel things they had done but had completely and honestly forgiven them in my heart. I shared how God had called me into ministry. The longer we talked the more I could see God was up to something. More on that later.

I drove back to Idaho a changed man. All the anger and hatred was gone. I had obeyed God. I had done the right thing, not because I felt like it, but because my King had asked me to. From that day on, I began to pray for both my parents. They were broken and dysfunctional. They needed the healing that God had given me.

My relationship with God was healthy again, and I began to grow spiritually again. God could see that I was healthy enough for a new chapter in my life.

Wee Wittle Wog

I'm a tall guy, and yet I met this tiny little girl in college. As it turned out she would play a very large part in my maturity, as a Christian, as a man, and as a pastor. Her name was Jill Benefield, and my pet name for this small little dynamo was the Wee Wittle Wog or Wee Wittle One.

To say that we came from different worlds would be an understatement. Her parents were very wealthy. Jill came from a high-society family. Her family was from the other side of the tracks from the "trailer court world" I came from. Dating me was a cultural shock for Jill. Yet we became the best of friends.

The struggle was with her parents. They viewed me as a poor, backward redneck. They had a visceral hatred of "my kind!" They detested "Trailer trash!" This was especially true of Jill's mother, who couldn't stand me and where I had come from.

When Jill's mother found out that I was going to be a pastor, she informed both of us, that we must break off any relationship, immediately. She scolded Jill right there in front of me. "You have been raised with privilege; this boy is nothing more than trailer trash. What is worse, as a pastor, he will drag you down into the abject poverty he is used to! You will learn to hate him."

I had seen movies of such women, but always thought they were something Hollywood created. This woman was yelling at her daughter, for being naive and ridiculous, right in front of me. As if I didn't exist. In her mother's mind, I was a none entity. It was awkward to the extreme, and of course, Jill was mortified. Jill tried to defend me, but her mother wouldn't hear of it. A rift formed between Jill and her mother. Which of course I was blamed for. I was accused by her mother of dividing the family, and wrecking Jill's life.

Level of Hatred

Over the several years we dated, Jill tried to reason with her parents, and assured me, that when we were married, it would all change, and they would love me as part of the family.

That changed the day we announced our engagement. We arrived at their house, and when we walked in, Jill's mother and grandmother were waiting to end our relationship, once and for all. As soon as we entered, they began the verbal onslaught. It got so ugly, they began screaming and threats were made. Finally, in a fit of rage, her mother ran up to me, and with all her might started slapping and punching me, screaming for me to get out of her house and never come back.

I walked out in a state of shock. Jill and I drove away and she apologized and admitted she was utterly embarrassed. She was dumbfounded at the level of hated her mother had stooped to.

In an effort to get Jill to reconsider, her parents threatened to disinherit her.

Her parents eventually moved to Houston Texas. Just prior to the planned wedding, Jill wanted to fly down, and try to heal the rift between her and her parents. Jill assumed, that if the voice of reason were used, she could win them over. Her thoughts were; that if they could just spend some time with us, they would come to realize that they were wrong about us. Up to this time, they refused to spend any time with us.

We were told they would receive our visit. We assumed that perhaps they were finally accepting the fact we were getting married.

Oh, but they had other plans!

When we arrived at their mansion in Texas, we were ushered into a room and seated. We waited for her mother and father to arrive. When the two of them came in, they sat down. The greeting was cold and stark. I could tell this was not going to go well. They immediately launched into a diatribe, explaining why they would never bless such a marriage.

We listened politely, trying to earn the right to be heard. But in the end, we were told in no uncertain terms, that they would never accept me as part of the family. Her father told Jill that they would not attend the wedding and that he would not lead her down the aisle. He insisted that "The plans for the upcoming marriage must stop immediately! This foolishness had gone far enough!"

Their stance had not changed. We had hoped for the best, but half expected this, so we had agreed beforehand not to react.

We stood and politely excused ourselves. As we were leaving the room, we were told to dress for dinner, we would be dining out. We held our tongues waiting for our opportunity, perhaps at dinner.

We were taken to a very high-end French restaurant. If they were trying to make me feel uncomfortable, they were succeeding. This place was something out of a French movie. Everything was in French. I had no idea what was on the menu. I believe that was the intent.

Jill and her family could read and understand all that was going on. Jill's mother knowing full well I couldn't read French, insisted she would have to "help" the poor boy out. She ordered me a shrimp cocktail, and I quickly informed her I didn't drink. They all burst out laughing including Jill. She informed me that it was an appetizer, served in a cocktail glass. When it came, Jill's mother started mocking me, because I was using the wrong fork to eat the Shrimp cocktail. (They had 5 different forks at this restaurant). You can only imagine the scolding her mother gave me.

The Shrimp cocktail was served in a cocktail glass, over fresh lettuce. I had just assumed the lettuce was to be eaten. Her mother was watching me and as soon as I had taken a bite of the lettuce, she brought it to everyone's attention, that "the poor fool had eaten the garnish." I knew then that dinner had been set up. She was relishing the opportunity to mock my lack of High social graces.

I finally leaned over to Jill and asked her to order for me. When the Maître D arrived, her mother jumped in and mockingly told him, she would have to order Filet mignon for the poor boy, who had never been to a nice place before. I of course had heard of Filet mignon but didn't know what it was. Jill pointed it out on the menu and told me it was steak. I had always thought it was fish, but I dared not say anything. All I could do was stare at the price. Although the words were in French, the prices were American. To this day, that is still the highest-priced steak I have ever eaten.

The point of the meal was to show Jill that we were from different worlds. Jill already knew that, yet she also knew the authentic man she was marrying, and the shallowness of her own parents.

We tried in vain to talk to her parents, but they were on a mission, and they had no intention of listening to anything we had to say. We flew back to Idaho; the trip was a complete failure.

Over the two years, we had dated, God had used Jill to refine my rough edges. It proved invaluable in the ministry. She taught me manners and etiquette. She taught me to see the rich, as just normal flawed people, and not to place them on a pedestal. I will be forever grateful for those lessons in life. In time I felt comfortable with the poorest of the poor, to the richest in the world.... all thanks to the wonderful relationship with Jill. God used those two years to prepare me for all forms of ministry. It also prepared me for the woman I would eventually spend the rest of my life with. But it wasn't to be Jill. More on that later.

Where's Waldo?

There is a tradition in the Treasure Valley which has been going on for over 80 years. On top of Lizard Butte there is a large white cross, and on Easter Morning, folks from all over, come to celebrate a sunrise service. The local pastors lead the multidenominational service. The highlight of the service was of course the reading of the resurrection story from the bible.

The problem is that Easter falls near April first and the weather can still be winter in Idaho. It can be extremely cold and miserable. Yet hundreds of students from the nearby colleges, and the entire community, do brave the elements to attend. I had attended it for a number of years myself. Every year we made the pilgrimage. We would climb up the hill to sit on the frozen ground. We would sit in ice-cold conditions, waiting till the sun came up.

Every year a cheer would erupt just as the sun peaked over the horizon and the services started. Immediately one of the honored pastors in the Treasure Valley would begin reading the resurrection story.

This particular year it was bitterly cold. It was because of this very reason, that after several years of attendance, I decided not to go.

For several days before Easter Sunday, my roommates and friends begged me to go. I was adamant, "I am NOT going! Not this year! I don't enjoy freezing"

Even my fiancé Jill kept hounding me to go. Early Easter morning my roommates got up and again begged me to go.

"NO, I insisted!"

But they were relentless… "You are already awake, come on just one more time?"

Finally, I relented, with a less than stellar attitude.

We drove over to the girls' dorms and picked up our girlfriends and headed out to the mountain.

When we arrived, it was brutally cold, but this time I had come prepared, with blankets and warm clothes. We made our way up the mountain, and in the dark, finally found a place to sit. It was freezing cold. I sat under my blanket brooding my decision! How had they talked me out of a warm bed?

We watched as the sky turned light and the sun began to peek above the horizon. A cheer went up from the crowd. Finally, I thought, "let's get this over with. This is torturous. I hate cold!"

Just my luck, this year, there was some glitch, and the service did not start at sunrise! I was so angry with myself for not sticking to my guns. I stuck my head under the blanket again, for another 20 minutes, waiting for the service to start. People were beginning to grumble all around us. Finally, I couldn't stand it any longer, furious that they were delaying the service, I told the group, I would go down and find out why the service was delayed.

When I got down to the makeshift stage, I curtly asked what the holdup was, and suddenly a cheer went up and someone on the stage yelled out "HE'S HERE, let's get started!" One of the organizers tersely scolded me "Where in the world have you been?"

"What are you talking about?" I asked.

She snapped back, "We've all been waiting for YOU!"

They handed me a bulletin. There was my name at the very top: Scripture reading of the resurrection…. Pastor Perry Arbogast, youth pastor of the Deer Flat Free Methodist church!

Utterly confused I asked someone to lend me a bible because I hadn't brought one. Now everyone was glaring at me as if to say "What planet are you from?" They were genuinely upset with me, but I was still stunned to see my name in the bulletin. No one had approached me! No one had asked me if I would be willing to do this. No one had ever talked to me about this. I hadn't even planned on being there that morning.

I didn't have time to explain this, and I didn't want to make a bigger scene, so I humbly apologized, stepped to the mic, and read the resurrection story.

Later that morning when I arrived at church for our services at Deer Flat Free Methodist, I was approached by one of the ladies who helped organize the sunrise event. She was extremely apologetic. "Perry I am so sorry, the committee chose you to be the scripture reader this year, and I told the committee you would be more than willing to do it. The committee tasked me with informing you. I was so sure you would do it, to me it was a foregone conclusion. I was so confident, I simply put it out of my mind, and didn't worry about it. The problem is, I forgot to tell you. I am so embarrassed. It was my responsibility to tell you, and I completely forgot. Thank you for being so gracious this morning, and not causing a scene. After the sunrise service, I confessed to the team what I had done, so they are not angry with you anymore. I totally blew it; can you ever forgive me?"

I did of course, but I was also thankful that my roommates insisted I go!

Senator's Dog

Senator Simms of Idaho and his family attended our church. His daughter was in my youth group. They lived just a few miles from the Church.

One day during the summer months, I was helping a farmer in our congregation, driving a silage truck for him. Silage is harvested with a giant combine, which cuts the corn stalks and shoots it into a large truck. This silage is then dumped into large piles, and fed to the cattle.

Several college students, from our church, were making a little extra money, driving those big silage trucks during the harvest, and I joined them.

I was following another truck down the highway when out of the corner of my eye, I saw a big dog come racing out to chase the truck in front of me. I slammed on the brakes but the dog went under my truck and was killed instantly. When I came to a stop, I ran back to drag the dog off the highway. As I walked back to the truck, I felt a duty to notify the owners, if I could locate them.

I drove up the long dirt drive to the nearest house and was stunned to see who came out to greet me. It was Mrs. Simms! I asked her if they owned a big yellow dog.

It was then that I realized, that the worst part of the job for law enforcement, has to be notifying the family of a death. It was a terrible gut-wrenching ordeal, especially when I had to take them to see their dead dog. I know intellectually it was NOT my fault, but I still felt guilty. I love animals and grieved for them, and with them.

They were gracious of course, but it was a horrible day all the same. Of all the dogs to run over it had to be the senator's dog. That wasn't the only horrible thing that happened that summer. Several weeks earlier, I had really messed up.

Brain Lock

One of the delights in ministry is when someone in your sphere of influence, is inspired to serve in ministry. This is especially humbling when they have a servant's heart and choose the selfless and difficult task, of serving in a third-world country. It can be very difficult and even dangerous.

One of the young men in our youth group felt that calling and challenge. I was extremely proud of this young man's character.

On the day of his departure, I had asked for the privilege of buying him lunch and praying for his safe trip.

I put the date on my desk calendar and grew more excited as the day approached. The week he was to fly out, we were in the middle of Vacation Bible School. Several hundred kids, came from all over, to participate in exciting activities, every day for two weeks. Culminating is a grand showcase of their accomplishments and creations.

On the Sunday before his departure, I touched base with "Mark" (not his real name) and reiterated my plan to take him to lunch that Wednesday before he flew overseas.

That Wednesday morning the pastor asked me to prepare the fellowship hall for evening services. So, after the VBS activities, I was responsible to tear down the tables and stack the chairs. He insisted that it be done before I left for lunch. Of course, I told him I would do it, no problem.

I got into the VBS schedule for the rest of the morning, and I had lots of responsibilities. The place was a madhouse of activity. The chaos of fun was everywhere. It was a zoo!

The last twenty minutes was chapel, and then just like school, the kids all rush out to a sea of cars and moms. On this particular Wednesday at around 10 minutes till the end of Chapel and lunch, I was greeted by my fiancée Jill and her friend. This was a really unexpected shocker. She had gotten off work and driven all the way out to the church, to surprise me. I was thrilled. They came to take me to lunch, and I was so taken aback at seeing her, all I could think about was the pastor's request to get the tables put up before I left. They were on a tight schedule to make it back to work, so I asked some others to help us.

When I caught sight of "MARK" my only thought was my good fortune because I knew he had a servant's heart and would be delighted to help, which of course he agreed to do without a moment's hesitation.

So, I quickly enlisted a few others, and off I ran with the girls for a delightful lunch.

When I got back to the office, I was exhausted, so I sat back in my chair and began planning in my head the agenda for the afternoon. I glanced at the calendar on my desk and saw Marks name. My first thought was, that's funny, I wonder why he didn't show up. Then like a ton of bricks smashing on my head, it hit me! He **HAD** come, and I had completely **forgotten!** Worse yet, I had **put him to WORK!** It was another time in my life I wished I could have pushed rewind.

I called his home and his mom answered. I asked if Mark was there?" She said, "No," that he had gone to the airport and was on his way." She scolded me, and said he mentioned that he had shown up at the church for lunch, but that I put him to work, and then I disappeared. I was utterly devastated. He showed up expecting to be honored with lunch, and I had put him to work, then ducked out.

We didn't have cell phones in those days, so I jumped in my car and raced towards the airport. I was almost at the airport when my front tire blew out. I raced to change the tire, but it was too late, I had missed his departure. I had to live with the horrific guilt for the rest of the summer.

Ever since that day, I have given grace, when people miss their appointments with me. I will never have room to point a finger at anyone, after what I have done.

The day Mark returned, I drove over and apologized for the hurt I had caused.

Nicki

I have experienced many heart-wrenching moments in my walk with God. One of the most profound was Nicki.

My fiancée Jill had a brother about my age, Kab Benefield! Kab was a youth pastor in another state. He had developed a youth Choir, and they were traveling around to churches and performing. They were on their way to Deer Flat, where I was the youth pastor.

Kab was driving a pickup and pulling a trailer with all the sound equipment. Following him, was the bus full of kids from the youth choir. In the front seat of the bus was Nicki's mother, who was an adult chaperone. Nicki was her eight-year-old daughter.

Traveling down the freeway, the pickup began to jackknife and flipped. Nicki's mother watched in horror as the pickup rolled and flipped off the freeway. Eventually, it came to rest on its roof. The contents of the trailer were scattered across the lanes of traffic.

The bus stopped and everyone rushed off the bus to help. Nicki's mother, of course, ran to find her only daughter. They pulled Kab out, and he was still alive, but no one could find Nicki. It was night and everyone spread out with flashlights running up and down the freeway, looking for her body. She had been thrown out of the truck as it rolled.

By this time, truck drivers had also begun to help in the search for the little body. She was nowhere to be found. They doubled their effort and searched the brush alongside the freeway. Still no Nicki!

Finally, one of the truck drivers suggested, that all the men help him to roll the truck over; perhaps her body was crushed under the wreckage. When they did, they found her dead body lying under the cab of the pickup. She had been thrown from the pickup and the truck had rolled over the top of her. She had no heartbeat. They tried CPR but to no avail.

Everyone was in a state of shock. Kids were openly sobbing; Nicki's mother was understandably crying out to God. Everyone began to pray. Eventually, the ambulance arrived and they loaded Nicki's tiny lifeless body into the ambulance along with Kab. They rushed them to the nearest hospital.

On the way, one of the paramedics who was still performing CPR according to protocol thought he detected a faint heartbeat. Sure, enough her heart had started beating.

At the small hospital, they had no trauma unit. So, they ordered Life Flight to fly her to a larger hospital. As Life flight was getting ready, the Doctors feverishly worked to keep Nicki's heart beating.

The x-rays showed the full extent of her injuries. Her brain was so badly crushed that it hemorrhaged. She had such badly broken ribs that one rib had punctured her tiny heart. One of her lungs had collapsed.

Nicki's mother was approached by the team of doctors and given the bad news. The message relayed to her was this: Your daughter has no chance of survival. By the time the life flight gets here, it will be too late. The only reason she is still alive is all the life support machines she is hooked to. Even if she would happen to live long enough for the plane to arrive, she is too badly broken to survive the flight itself. The turbulence alone will kill her. You need to say goodbye to your daughter.

At the same time, they are also tending to Kab. His injuries were not as life-threatening, but they were going to send him on a separate flight, after Nicki's trip.

Kab called Jill (his sister) and asked her to have everyone pray. I got a call late that night and began praying for a little girl I had never met. The word went out across the college campus; the churches in the treasure valley began to have prayer chains enlisted to pray. Everyone was praying for a little girl they didn't even know.

When the plane arrived at the small hospital, Nicki was still alive. So, they loaded her on the plane, and it took off.

Somewhere in that flight, God did something amazing. When the plane landed, they rushed the little girl into the trauma unit. Something unthinkable had happened.

The Doctors at the large city hospital called up the first hospital and delivered the shocking news. "Somehow you sent the wrong little girl," they insisted! "The girl who arrived on the plane is perfectly fine!" "We've done a thorough examination, and we find nothing wrong with this girl, we think it's possible, you inadvertently placed the wrong girl on the plane!"

That started a screaming match between the doctors. "That's impossible; we loaded her on the plane ourselves". The argument got so heated that later when the plane arrived back at the smaller hospital, to transport Kab to the big city hospital, several doctors, and Nicki's mother herself; went along with copies of the X-rays.

Kab told Jill and I personally, what happened next. The accusations and finger-pointing continued and tempers flew. As they wheeled him into the emergency room, He and Nicki's mom and all the doctors looked on as Nicki was jumping up and down on the bed, holding the hands of a nurse, squealing with childlike delight.

The doctors looked at both sets of X-rays. The ones from the first hospital clearly showed all the broken bones, punctured lungs and heart, and the oblong head with the crushed brain. Yet God had utterly healed her on that flight. When they landed, she was perfectly fine!

The second set of X-rays was just as clear. No injuries whatsoever.

To the logical, physician's mind, it was impossible. They would not accept what was right before them. God doesn't fit into their paradigm, so they fell back on a more logical rationale. Either it was a prank or a mistake. Yet to those of us who know there is a God, we who have seen God perform many miracles, it is simply an answered prayer.

Kab, and the youth choir, made their way to our church. I met Nicki later that week. I saw the miracle with my own eyes. One of the most profound healings I ever had the privilege to witness personally. I've seen many miracles since then, but none quite as amazing as Nicki's! Somewhere in the middle of a life flight, God healed every broken bone and gave a little girl back to her mother.

I am just one believer that has seen miracles like the healing of Nicki. I have seen many miracles since then. There are thousands of stories like these.

Unfortunately, there are charlatans on T.V. that stage "Healings" in order to fleece the gullible sheeple. This has caused a reasonable skepticism in thinking people. Yet there are legitimate miracles that happen every day, like Nicki's! It saddens me deeply to see these counterfeiters undermining these authentic miracles. The damage they are doing is incalculable!

I have seen true, legitimate, miracles. I have talked to doctors that can't explain these Devine healings. I have visited hospitals with non-Christian doctors who admit, what they have just experienced, leads them to believe there must be a God because they can't explain what just happened. One minute there is a broken bone, and the next it is perfectly healed. One minute there is a hole in the heart, and the next it is gone! One minute there is cancer throughout the body, a large mass, and then nothing! Gone! It defies logic, and yet it happened.

These counterfeiters and their sleight-of-hand magic tricks are undermining the legitimate miracles that God is doing.

I understand if the reader is skeptical. In some ways, it's admirable that you are not easily taken in. Authentic Christians are just as repulsed and disgusted with these simple-minded "sheeple", (Sheeple are naïve people who blindly follow without question.) that fall all over themselves, propping up the counterfeiters. Yet I encourage you to also leave room for real miracles. Please don't let the scammers, and con men, destroy your faith in these authentic miracles. I have seen so many genuine, real, and unexplainable miracles, that I can say with certainty that God answers prayers and performs miracles.

A few sex offenders don't make all men sex offenders. A few bad cops, don't make all law enforcement corrupt. A few mailroom shootings don't make all mailmen go postal. A few sexually depraved priests don't make all pastors deviates. A few counterfeiters don't make God's miracles any less real.

That summer I experienced Nicki's miracle, and I also experienced another life-changing event.

Flip of the Coin

Jill and I had been dating for two years, and we were within weeks of the wedding. We were in the process of finalizing the last arrangements for the wedding. She had her dress, and the rings purchased, and we were about to send the last of the announcements out.

I could tell that something was bothering Jill. It was not just the pre-wedding jitters. I asked her what was wrong. She shared that she had always dreamed that her dad would lead her down the Aisle. It would be the happiest celebration of her life. Instead, it was going to be a bittersweet day. She also made a statement that caught my attention. She was commenting on the ridiculous insistence of her mother, that we would end up pastoring some tiny church.

I told Jill, I didn't care what size of church God called me to, that every size church needs a shepherd.

Then Jill looked straight at me and said "I will not go to some Podunk little town in the middle of nowhere!" I knew in that instant, that Jill was not as committed to pastoral ministry, as a pastor's wife would need to be. She was having second thoughts. She was hearing the voice of her mother's warnings. Jill was wondering if indeed, she would regret living in poverty.

Jill was a devout Christian, but being in ministry, in the role of pastor's wife is intimidating to any woman. We were seeking God's will. We both came to the conclusion in those hours of discussion, that we needed to be 100% sure this was God's will for our life. We weren't being flippant or argumentative. Quite the opposite, we were seeking, with all the wisdom we had, to be sure we were doing the right thing. We genuinely loved each other, so much so, that we were looking for the best life for the other person.

We prayed that God would show us without a shadow of a doubt. We had also been studying a scripture that says "The lot is cast into the lap, but the outcome is in the Lord's hands." In other words, it might seem like chance, but even the flip of a coin is in God's hands. There are examples of men in the bible who put out a fleece, to determine God's will.

So that we might know fully and without question, we decided to Pray and ask God to let us know, with the flip of a coin. I will also tell you, that I have never made decisions in my life, by the flip of a coin. Yet that night alone with Jill, we both felt it was the right thing to do. We realized that if anyone in the world, ever found out that we were flipping a coin, we would be institutionalized.

That night though, we were as genuine and sincere as two Christians could be. We felt we were sitting in that room, with our loving Father at our side. We knew that He was with us. He could see the utter faith we had in Him, we trusted Him to make this decision for us. Both of us were determined to be in the center of His will. It was a sacred moment between the three of us. He made it clear beyond any shadow of a doubt, that we were not to merry.

We both left feeling relieved. We have remained friends. There were never any harsh feelings whatsoever. We were good for each other, for the season that God had us together. Yet in the end, He had chosen others to be our life's partners. We can see it clearly now in hindsight. The wife God chose for me, has been a better pastor's wife, than I have ever been a pastor. She was born to be a pastor's wife.

That Divine appointment would not come for a while though. So, for some time after we parted ways, I didn't date. I took some time to reflect on all that I had learned and grew closer to God.

Sawtooth Mountains

As a fellow youth pastor, I can tell you we youth pastors are always looking for exciting adventures to involve our teens in. When an opportunity came to take a team into the Sawtooth Mountain range on horseback, I jumped at it. An outfitter from Oregon contacted me and wondered if I would be interested in taking a number of young men into the wilderness for a week. He would provide the horses as pack animals. I found the idea very intriguing. All I had to do was sell the idea to others.

Being a youth pastor is not for the faint of heart. You are viewed by the congregation, as little more than an overgrown adolescent, yourself. Any time you have an idea, you have to sell, sell, sell, that idea to everyone. The pastor, the board, the treasurer, the kids themselves, and the hardest sell is the parents!

After the stabbing incident, my "Trust me…what could go wrong?" account, was at low ebb.

For several months, plans were put in place to take around 10 to 12 boys out into the wild to experience raw nature. We needed a van to transport them, but the church van was not available. I made a plea to the congregation. No one came forward. So, in desperation, I pleaded with a couple in our church to let us borrow their custom van.

This van was very nice. It was carpeted on the inside and a beautiful custom mural was painted on the outside. In the 70s and 80s it was the "in thing" to have an airbrushed scene painted on the Van….and very expensive. I finally talked them into letting us use it. To say they were hesitant would be an understatement. I don't remember all the promises I made, but I do remember telling them I would be extremely careful with it.

I knew it was their pride and joy, so I promised to keep it immaculate and wash it before we brought it back.

I also spent a considerable amount of time calming the parent's fears about taking their boys for a week into the wilderness. Yet in the end, I had convinced everyone that we could do this.

I also tried desperately to enlist men from the church to help and become chaperones. No takers. So, in the end, I was on my own. At the time I thought that the Outfitter and I could easily handle a dozen boys. As the time came to leave on the trip, I was relieved to find only one "problem" kid was going anyway.

The day finally came, and we loaded everyone into the van, and off we drove into the mountains. When we got into Idaho City, we filled up the vehicles with fuel, because this would be the last civilization we would see for a week. From that point on, it was dirt roads and no gas stations or services.

I had no idea where the Outfitter was taking us, but I trusted him and he knew the country well. We made a deal that because I was utterly lost, he would lead and I would follow. I told him that I would follow right behind him.

He took us deep into the Saw Tooth wilderness, in the heart of Idaho. We would travel miles on a dirt road, then turn onto another dirt road. A few more miles and another turn. I was utterly lost. What made it even more miserable was the thick choking dust. The boys complained about their breathing. At times I would have to slow down and back off, just to see the road. I was actually using the wipers to clear the layer of dirt that was accumulating on the windshield.

Unfortunately, the inside of the van was getting extremely dusty. This caused my stomach to tighten with anxiety. I would have to vacuum out the entire van before I could return it.

We finally made it to Atlanta, an old mining settlement long since abandoned. Atlanta was where the dirt road dead-ended. We were in the wilderness area, and motorized vehicles are prohibited from that point on. We would make the rest of the trip on foot.

We all unloaded our stuff and put it in the Manny packs. Manny packs are used a lot, by old prospectors on the backs of a mule. Manny packs are large canvas sacks that carry one large box on each side of the horse. We put the boxes inside the packs, then filled the boxes with our provisions for the upcoming week. We then secured the Manny packs onto the pack horses.

I locked the van and began the long and grueling climb up into the mountains.

As the evening approached, we made camp. We sat around the fire and ate campfire food. I was in heaven. The boys were having a blast. Everything was working out according to plan.

The next morning, I heard something outside the tent. As I waited for the sun to rise, I saw what was making all the racket. It was deer. A whole herd of deer were meandering around our camp. They were licking the salt off of the saddles. I stood perfectly still, next to a tree. They walked so close by me, that if I had wanted to, I could have reached out and swatted them. I was thrilled. I had never been so close to wild deer. I was the only one up, and I must have watched them for a 1/2 an hour or so.

Eventually, the boys began to stir in their tents and the deer scampered away. The rest of the day was spent hiking further in and further up. We finally arrived at Greylock Mountain which is over nine thousand feet. There were three lakes and we set up camp next to the largest.

The rest of the week was spent exploring the mountains and fishing. We had very little sleep. By the end of the week, we were exhausted, and I had a new appreciation for the pioneers. Everything is hard work.

On the last day, we were up at dawn and spent the morning packing up the tents and loading the horses. We began the long and arduous hike back to the trailhead. The trip up had taken two days because we hadn't gotten to Atlanta until the afternoon. The trip back started early and so we arrived back at the vehicles around midafternoon.

When we arrived, one look at the van told the story. Someone had broken into our vehicles and ransacked them. My heart sank. They had broken out one of the windows and taken everything including the spare tire, off the back of the van. I was barely able to think, I was so tired. I had not bathed in a week and the pack of us smelled like a gym locker. Our hair hadn't been combed and we hadn't shaved since we left. We looked as ragged as the old miners who used to live in this ghost town.

I talked to the Outfitter and guide and explained that I was utterly lost, and had no way of finding my way back to Idaho City or even the main highway. I didn't have a map. In those days no one had cell phones or GPS. I was completely reliant on following him. I told him the dust was so heavy, that I would be forced to follow at a distance. He would have to wait at every intersection until I caught up. I would hang back so I could see the road. When I caught up with him, we would give the thumbs up and he could continue till the next turn, and I would wait till the dust settled to continue. I made it abundantly clear that if he were going to turn at an intersection, he would have to wait till I arrived. I had no idea which turns to make.

In addition, I told him that if on the off chance, I had some mechanical issues and did not make it to the intersection, turn around and come back for me! I went a step further, I told him (and he agreed) to wait at Idaho City until we arrived. If I don't show up after the last turn, STAY THERE or come looking for me. I was adamant....and made myself crystal clear!!!!

I warned him, I was completely dependent on him to get me home because I had no idea where we were in the mountains.

I told him to start driving and I would wait 5 minutes for the dust to settle and then I would follow.

He drove off. I waited in the warm van and started nodding off. Some of the boys were so exhausted they fell sound asleep. I began driving but struggled to keep my eyes open. I was thoroughly and completely spent. I began to nod and realized the true danger of the situation. It would take hours to get back to the highway and I couldn't stay awake. I tried everything, opening the window, slapping myself, throwing water on my face, everything was futile. I had to stop. I had barely slept in seven days. I thought if I could only get 20 minutes of sleep, I would be fine.

One of the boys, who was a senior in high school, had been driving for a couple of years. He suggested he drive for a short time and give me time to cat nap. I didn't want to keep the Outfitter waiting up the road, so I decided to let him drive for a short way. I knew that it would have been far more dangerous to keep driving myself.

I fell asleep immediately! The next thing I knew, was a crashing sound, and a violent bouncing around. He had crashed into a bolder and flattened the passenger's side tire. I was sick.

I took the wheel off and waited for the Outfitter to come back and get me. I asked the young man that had been driving; "Had he seen any roads that turned off this road?" He told me that yes, there had been a number of side roads! I asked him; "How long I had been asleep?" He thought perhaps half an hour. So, I figured that the outfitter would be there within 30 minutes or so. The kid assured me that he had not taken any turn-offs. He said that Atlanta was straight back up the road behind us. I reasoned that even if the outfitter had taken a side road, he would simply drive back up to the trailhead, and not finding us, would simply drive down till he came to the van. So, I wasn't really worried that he couldn't find us.

Several hours passed by and no help came. Not even one car. We were in a very remote area. I was irritated at the Outfitter.... where was he? I had made it extremely clear to wait for me at the first turn off and if I didn't show up.... COME LOOK FOR ME!

By 6:00 pm he should have been there several hours before. So, I wondered if he had fallen asleep like me and had an accident.

Several more hours passed and at around 8:00 pm, an old prospector finally came rumbling down the road in a raggedy old station wagon. I waved him down and told him our situation, and that our spare tire had been stolen. I asked him if he could take me to Idaho City. I assured him, that there would be an outfitter waiting there for me.

My thought process was, if we saw the Outfitter coming up the road looking for us, I would just hop in his truck, and he would take me to get the flat fixed. Naturally, I figured at worst he would be waiting for me in Idaho City, as we agreed, or sitting beside the road broken down himself.

I knew I couldn't send two of the kids with this stranger, so the logical thing to do was go myself. After all, the group had plenty of water and food left over in the van. So, I gathered all the guys together and gave them my instructions. Stay by the van! Don't wander off! I would be back later that night. If the Outfitter shows up let him know I will wait for him in Idaho City.

The last thing I said was, "Stay with the van!"

(I should tell you that Idaho City is a one-horse town. One dilapidated old gas station. City it was **not**!)

I also thought that it would be wise to take the one "problem" kid with me. Two reasons: Keep him from causing trouble back at the van, and it would be smart to have two of us traveling together, rather than by myself. I still had the hope that the outfitter would be looking for me.

So, we put the tire in the back of the broken-down station wagon, and off we went. We hadn't gone 10 miles and BOOM one of the old codgers' tires blew out. I couldn't believe my bad fortune. This was turning into a nightmare. Little did I know it had only just begun! The true nightmare lay ahead.

I have often stated that true life is more unbelievable than any Hollywood movie script. I want the reader to know that absolutely everything I am about to reveal is true. It happened exactly as I am about to share it.

We found ourselves sitting on a dirt road, high in the Sawtooth Mountain range, with two vehicles with blown tires. The Van ten miles back up the road, and here with this old man and his junk mobile. Of course, he didn't have a spare tire either. So now we waited together.

I don't remember how long we waited, but I do remember how cold it got when it got dark. Then came the rain. Thunderstorms were battering the mountains. Lightening flashing and thunder.

Finally, another car came along, picked us all up, and took us as far as the highway. Then the driver told us to get out! He said "I'm sorry but I'm going the other way"

I implored him to take me to Idaho City. But he refused. I was so bewildered by his attitude I asked him, "You're kidding aren't you; you can't just leave us here by the side of the highway!" But he did, and we had to wait to hitch a ride from a passing car.

Now I understand how scary we must have looked, and I understand that it was nighttime, but seriously who stands by the road holding two flat tires? Come on people, it's obvious we need help.

Finally, someone came to our rescue. He dropped us off at the gas station and of course, it was closed. I looked around for the Outfitter. Where was he? Why hadn't he come looking for us? I used the payphone and called the church. The parents were all waiting at the church. They had expected our return earlier that day, so I assumed they would be glad to hear that we were all ok. They were not!

The pastor was angry because he had been taking the heat all day, from the anxious parents. He was miffed that we had damaged the van. He was ticked that the boys were all alone without adult supervision. They questioned every decision I had made that whole day. He was especially disgusted because it was Saturday night and the tire shops were closed on Sunday. The earliest they could get a tire and wheel would be Monday. So, he finally said, "Let me call a friend who lives up in that area, and see if he will come to pick you up?"

So, I waited in the frigid cold night with a teenager who himself was not a happy camper. It seemed that everyone was angry with me. "How much worse could it get" I remember thinking.

Finally, we saw headlights and up screeched an open-air dune buggy. That's right, a dune buggy with roll bars like you would see in a Disney movie. And worse yet.... the guy driving was drunk out of his mind! STAGGERING DRUNK! But most shocking was his attire.... A TUXEDO! The man was dressed to the hilt!

He yelled out in a drunken slur, "Yous two the ones what needs a ride? Pasther says come wiff me."

I was in a state of disbelief. Had I entered the twilight zone?

I was genuinely terrified to get in an open-air dune buggy, with a drunk. What if it rolled?

But I had no choice. Then he peeled out, screeching his tires, I feared I was going to die. Making me even more miserable, was the wind chill. I was already shaking with wet cold, now we were hurtling down the highway at a terrifying speed with ice-cold wind and rain slicing at my body.

The whole time he was trying to tell me why he was dressed up. Because of the wind, he was yelling at the top of his lungs, but I was only picking up some of the words. When we finally pull into his place it was packed with limousines and expensive cars. At first, I assume it was a wedding.

"Zisss iz my humble abode!" He stammered out.

I was shocked at the size of the mansion. It was beautiful. I had no idea there were estates up in the mountains of this magnitude. He was clearly a wealthy individual.

We climbed out and all I could think was how filthy I was, and how putrid we smelled. I begged him to slip us quietly into the back door, but he was drunk, and as we walked into the foyer, he is screaming out at the top of his lungs...MAKE WAY, MAKE WAY, WE HAVE SOME HUNGRY BOYS HERE!

I was horrified. Here I was, looking as bad as I had ever looked, in my entire life, amongst beautiful women wearing long flowing gowns and men in tuxedos'. A drunk dragging me to the front of a long line, waiting for food. All the time screaming out, in the most obnoxious voice. I have never in my life been that embarrassed.

It turns out that the historical society of Idaho, had discovered a time capsule in Idaho City, and this was the very night of its unveiling. There were dignitaries from the Idaho legislature, Judges, and the filthy rich. Anyone who was anyone was there that night, to see what must have looked like two homeless hippies being led by a lush. My only solace was, they would never recognize me, after a shower, shave, and change of clothes.

That night after we were in bed, I was so tired I couldn't sleep. I was anxious and scared. I was in anguish about the boys left back at the van. I was hurt that the pastor was so angry. I was fearful of the parent's anger. I was also upset about the condition of the van.... how could I ever face them?

The next morning was Sunday. I called the pastor and asked what the game plan was. I also asked if anyone had heard from the Outfitter, I feared for his safety. Only later would I find out that he had returned to Oregon without even so much as a glance in his mirror. Once he left the trailhead he headed back home, completely ignoring our agreement. He never gave us a second thought. He had his money and left us in the dust.... literally! I was heartbroken.

That Sunday afternoon, the parents of two of the boys, whom I had left back at the van, showed up at the Mansion. They were not amused.

The mom just started berating me, insulting me, scolding me, and yelling at me, she was relentless, and the only time she would stop, was to come up for air. She was livid! All I could do was bite my tongue and take it.

When the dad asked me where the Van was, I told him, "I had no idea," He came uncorked. He was beside himself in anger. I told him, "If we can find Atlanta, then all we have to do is follow that road down, till we found the van.

The ride with these two angry parents was pure torture. Both parents kept up the constant attack. Of course, I could understand that they were worried for the safety of their boys, but after several hours, I was seething in quiet anger. I was simply a victim of circumstances, beyond my control. I was really angry, at the betrayal of the outfitter.

We finally made it to Atlanta and turned around. I was just hoping that the van was indeed down this road. Every time we came around a corner, and the van is still not in sight, the verbal attack would continue.

They kept asking me "How much further?"

"I don't know, I was asleep." I would remind them.

"You said you only napped for 30 minutes! We've been driving for over an hour!" They complained.

"No" what I said was, "The driver assumed I had been asleep for approximately 30 minutes." On and on it went.

When we did eventually come to the van, the nightmare turned hellish. Not one kid was there! Not one! They had completely ignored my instructions. So now we start the search for the boys.

We drive down the road a few miles and finally spot one boy. We pick him up and what he tells us crushes all hope.

It seems that after I didn't return to the van when it got dark, some of the boys convince the others, that the old codger looked criminal. He reasoned that the old man must have bludgeoned me to death, and left my body in the ditch, otherwise I would have returned. They decide that if they could, they were going down the road and try to find me. So, some of the boys left in that group.

One of the boys that was left at the van thought he knew where he was and was convinced, he knew a shortcut and took off over the mountains.

Another kid hitched a ride into Boise and without calling his parents, hooked up with a friend and partied.

The rest of the teenagers left the van, when a lightning strike, from the thunderstorms, started a fire near the van, and they all thought they should try and outrun the fire. The smell of smoke sent them into an unreasoning panic. The lightning strikes started Fires all over the mountains that night, but the rain doused them quickly.

All I could think was "Please God, no loss of life."

When we made it back to Deer Flat, the parents were waiting for us, expecting the boys to be with us. They were not.

If they could have found a rope, and it was the early years of this country, they would have hung me and danced!

We waited at the church hour by agonizing hour waiting for news.

The sheriff's department organized a search party and one by one they began finding the boys. Eventually, they were all found safe.

Needless to say, the pastor had a chat with me after the last kid was found. He informed me, they no longer needed my services, I was let go, outsourced, sacked, fired, going in a different direction, yada, yada.

I am much older now, and I have gone back over that whole ordeal, and I have evaluated every decision I made those few days. Sometimes you only have two options in life and both come with risks. They are both far from optimal. Some of the options I had to choose from, were all fraught with potential downsides. Yet in life, we are faced with these decisions.

With wisdom and discernment, you have to choose the one with the least probable consequences. Sometimes in life, you can make the right decision, and circumstances change in an instant. You can't have do-overs. The decision has already been made!

The opposite is also true.... there have been other times in my life, I made horrible decisions, and God worked circumstances so I came out smelling like a rose. I have made decisions that should have cost me my life, but by God's graciousness, He was there, to change circumstances in my favor. Solomon was right "life oftentimes comes down to timing and chance." Ecclesiastes 9:11

Sometimes in life, both options stink, but you simply hold your nose and chose the lesser of two skunks. I have found this especially true in elections!

On that fateful trip, I made wise decisions. Circumstances worked against me. This same thing happens in war. Leaders make decisions based on the most probable outcomes. When circumstances change, they can't go back. They are forced to make decisions on the fly and use everything at their disposal to make the right decisions. Sometimes the battle comes down to pure chance. Life is unpredictable. You can go with the odds, but sometimes that impossibly rare exception happens.

When that happens, there will always be an armchair quarterback, second-guessing your decision, and mocking you. There will always be talking heads, ready to ridicule a leader. If you're a leader and you care what others might think, you will never be a good leader. You will be paralyzed to make the right decision, fearful of what others might think if something goes wrong.

I have met people that live in a constant paralysis of fear. "But what if...?" is their mantra. The problem with this approach is the "What if's" are endless. You can always come up with another "What if."

Even though things didn't work out on that trip, I refuse to live my life in constant fear of making a wrong decision. A leader's gift is the ability to make a decision, learn from their mistakes, and have shoulders large enough to carry the constant criticism.

Bobby and Bruce

Even though the end of the week turned sour, the week in the mountains was amazing. I heard a story around the campfire that forever enhanced my understanding of the Bible, God, and his son, Jesus. I used this story for the rest of my forty-plus years of ministry.

In the mid-1800s pioneers were pushing west. Many times, the trip proved too difficult and people would stop along the way and start a new settlement.

Imagine how hard it would have been for young boys who for two years were experiencing the adventure of a lifetime, moving across the wild unexplored territory of the west. Every day was a new experience. Only to be thrust into a classroom. It had to be pure torture, forced to sit in a school building behind a desk.

This is a story of just such a group of kids. They were a rowdy and rambunctious group. They were used to freedom and adventure. But their parents settled in a small town and felt that education was important.

Several times that first year, the school would open, only to close when the teacher would quit. Then came the second year.

The first day of school arrived and the children filed into the little one-room schoolhouse. They were full of mischief and had already made plans to get rid of the new teacher. The fact was, they had run off a number of teachers in the months previous. But this new teacher was different.

The teacher was a tall, thin man; and as the children found their seats, he turned his back to them and wrote on the chalkboard "Mr. Williams."

"My name is mister Williams." He said with a cheerful grin. And I just want you to know in my classroom there are NO rules!

The room suddenly got totally silent; did they hear that right? .... No rules? The children glanced at each other, trying to absorb this new development. This was not how the other teachers had started. They had laid down the law, filled with threats. This new guy was smiling and obviously serious.

Mr. Williams continued; "If you want any rules, you will have to make them yourselves."

Finally, one little girl raised her hand, "Mr. Williams, I don't think there ought to be any cheating." "Good, Good," said Mr. Williams as he wrote the rule on the chalkboard. Then he turned back to the classroom and asked once again, "Are there any more rules."

Now there was a little boy in this class named Bobby. Bobby had a very rough life. His mother had died giving birth to him. His father took the death very hard and blamed Bobby. His Father had become the town drunk; unable to hold down a job. If any money did come into the house it was spent on booze.

Bobby grew up malnourished. He also had to endure the brutality of his abusive father. He often came to class with bruises on his body.

From the little desk in the corner, Bobby said, "I don't think that there otta be no hitting." "That's a good one young man." Mr. Williams said as he wrote it on the board. Everyone could understand why Bobby would want this rule since Bobby was small for his age. The lack of food had stunted his growth.

Mr. Williams once again asked the class, "Do you think we need any more rules?" Now in the very back of the room sat the biggest student in the class. His name was Bruce. He was almost a foot taller than his peers. He stood to his feet and in a loud voice said, "Mr. Williams, my dad says, anyone what gets caught stealing, otta be strung up."

"Ok," said Mr. Williams, "What rule are you Suggesting?"

"There ain't otta be no stealing," Bruce responded emphatically.

Mr. Williams turned to the chalkboard and wrote "No stealing." As he turned back to face the class, he said, "These are some good rules, but for every rule, there must be a punishment, or there would be no deterrent for breaking the rule."

"I'm not going to make the punishment; you will have to determine the punishment." Said, Mr. Williams

Bruce spoke up from the back of the classroom, "I think that anyone what gets caught stealing otta get 10 lashes with a horsewhip."

"Hold on, let's start with the first rule," said Mr. Williams. "How many lashes for cheating?"

Bruce said, "How 'bout one lash?" Mr. Williams asked the rest of the class if they agreed. No one dared voice any objection. So, Mr. Williams wrote a "1" next to "No Cheating".

He then asked, "What about hitting?" Bruce hesitantly suggested "How 'bout just two lashes for hitting." So, Mr. Williams wrote a "2" next to the rule "No Hitting"

All right, what about your rule young man? Without a moment's hesitation, Bruce thundered, "TEN LASHES!"

"That seems pretty harsh, are you sure? What do the rest of you think?" Mr. Williams asked the class.

"Mr. Williams I'm the one, what made that rule, and I'm the one, what gets to make the punishment," said Bruce defiantly.

So, Mr. Williams hesitantly wrote "10" on the chalkboard behind the words "NO STEALING"

Mr. William's wisdom had won them over. The kids really liked him. He would often play at recess, right along with them. He had also seen the leadership potential in Bruce. Mr. Williams recruited him, to be the assistant teacher, and had Bruce, teaching the youngest kids. Mr. Williams also knew that this would also help Bruce to begin caring for them, rather than picking on them.

As the school year progressed, things went very well at the school. During the next few months, Mr. Williams learned a lot about little Bobby and his father. Many times, the boy didn't have enough to eat, because his father spent in on drink. Mr. Williams felt sorry for the child but wasn't quite sure how to go about helping Bobby's situation.

Things finally came to a head after recess one day. Bobby hadn't had anything to eat in three days. He was so hungry and dizzy that he stayed inside for recess. As he sat at his desk his eyes wandered over the classroom until they came to rest, on the bench in the back of the room. This bench was where the children's set their lunches.

Bobby noticed that one of the lunches had three extra sandwiches. "Who could eat that many sandwiches? He reasoned.

"Surely they won't miss just one!" He thought to himself.

He looked around and no one was in the room. So, he slowly walked to the bench and glanced around, then quickly grabbed one of the extra sandwiches. He devoured it as fast as he could and wiped the crumbs off his face. He then made his way outside, so no one would suspect him.

After recess, the children cheerfully filed into the school and sat down at their desks. They got busy doing their schoolwork. It was somewhat quiet when suddenly Bruce cried out, "Mr. Williams, someone has eaten one of my sandwiches!" The room became perfectly still, no one moved. No one spoke. Who would dare steal Bruce's sandwich? They wondered to themselves.

Mr. Williams realized that this was the first time anyone had broken one of the rules. He said, "All right…. I want everyone to put their books away and put your hands on the desk."

As Mr. Williams quietly surveyed the room, he said, "I want the person who ate Bruce's sandwich to raise their hand." No one moved.

Mr. Williams was very wise and began to walk down each row looking straight into each student's eyes. When he came to Bobby's desk, Bobby couldn't look at him…. Mr. William's heart sank. Not Bobby he thought.

"Bobby, did you eat Bruce's sandwich?" asked Mr. Williams. Bobby's eyes welled up, and he nodded his head. Do you know what I must do? Mr. Williams asked quietly. Again, bobby nodded…. "I want you to come to the front of the classroom, and bend over the desk," said Mr. Williams.

Now Mr. Williams did not want to give these lashes. He suspected that Bobby hadn't eaten in a couple of days, and had been tempted to eat the meal because he was hungry. But Mr. Williams also knew that if he didn't punish Bobby, everything he had worked so hard to accomplish, would be wasted. The children would not respect his authority. Mr. Williams had always been a man of integrity.

The tension grew in the little schoolhouse as Mr. Williams pulled the horsewhip down from the wall. Many of the students felt sorry for Bobby. Mr. Williams had Bobby bend over, and place his hands on the desk. As Mr. Williams drew his arm back to give the first lash, Bruce suddenly stood up and shouted, "STOP!" Mr. Williams, you give those lashes to me, and you let Bobby go."

"But Bruce you made this rule…," said Mr. Williams, "….and you're the one who made the punishment 10 lashes!"

"Yea, but I ain't never said, who had to take them lashes," Bruce said in a gentle commanding voice.

So as Bobby stepped back, the class watched in silent amazement. Bruce walked up and bent over the desk. Mr. Williams began administering the whipping.

When it was over, little Bobby stood there with tears flowing down his face. He knew, he had deserved that whipping.

The Point: This illustration is clear. Bruce made the rule, he defined the punishment, and then Bruce paid the price and took the punishment for Bobby. Bruce showed unconditional love, even though Bobby stole **his** sandwiches, and sinned against him.

In the same way, God made the rule, **don't sin.** God defined the punishment. **The price of sin is death.** Then God paid the ultimate price for our sins, by **dying in our place.** Even though we sinned against **Him**, and broke **His** laws. This is why Christians love Jesus with all their heart, soul, and mind. He voluntarily died in our place and took our punishment.

What a tremendous show of unconditional love. Jesus took the whipping and death for our sins. Man is powerless to make himself pure. A payment is required to remove our sins. Jesus paid the price! He sacrificially carried all mankind's sins to the cross. He died in our place.

Bruce voluntarily took Bobby's whipping for him. It was a gift. Bobby didn't earn it. In fact, Bobby deliberately earned the punishment. We are all Bobby. There is no one on earth that is pure, we all fall short of perfection. But God knew that fact when he created the human race. So, He came up with the plan to die in our place, at the beginning of time. The Old Testament tells the story of how God set the stage for Jesus to come. The New Testament is the complete story of how God died for us.

This simple story of Bobby and Bruce, did more to explain the theology of the Bible, than most of my classes in Theology. I would not have heard that story if I had not gone on that trip into the Sawtooth Mountains.

The challenges during my college years never stopped. The learning curve God was taking me on, never stopped.

Resident Assistant

On every wing of a dorm at NNC, there is an R.A. A Resident Assistant helps the Resident Director. They help serve the men on their wing. They are a friend, counselor, encouragers, tutor, helpers, organizers, leaders etc. etc. A combination of many things.

In my third year, I became that R.A. in Southerland Hall, a men's dorm for upperclassmen. The very first night should have been a clue, to abandon all hope.

I was in my room, with the door open, and a policeman walked in. He asks me to step out into the hallway. At the end of the corridor is a life-size statue of Ronald McDonald. The Policeman asks me if I know anything about it.

It turns out that someone driving by the dorm saw a couple of guys carrying a body inside the dorm and called the police. The "body", as it turned out, was this statue of Ronald McDonald, that someone had taken from a nearby McDonalds'. I had my suspects, but I couldn't prove, who on my wing had pulled this prank.

College is full of characters, who love to pull pranks. I am one of them. I am pretty sure we are beyond the statute of limitations, but I still plead the fifth!

Campus Security

One night while I was working security, one of my friends strongly suggested I walk to the other end of campus and stay there. He said; "Trust me, keep walking, don't look back, you don't want to know....and you will want to plead plausible deniability."

Their practical jokes were always harmless, but always humorous. It turns out the next morning, that they had taken a small row boat, and placed it atop the admin building. It was hanging out over the front of the building, and in the front of the boat is the bust of George Washington. (Borrowed from the library), reminiscent of the painting, "Crossing the Delaware."

One day while I was studying in my dorm room, I heard some commotion outside my door. I jump up to open the door, but I discovered, I had been penny locked into the room. Now for the uninitiated "penny locked" means that a number of guys push against the outside of the metal door, while someone else wedges pennies tightly between the metal frame and door. When they release the pressure, the person inside is locked in. The door is bound so tightly that turning the knob is futile.

Now I knew exactly who it was because, even though they were whispering and trying to be covert, their giggling betrayed them. What they did next was pour Desenex Foot Powder into piles, filling the gap below the door. Then they turned on hairdryers and blew the fine powder into my room.

We were on the upper floor, so escape out the window was impossible. The powder was so fine that it makes breathing impossible also. I had to lean out the window to catch my breath. From the street, it looked like my room was on fire with smoke boiling out of the window, above my head.

The powder worked its way into every crevice of my room. All my clothes were inundated. For the rest of that semester every time, I opened or closed my textbook in class, a little cloud of Desenex wafted in the air. On the bright side, I staved off any athlete's foot that term.

Even though I was pranked all year long, I loved the guys on that wing. We grew to be great friends. Some of them are still friends to this day.

Turning of the Tide

As I have already stated, when I became a Christian and my grandfather rejected me, the rest of the family joined suit. For the most part, I was the only Christian in the immediate family.

I had been praying for the family since I accepted Christ. It was sad to me, that the family made fun of something, they had no idea about. It is a tragedy that haunts America, utterly no clue what authentic Christianity is. It's like looking at a hospital, and concluding it doesn't work, because it is full of sick people. They have no idea what they don't know!

Then came the day my grandfather died. The great antagonist had passed. He had spent his lifetime attacking something, he knew nothing about.

Several years after he died, I came to visit my grandmother. She greeted me at the door and gave me the biggest hug. She had that mischievous grin on her face and I could tell immediately, something was up.

I said "What's going on? You are up to something I can tell; your eyes are positively beaming."

She said, "Sit down I have a surprise for you." What she said next blew my mind. I was utterly speechless.

She took my hand and delightfully exclaimed, "I have become a Christian and I was just baptized! I was waiting for your visit to tell you personally."

All I could think of at that moment was what Granddad would have thought if he knew his own grandson was now a pastor, and his own wife had become a Christian. His head would explode.

God was working in this family that had utterly rejected Him. Why, of all people, had he loved and called us to be a part of His eternal family? His love has absolutely nothing to do with worthiness because if it did, our godless family would have been lost forever.

Rene'

Later that same year I was walking out of an evening service at Nampa First church when I suddenly felt lightheaded and thought I was going to pass out. A beautiful woman, who was standing near me, could see I was in trouble. She came up to me and had me sit on the curb. She told me to put my head down between my legs. I thought she must be a nurse, so I complied and within a few minutes, I felt much better.

A number of people came to see what all the commotion was about, and I began to feel self-conscious. Since I was feeling so much better, I thanked everyone and told them I was ok. I would be fine.

One by one they walked away and I was left alone with the young woman. Even though I had nearly fainted, I noticed how strikingly good-looking the woman was. This added to my awkwardness. I told her I would be fine, but she insisted on helping me to my car. I introduced myself and apologized again, for being such a bother.

She just smiled and I marveled at her beauty. She was truly one of the most beautiful women I had ever talked with. As I looked into her eyes, I saw a degree of tenderness and warmth that made my heart skip a beat. She was so poised, and confident. She was totally out of my league, but I noticed she didn't have a ring on her hand. I asked her if she were a nurse, and she laughed. She told me she worked in the corporate offices of Safeway, in Boise. That started a long conversation, as we shared our common bond of working for the same company.

As it turned out we shared a lot in common. She was also a devout believer in Christ.

I kept waiting for her to make some excuse and walk away, but the more we talked, the more we enjoyed the conversation. Finally, I invited her to have a bite to eat and she cheerfully took me up on it. I do remember thinking to myself, what in the world is she still talking to me for?

We discovered we were the same age, but she was not a giggly girl, she was a mature woman. I was in my sixth year of college and far beyond the silly dating games that come with youth. Our conversation came easy, not forced or awkward. We talked for hours.

We began seeing each other, and we both knew this was different. I found myself treating her with a depth of honor, I had never had with anyone in my life. She also went out of her way, to protect my reputation. We would only meet in public places, or with a number of others. She knew I was going into the ministry, and could ill afford the appearance of impropriety. We would not put ourselves in compromising situations.

We dated and grew deeper in love as the months went by.

On one particular Wednesday, I was walking across campus, when I was approached by a messenger and received a note from one of the psychology professors, professor Simpson. He wanted to see me immediately. I had a number of classes with him in the past but was not currently taking a class from him, so I was puzzled.

In addition to this, I had always found Psychology professors to be a little odd. They were always a little peculiar. I truly felt uncomfortable and awkward around them. I always thought they were analyzing me, judging what I said, watching my body language. They creeped me out.

As I walked to his office, several questions were running through my mind. What in the world would Professor Simpson want with me? With several thousand students, how did he even know me? His note was handwritten and he used my first name, "Perry I need to see you immediately, could you come to my office?" Normally a professor would address me as Mr. Arbogast. This was definitely weird.

When I arrived, his secretary warmly greeted me with, "Hi Perry, go right on in. Professor Simpson is expecting you." How did she know me? What was going on?

When I stepped into his office, he jumped to his feet and greeted me with a handshake and a broad smile. This was getting stranger by the minute.

He asked me to have a seat and was genuinely warm and kind.

"You are dating Rene' and she speaks very highly of you. She tells my wife and I; you treat her with the utmost respect, and that the two of you are growing deeper in love by the day.

How in the world, did Rene' know this professor? She had never told me she knew anyone on campus. She wasn't even attending college.

"I can see you're confused," he said, "Let me explain. Rene' is my daughter!"

WHAT???!!!! I was completely blindsided.

I'm truly ashamed to admit this, but I still remember one of the thoughts that ran through my mind, in that nanosecond…., How could someone so poised and beautiful, be related to a professor of psychology?

The thoughts were running through my mind so fast at that moment, that it was hard to remember all I was thinking, but I do remember thinking Rene's last name wasn't Simpson, and immediately put two and two together…. Rene' must be adopted.

Professor Simpson continued; "Rene' told us that she has treasured the many hours of conversation and that you have made her feel so at ease. You have been the consummate gentleman. She also tells us, that you two are starting to talk more deeply about the future. She has asked me to share something with you."

I was listening intently, yet my mind was racing. Was this the "What are your intentions with my daughter" grilling?

Then he paused. "Rene' has been trying to tell you something for months now, but every time she starts to say it, she is overwhelmed with fear. She has asked me to tell you something you should know…. Rene' is married!"

I felt like I had been hit by a bolt of lightning. Did he say Married? That's impossible. I had so many emotions running through my body, and so many thoughts in that few seconds, that I was speechless. I was in a state of shock. Too numb to speak. I couldn't breathe, and I wonder if my heart stopped beating.

Then it flashed through my mind that perhaps he was angry and that he thought I was a homewrecker! The first words out of my mouth were almost a defensive shout; "But she doesn't wear a ring!?"

He put his hand on my shoulder and gently said "Perry I'm so sorry, you couldn't possibly have known."

As I sat there, I felt like I was falling through the floor.

He leaned back against his desk and over the next few minutes explained the rest of the story.

Several years before, Rene' had gone to work and when she returned home that evening, the front door was open, the breakfast food still on the plate. His car was still in the driveway. He had simply disappeared. She called the police and over the next few months, they conducted a homicide investigation.

They surmised that the murderer may have been someone he knew because there were no signs of forced entry. He had evidently been interrupted from eating his breakfast because it was only partially eaten.

The problem was they couldn't find the body, and in Idaho, it takes seven years before a person can be considered single. Rene' was technically and legally still married. It was still an open case, and the investigation was still active.

Professor Simpson then shared this with me; Rene' went into a deep depression after the death of her husband. She eventually took off her wedding ring and began living as a widow. One day she meets you, and you were so cheerful and outgoing, it made her want to live again. She had a reason to want to wake up and get out of bed. You have been the best thing to come into her life, and she was afraid that if she told you, she might lose you. She wasn't brave enough to risk that. She loves you, and she could tell, you were about to ask for her hand in marriage.

She tried a hundred times to share this with you, but she just couldn't. She understands that this breaches the core trust, you two have built. She also fully understands why you may not want to speak with her again. Yet, she is at her home, and if you want to talk with her, she is waiting for you.

I thanked Professor Simpson, and in addition, I expressed to him my gratitude for sharing all this with me, and I acknowledged it couldn't have been easy for him, to be put in that position.

I drove over to her home and she came out the door to greet me, tears freely running down her face, she had obviously been crying for hours. We sat on the porch talking until late that night. We prayed together and asked God to help the police recover the body.

I had a trip planned that weekend and left on Friday. Saturday morning, I found myself in a frustrating situation. I had planned on doing my laundry earlier in the week, but with the situation with Rene' I had put it off. I found myself in a strange city, looking for a laundromat.

As everyone knows, the worst time of the week to do laundry is Saturday morning. The place is packed with undisciplined, noisy kids and you have to fight to find an open washer.

Let's face it, another downside is the dirty neighborhoods and filthy condition of most laundromats. And there are some real characters to enhance the experience. I normally sat in my car, trying not to be accosted. Frankly, I loathed doing laundry! It was one of the worst chores of the week for me. I hated it with a passion, especially at a laundromat.

The only redeemable thing about doing laundry was I could study, while the clothes were being washed and dried.

I finally found a laundromat but it looked closed. There was not a single car in the parking lot. Yet, just to make sure, I got out and checked the door. To my shock and amazement, it opened. I quickly grabbed my clothes and threw them in the washer. I grabbed my books and sat on the washer to study. In the back of my mind, I was wondering if perhaps it was empty because it was a seedy neighborhood and dangerous.

Eventually, the door opened, and in walked another customer. Just as I had done, he looks around and asks out loud "Where is everyone, this IS Saturday morning isn't it?"

We both laughed, and I explained that I was just passing through this city, and this was the first laundromat I could find.

He put his load in the washer across from mine, hopped up, and sat facing me while he chatted away. I was a bit irritated because I could tell I wasn't going to get any studying done. I could tell it was futile to try, so I put the books down and engaged in chit-chat. We marveled at our good fortune.

Somewhere in the conversation, he confides in me that he doesn't normally get caught up in talking at a laundromat, because of the riff-raff that frequents the establishment.

I nodded my agreement, and off he goes into more monologue. He shares with me his childhood and that he was once a Christian. That perked my interest, but I don't tell him I'm a Christian, I just listen.

He explains that when he was younger, he met this gorgeous Christian girl, who attended church all the time. They had gotten married, but he got restless. Then he stops and looks at me as if to study me. Then he continues.

He explains that he was living a double life. He was watching me to see how I was responding, and I acted unfazed at his confession.

He can see that he is safe and that I am listening intently so he continues. "One morning while I was eating breakfast, I just decided I could no longer live the lie." He decided that the best thing to do was just walk out of Rene's life.

For the first time, he had called her by name! He explained that she was a genuine Christian, and so innocent. He simply felt he couldn't do that to her.

This was Rene's Husband!

He explained that her whole family were devout Christians and that her dad was a Psychology professor at a Christian college in Idaho.

I felt a chill run up my spine!

What were the odds that less than 72 hours after hearing about this guy, I was sitting across from him? If this had happened the weekend before, it wouldn't have even entered my mind, that Rene' was my Rene'! I wouldn't have even considered a connection. Yet God had set up a Divine appointment at just the right time. He had emptied the place so we would talk. Out of the many cities and towns, He had guided me to this city. Out of the many laundromats, He had guided me to this one.

I didn't want to let on who I was, because I wanted him to continue to talk. I continued to ask questions as if I knew nothing. I innocently ask what she did when he finally told her as if I didn't already know he had never spoken to her. He considers my questions quite normal and continues to pour out his life. At one point he even apologizes, that he isn't normally such a chatterbox, but that I was easy to talk to. He confessed it felt good to talk to someone about this.

I asked him what Rene' was doing with her life now. He said he had no idea.

I asked if Rene' knew he was dead or alive. He said he had never considered that, but that he should have thought of that before.

I ask him if she was able to get on with her life. He just assumed I was simply curious. We talked for several hours and I felt that I had been walking on holy ground. This was a profound and God-ordained conversation. This appointment was a direct answer to Rene and her family's prayers.

In the end, I encouraged him to call his wife, and share as openly as he did with me, a total stranger. I never let on who I was or that I knew Rene'. He thanked me and told me, how appreciative he was, that I had challenged him. He told me he hadn't considered some of the things I had brought up.

The Bible teaches that "A man plans his way, but it is the Lord, that directs our footsteps." In the book of Proverbs, it says that a man's steps are directed by the Lord. This was the first Divine appointment that I became aware of. I would later come to realize I had experienced many Divine appointments, but this is the first one that I KNEW, without a shadow of a doubt, that God set up.

The mathematical chances of meeting this man, at just the right week, were astronomical. I had lived over 1,200 weeks in my life, at that point, and God chose that precise week. I could have stopped in any of a hundred towns, God had me stop in that city. I could have found any number of Laundromats, but God directed me to that one. I could have gone in at any time of the day, but I was prompted to get up early that morning.

How was God going to get these two strangers talking? Yet He worked it out.

I wanted to tell Rene' all that had happened, but I wanted to do it face to face, not on the phone. I finished my trip and returned to Nampa.

When I drove up to Rene's house she came running out into my arms. Before I could say a word, she burst into a rapid succession of statements. "You're never going to believe who called! He went into a laundromat of all places, and God sent someone to talk with him, and whoever it was, told him to call me! My husband's alive. He said there was no one else in the laundromat, just this guy, and on a Saturday of all things… she went on and on…not coming up for air. Finally, she slows down enough for me to speak and I tell her my side of the story.

Over the next few days, we processed the situation. Because we both were devout Christians, we agreed that she should hold to her vows, even when it was no longer convenient. She had made a vow to God, that she would remain faithful, for better or worse, until death do us part. I deeply respected that in Rene'.

I knew the moment I realized her husband was alive, I could not marry another man's wife.

Even if the other half of the marriage, breaks their vow with God, that does not give us the right to break our vow with God. The marriage vows are to God, not the other person. God teaches us, that a person of integrity, who fears God and honors God, does not break vows with God.

Rene' and I have remained friends to this day, in fact, I grew to love Professor and Mrs. Simpson as well and found them to be dear and wonderful people. They opened their home to college students and invited us over for wonderful times of food and fun. Rene' also open her house. She would have college students over to her place, for parties of Trivial pursuit, Bible trivia, and other games.

She stayed true to her vows. I saw her many years later and even though her husband had divorced her, she remained true to her vows.

The Kitten

That fall I entered my senior year of college. It had taken me six years to finally enter my last year of college. Partly because I could only afford the minimum class load and partly because I worked all through my college years. One evening, as I was walking out of the dining room, on campus, a beautiful freshman girl walked up to me with a kitten in her hands. Both were extremely cute. She states matter-of-factly, "Your Perry, aren't you?"

Again, I wondered, how was it that she knew my name? Yet before I could respond she continued. "I found this tiny kitten outside, in the frigid cold, crying. It can't make it through the night, and I looked everywhere for its mother, but have had no luck. I know you live off campus, and I was hoping that you could take it and care for it. I would," she said, "but they don't allow pets in the dorms."

Several thoughts ran through my mind in that brief instant. How did she know I lived off campus, my initial humorous thought was "I will take the kitten only if you are a package deal!?" I didn't say that of course, but it had flashed in my gray matter.

I love animals, but I am allergic to cat hair. I was not interested in the least, but when I looked into the young ladies pleading eyes, I couldn't say no.

I had seen this girl on campus, as had most of the men. Her beauty was hard to miss. She was one of those women that when you see her you simply say "WOW, she's cute!" Just like Rene' she was a 1% percenter. A term for the rare "drop-dead gorgeous" women in the world. The kind you see in magazines, the model type. You notice them, but just keep walking because they are out of your league.

What good fortune to find myself talking with her! Not only that but doing her a favor. She had come up to me, so I felt the courage to ask her if she was doing anything that evening. It just happened to be Friday night, and a bunch of us were headed to Rene's house for game night. I asked her if she would like to join me at a party. She flatly turned me down!

Just then, another friend, Debbie, came up to us and said to her "Ah Michelle, I see you met Perry. Has he invited you to the party?"

Michelle was from Southern California, and she would later confide in me, that whenever some boy found out she was from California, they just naturally assumed, she was a party girl. The only parties she had ever been invited to, were full of free-flowing alcohol and drugs. She had assumed, that was the kind of party, I had invited her to. Oddly enough, just the week before, she had been invited to a party, and some guy tried to accost her. So, when I asked her to a party, she leaped to the wrong conclusions.

It turned out that Debbie knew Michelle. Debbie explained that every Friday, we had a fun Christian party, where the Pepsi and root beer flowed freely, and popcorn was all the rage. We loved to play the game Trivial Pursuit. Debbie went on to explain to her, that I was the one who set the party up!

It was for those who wanted innocent fun, without the vices that normally entrap young college kids. The truth was, Rene' and I had been having these parties since school had started that fall. Partly to give the college kids an alternative on a Friday night, and partly to give Rene' something to look forward to. Sometimes Professor Simpson would invite the party to his house.

With that explanation, Michelle agreed to attend, provided that Debbie come along with her. So that night the three of us went over to Rene's house and I introduced Michelle to Rene'. Rene' took me into the kitchen and encouraged me to sit next to Michelle. Rene' was becoming a little matchmaker.

We had an incredible night of fun and as it turned out, "Michelle and I" as a team won the game. She was not only stunningly beautiful, but she was also smart. What I remember, is that she was strong in areas in which I had little knowledge, and I was strong in areas that she was weak. Yet as a team we dominated.

When I returned to my little house, I told my roommate, "Tonight I met my wife," he burst out laughing. What we could not have known that night, was that within ten months, he would be the best man at my wedding, and I would be his best man at his.

A few months after the party, I asked Michelle, how had she known, that night when she brought the kitten up to me, who I was. It turns out, that I had dated a girl on Michelle's wing, several weeks before we met.

Michelle explained; "I was walking down the hallway and I heard this girl crying, I stepped into her room and some other Girls were already in the room with her. They were all talking about this senior student, named Perry. That he was a leader on campus and a ministry student. But what caught my attention, was they were talking about your purity, and that you had a strong moral standard. That your character was authentically Christian. That you were saving yourself until marriage. It turns out this girl had slept with her previous boyfriend and realized that she had no chance with you."

What Michelle went on to say is that "She herself had remained pure, and wondered if she was the last pure woman on earth. She was determined to meet this man, with these ideals. She wanted to know this man with a kindred spirit! She had asked the girls to point Perry out to her, and had been looking for a way to meet me,"

I was stunned at what she was telling me. Wow, who knew?

You're probably wondering about the kitten. Well as it turned out my landlord, who was an elderly woman with dementia, saw the kitten, and thinking it was her cat, decided she didn't want a cat anymore and gave it to a little girl, who just happened to be walking by.

The next day I am looking for the kitten, and my landlord told me, it was her cat, and she had given it away. What makes this even more hilarious, is my landlord, never owned a cat.... ever! Thank you, Lord, for Dementia.

I was utterly relieved! What was I going to do with a kitten anyway? Once again God had divinely placed a kitten, so that only one woman on the entire campus saw it, Michelle! This had given her the opening she needed, to introduce herself to me. Then He placed me in the right place, at the perfect time. Even better, when God was finished with the prop (the kitten), He gave it away to a good home, through a confused old woman.

Circle K

One of the many jobs I had, working through school, was working the night shift at Circle K. On one of my nights off, I received an urgent call. They needed me to fill in at another store. Now normally I had a Circle K smock and name badge, but they told me to forgo picking up those things, at my store, and come right in! They needed me immediately.

So, on that particular night, I was simply in my street clothes and had no badge. Around three in the morning, a couple of young men my age came in. They picked up some junk food and walked up to the cash register. I rang up their items and was in the process of grabbing their change out of the till.... when suddenly the front door burst open, and a number of policemen came in, guns drawn! They were screaming at the top of their lungs "GET DOWN, GET DOWN! GET DOWN ON YOUR FACES, NOW!"

They tackled us, and brought all three of us to the ground, all the while screaming orders. "PUT YOUR HANDS ON TOP OF YOUR HEAD! DON'T MOVE!"

They thrust their knees into my rib cage so hard, it knocked the wind out of me. They genuinely injured my rib cage. They put us in handcuffs, as more police entered the store.

They jerked me to my feet, and ask me, what I had done with the store clerk.

I told them, "I was the store clerk!" and they became very agitated. They start shouting at me, to wise up, or this was going to go very badly for me.

Meanwhile, the other officers are yelling to one another, "Search the back room!" "Check the freezer!" "Look in the dumpster outside, in case they put the body out there!"

I tell them I work there, but one of the policemen calls me a **liar**! He told the other officers, that he came in there all the time, and knew all the cashiers.

Another officer mocks me, and asks me, "If I work there, where's your smock? I told him it was at the other store, and he said "Convenient for you, and I suppose you missed placed your name tag as well?" They all laughed.

"If you work here, who's your manager?" They demand!

It struck me, that I had no clue who the manager was or the names of anyone in this store.

All the while, they brought in a canine unit, and thoroughly searched the back room. They are interrogating the other two young men, who are just as confused, and unhelpful as I was.

One of the leading officers showed up, and I overheard the conversation. "We haven't located the clerk yet, sir, but she had time to set off the silent alarm before they took care of her."

As he pointed toward me, he sneered, "That one was cleaning out the cash register when we arrived,"

It became apparent that I had inadvertently set off some silent alarm system, without knowing it. We didn't have one at our store, and I had no clue how it happened. I begged the officers to call the manager of the store, but of course, I couldn't give them a number or name.

We were threatened, "If you've done harm to the clerk, and you're letting her suffer, while we're wasting time finding her, you will have a number of extra charges added on. And if she dies...," they warned us, "...because you three won't tell us where she is, I hope you all rot in jail the rest of your lives."

I asked them to check with the store I worked at! "They will know me," I pleaded!

One of the officers responded to the commander, "Perhaps that's how he knew how to get into the till, sir!

The more I tried to convince them, the bigger the liar, they thought I was. The more I said, the guiltier I looked. They were not buying, what I was selling.

In total frustration, I begged them, "Go to my store, get the phone number of my manager. She will know the manager of this store! Please, wake them up and get them down here. They will vouch for me."

Partly because they couldn't find a clerk, and partly because a lot of time had passed, they finally found a way to contact the manager of the store.

The police insisted she come to the store, and identify me. The problem was, I had never met this manager. When she arrives, she can't definitively say I worked there.

Yet by now, it was beginning to look like I am telling the truth. The manager contacted my regular manager and gets a description of me. Finally, the police are beginning to realize, that I was not lying.

They get it all sorted out, and eventually take the handcuffs off.

I apologize to the two other poor young men, who just happened to come in to buy something. My wrists were sore and my ribcage was injured. I was just glad they didn't get trigger-happy.

It taught me a lesson: When someone is convinced of something, they make all the evidence point in that direction. No matter how plausible another story is, if they are convinced in their heart they are correct, their mind will connect the dots toward their conclusions. They become blind to other possibilities. I can truly feel for those in jail on circumstantial evidence. This theme will come up many times in my life. Edgar Allen Poe was correct; *"Believe nothing of what you hear, and only half of what you see."*

I have since watched quite a few documentaries, and science has proven, beyond any doubt, that even eyewitnesses are often wrong. Watch "Brain games" on Netflix sometime, and you will never again be dogmatic about reality and perception. I think that may be why God encourages us to show mercy. Be forgiving. It may be us, who are convinced that we saw something, but we are mistaken.

Dr. Kinderman

When I worked at Circle K, I worked almost exclusively at night. I met some very interesting people, but none were as amazing as Dr. Kinderman.

One night he walked into the store after midnight. The store was very slow at this time of night. Normally only a few customers an hour. We began to talk, and immediately, he struck me as a very brilliant man. He was perhaps in his late 70s or early 80s. He looked to be East Indian or Arabic. He introduced himself as Dr. Kinderman. He told me he was a retired Physician.

We had such a delightful and intellectual talk, that he began showing up every night after midnight. We discussed deep subjects. After a few visits, he found out I was a student at NNC and was preparing for pastoral ministry. We talked for hours about my area of study. I told him the name of my classes, and how difficult the upper-division classes were.

Several nights later, he entered the store at the regular time and had this funny-looking grin on his face. "What have you been up to?" I asked. What he told me, blows my mind.

"You were mentioning that you were taking some hard classes." He interjected, "and I just happen to love Philosophy and the study of religion. So I went to your school, and bought all the books, in every class you're taking, and read them all. In addition, I read the Bible as well, so I could understand what you are so excited about. In my country, it was against the law to read the Bible. I come from an Islamic country."

When I asked him "What country?"

He hesitated, and simply said, "I would rather not say", and left me hanging. I didn't want to press, so I figured someday when he felt more comfortable with me, he would tell me.

I was somewhat skeptical, and asked him "How did he have the time to read all this material?" I was thinking to myself, the Bible alone would take weeks to read.

He told me he had a gifted mind, and the ability to read and retain. He possessed a photographic memory. I had already seen that gift, in Steve, my friend, so now I was intrigued. Was it possible, that I had met a second person, with this incredible gift?

Dr. Kinderman asked me to tell him what philosophical concept had me puzzled. He promises he would explain it to me! I shared one, and Dr. Kinderman began explaining the concept in great detail, quoting sources and page numbers. He used the names of those who introduced the philosophy, and those who propagated that thought, quoting specific statements, and

106

explaining what they were saying. He was having a delightful time and you could see the joy in his eyes.

Over the next few months, he helped me grasp concepts, that had stumped me for years.

We became great friends, and he began to confide in me. Eventually, I asked him, "Why was he taking so much interest in my education?"

What he shared with me, I had to promise to keep to myself, until after his death.

Now what I am about to share here, will be the first time I have shared this publicly. How much of what he told, Michelle and I, was true? I may never know. What I do know, is Michelle and I verified everything he told us. He also had a house full of documentation and pictures. Over time, we have become utterly convinced, that everything he claimed, was true. He showed us photos. Magazines, with articles about him, with accompanying photos of himself. He had books, with pictures, of all the artifacts in his possession. We were invited into his private world.

It was an ironic, and tragic world! On the one hand, he had more money than most people on earth, yet it was a world of utter isolation.

When we asked him, why he would trust the two of us, with such information? He smiled, and in a serious tone said, "Because your Bible tells me, you are forbidden to lie, and you have sworn not to say anything about me. So, I have to trust, that you are faithful, to your God. You both have shown yourselves to be authentic and devout. I have no fear, that the both of you, will keep your word."

We also knew, that if we did say something, it could cost him his life.

Dr. Kinderman was not his real name. That was a new identity the government had given him.

Back in 1979, the Shaw of Iran was deposed. "Dr. Kinderman" had been very close to the Shaw of Iran and his wife. Because of this, he had become wealthy. When the Shaw fled Iran, he had also been forced to flee. Yet before he did, he confessed to us, that he transferred his tens of millions of dollars, into offshore accounts. He had also secured his rare and priceless artifacts. (Many of these pieces of art, we were privileged to see, touch, and study. He showed us rooms full of artworks that he had ushered out of Iran.)

Michelle and I were taking an Art class at the time, and Dr. Kinderman wanted us to see some of the Pottery he had collected, while he had been a wealthy man in Iran. We were shown Porcelain Ceramics from the Ming dynasty. He would then show us pictures, in a number of books, of that very piece we were handling. In the books, it would say below the picture "Courtesy of ...." and it would be his real name.

How do we know it was his real name? Because of the many Photographs identifying him. His picture was in stacks of magazines.

Before his escape, he had been fairly well known. He was pictured with the Shaw and the Shaw's wife. He had been pretty famous in his own country.

Another striking thing about him was his brokenness. He didn't put on airs or try to put on a good face. He admitted his many crimes. He had not been a very honest man. He was in fact a notorious scoundrel. The reason he was now living in utter seclusion, was that many in his own country wanted him dead.

The first time he invited us to his house, I was intimidated by the house itself. He had all the doors and windows encased with steel bars. All the doors were solid, reinforced, security doors. Who does that? There were many pistols lying around, never far from reach. He was living in absolute fear for his life.

He explained that he was placed in Idaho, in this midsize town, because it was large enough to get lost in but small enough, that no one would look for him there. Who in the middle east, would think that this notorious friend of the Shaw of Iran, was living in Podunk, Idaho? He had lived his life large, before the coup. Now he found himself in a prison of his own making. "This is my jail cell." He would refer to his house. "It is dangerous to leave, and when I do, I have to hide my face."

He explained that was why he came into Circle K in the middle of the night. It was safer to come out of his house at night. He told me, that when he met me, I had challenged his perceptions of Christians. He found me intelligent and engaging. He told me that because of my age, he felt safe, and I was not a threat. He appreciated my cheerfulness and kindness, to an old man like himself. He marveled, that I would be so kind, to someone, who had nothing to offer, but conversation.

He confessed that reading my books, gave him something to do. He confessed that he was lonely and that all day long, he would look forward to our long visits at night. He told me that helping me, gave him generativity and made him feel useful. He genuinely enjoyed quizzing me and helping me to excel in my classes. I did get extremely good grades that year.

His photographic memory kept me mesmerized. He knew the bible better, FAR BETTER, than I knew it. He could simply call it to memory. Sometimes I would make a statement and He would challenge me: "How does that line up with the scripture in…." then he would proceed to quote the passage. It was exasperating, because sometimes, I could see the duplicity, but couldn't explain it.

Sometimes he, himself would show: "It only seems to be contradictory, if not taken in the correct context." Then he would explain and quote some Theologian, that had wrestled with that issue. He was absolutely amazing.

He knew more about John Wesley, John Calvin, or Martin Luther than I did, and I had been studying their teachings for years. You couldn't buffalo or blow smoke or he would call you on it. He has perhaps been the most interesting man, I have ever met in my life.

He came to the store one night and said "You at NNC are Wesleyan, Armenian in your view of theology, so I thought you might like to hold something in your hand that was actually written and touched by your heroes." Then he handed me an old book. I open it up and there on the cover, was a handwritten note, to Susanna Wesley, John Wesley's mother, in his own handwriting.

"You're probably wondering how I happened to have this original?" He smiles.

"One of my passions in life is to have originals." He bragged, "I have always wanted the first edition or the actual handwritten manuscript. I have been collecting them and preserving them for most of my adult life. It is my dream to create a library with the first actual writings of every important book in the world. That way, scholars can come to one central location, to read any originals in the world. "

He had rubbed shoulders with the rich all his life and had become friends with others with the same dream. He had acquired many books and he was trying to preserve them. Now I was holding one of them in my hand.

As an added bonus, he encouraged me to, "Take it to class, and show it to the other students. Let them experience the same thrill you just had."

He then cautioned me, in a humorous tone, and a wink, "Just don't let it out of your sight."

Dr. Kinderman received a great deal of pleasure, shocking Michelle and I, with some priceless artifacts in our hands. His belief was that to truly appreciate something, you needed to have a kinetic connection with it. Touch it, feel it, handle it, turn it over, and experience it. I asked him; "What if we break it, or drop it?" He burst out laughing and told me; "It's quite simple…. don't drop it!"

I have held in my hand, one of the sacrificial knives from the Mayan period. Porcelain Pottery dating before Christ. Music, handwritten by Beethoven.

I had the privilege of meeting one of the most interesting men on the planet. A house that was full of priceless art treasures. Paintings by the masters. Music scores, handwritten by the virtuoso themselves.

I have always regretted that I couldn't convince him, to put his trust in Christ, but I have secretly hoped that before he died, he had considered the things we had studied. God doesn't do anything by accident, and He had a purpose behind that Divine encounter.

Haters

Before I was hired at Circle K, I told them that as a Christian, I would NOT sell pornography. I always tried to live my life, as I thought that Jesus would live His. I couldn't picture Him selling something like porn.

There was a secondary concern for me as well. As a youth pastor at Deer Flat, I couldn't imagine, the damage I could do, for the cause of Christ, if one of the young people, that had been in my youth group, witnessed me selling pornography. The manager of the store and Corporate Circle K agreed to my terms and hired me.

Every night, the first thing I did, was dump the magazines into the back room. I worked hard for the manager and she grew to appreciate me.

Another thing she truly appreciated, was that I showed up for work every night and on time. My grandfather had lived through the depression when jobs were almost impossible to get. He taught me, "Back then, once you had a job..." he said, "...if you ever, even once, showed up late to work, you would be fired on the spot." You see, there were hundreds of others, sitting like vultures on a fencepost, hoping for your job, and **they** would be on time!

He also taught me, "Being on time is being late." A wise man, "Anticipates the possibility of unforeseen delays, on the way to work!" "By showing up ten minutes early, it would show your boss, you appreciate your job, and want to keep it." So, all my life, I have made it a practice to arrive to work early, just in case of a flat tire.

My fellow workers really appreciated the work I put in, getting the store ready for the next shift. One once told me: "When I check the schedule and I follow your shift, I celebrate, because I know everything will be done. That courtesy was returned one night when my co-worker gave me a heads-up.

"Joan" (not her real name) found out that I didn't sell pornography, and became irate. She felt that I was being treated special. It just irked her, that I seemed to have some special privileges.

A few weeks earlier, she confronted the manager about it. When she didn't get any satisfaction, she really became angry. The following day she lied about me and said I never put the magazines back on the shelf, at the end of my shift. She complained that she was having to work twice as hard, to cover for my laziness. She also inferred that I was cheating the customers, by not selling everything Circle K had available.

The manager told her that she had never heard a negative word, from any of the other employees, or any customer. In fact, every time she had shown up early in the morning, everything was done and the store always looked great. That was not what she wanted to hear, and it really set Joan off. Joan had made it her personal mission to get me fired.

When Joan didn't get me fired, she got vindictive.   She began to sabotage my work. Even worse, she threatened the manager. Joan told the Manager, that if something wasn't done, she would go over the manager's head. She even called the corporate offices and complained. The corporate office told Joan, that until a customer complained, there wasn't much they could do.

This informant told me, that she had overheard Joan bragging to the manager that she was going to get corporate to fire me. Joan and her husband had come up with a plan. He was going to be coming in for a magazine on my shift that night. If I didn't sell him one, he, as a customer, was going to write a formal complaint to corporate.

Sure enough, that night Joan's husband came in and requested a pornographic magazine. I let him know, that he was the first person that had ever asked me for one. I didn't want to betray the confidential "heads up" so I did not let on, that I knew who he was. I just explained that as a Christian, I didn't feel comfortable dealing with that kind of material. So, he left.

The next morning, when the manager came in, I had already decided to resign from my position, because I was putting her in an awkward situation.

Why are some people like Joan? Just mean and vindictive. What could she possibly gain by forcing me to sell Pornography? Why did she even care? There are just pure, evil, people. If they sniff out something that even hints of unfairness, they go on a crusade. Frankly, I'm glad there is unfairness in the universe, otherwise, I would have to die for my sins. Gratefully, Jesus unfairly took my punishment on himself and paid off my sins. I was unfairly set free.

I was almost relieved that I left my job at Circle k. I hated working graveyard shifts. Doctor Kinderman and I remained friends, and he grew to love Michelle as well. His long visits while I worked, were the only thing I was going to miss.

Meeting Marie

By Christmas break, Michelle and I were getting pretty serious, so I decided that it was time she meet my family. She of course knew all about Marie's mental condition and the stories of abuse. I tried to prepare her, but I could only do so much.

I contacted Bud and Marie, and let them know I was driving up to Oregon, for a visit with my girlfriend. When we arrived in Hermiston, instead of honoring Michelle, and taking the afternoon off, they were working at the Cabinet shop.

We drove out to the shop. Bud came out to the car, and I introduce him to Michelle.

The first words out of his mouth were, "I don't know what was wrong with the first one, I liked her." He was of course referring to Jill.

Then he told us, he was leaving, and he needed to run to the store. We had traveled all the way to Oregon, and he simply jumps in the truck and leaves us standing there. I am stunned. The moment we arrive he abandons us. We went inside the cabinet shop, to be near the wood-burning stove and I introduced Michelle to Marie.

I think it's important to understand at this point, even though Marie had always been cruel and mean, she always seemed to be drawn to the "spiritual." The problem was, it was always the outside fringes of the occult. Accompanied by the most wacko teachings, and always on the mystical side of the spectrum. It has been my experience, that the simple-minded and mentally challenged people of this world, seem to be drawn into the mysterious side of spiritualism. Marie was no different.

As we were warming up by the fire and chatting, Marie launched into the latest fad in her spiritual journey. She was somehow trying to prove to Michelle and I, that she also is connected to God. She starts telling us she has power, given to her by God Himself, and that she can demand anything she wants, and it will be done.

I look over at Michelle and give her that "I-told-you-she-was-crazy" look. Marie must have seen me, because she suddenly says, "Come with me, and I will show you."

She walked outside, into the snowstorm, and to my horror, she starts chanting and screaming at the snow to stop. Of course, it does not, so she continues.

Picture the scene. I am here at my parent's place to introduce my future wife to them, and Bud is so nervous he unintentionally insults Michelle and immediately leaves. That leaves Marie and she is standing out in a snowstorm, commanding it to stop snowing…. what else can go wrong?

Marie, embarrassed that she has not been able to prove she has power, comes back inside and tells us that she is so powerful, she can pick up red-hot coals and it will not burn her! Before I can yell, she has already grabbed one in her hand, and we hear this sickening, sizzle sound. Marie screams out in pain, but it is too late. She has melted her skin. When we ask to see it, she starts telling us it doesn't hurt. We can see she is in agonizing pain, but she is trying to be stoic, to protect her pride.

This is NOT how I saw this visit playing out. I am wondering if Michelle is having second thoughts. I ask God, "Why can't I just have normal parents?"

Michelle's mom Is a psych nurse. Michelle's dad is a professor and Chair of the sociology department at Point Loma Nazarene University. I can just imagine what they will think of me when she tells them this story.

I had not met Michelle's parents. We were planning on flying down to San Diego during Spring break. My thought was, it couldn't possibly go as horribly, as this visit with Bud and Marie!

Her Parents

Two months later, on valentine's day, we went and looked at wedding rings. I hadn't officially asked her, but we had talked about a summer wedding. We made plans to meet with her parents, over the upcoming spring break. There were actually several reasons, for the trip to California. I needed to meet her parents for the first time. I also wanted to ask her father for Michelle's hand In Marriage, and Michelle needed foot surgery. She had developed bone spurs marching in the marching band. She was in extreme pain and was struggling to walk.

She wanted to be able to walk down the aisle at our wedding, so she needed to have this surgery, during spring break. She also needed to get it done, while she was still under her parents' medical insurance. So, a few weeks later we flew down to San Diego.

I bide my time, waiting for the proper moment to talk to Nelson, her father. But before I had a chance, Michelle, her mother, and I had to meet with the surgeons and get the pre-op instructions.

When the doctor came in, he explained, that he planned to do the right foot first, then, when it has healed, later in the year, he would do the left.

Michelle interrupted him and informed him that she wanted them both done at the same time. The doctor strongly advised against it, but Michelle was determined.

When we left the office, Ruth, Michelle's mother, stopped us in the hallway and demanded to know "What is going on." She scolded Michelle for being so demanding, about having both feet done at the same time. We try to act innocent, but Ruth is determined to get to the bottom of this.

"What was that all about?" She demands! "Why can't you just have one foot done now, and the other during the summer?" She is very upset.

Michelle feels she is being backed into a corner. She doesn't want to lie to her mother, so she spills the beans. She is planning to be married in June, and she wants to walk down the Aisle. That I have come to ask dad for her hand.

Ruth immediately says, "We've known that since your first letter home. In fact, I saved that first letter!"

When we arrive back at the house, I immediately ask Nelson if I could have a word with him. He is gracious and kind but he was concerned. Three things he felt were noteworthy. Firstly, I was 25, and she was only 19. Secondly, she had not finished college. Thirdly we had only known each other for five months. Yet, he had no objections and was excited to give his blessing.

I could tell Nelson liked me. Michelle's mother on the other hand…. not so much.

Nelson and I couldn't have been more different! He was a short, round, baldheaded, soft-spoken, intellectual, and somewhat effeminate. I was tall, athletic, outspoken, comedic, and pure masculine. He liked poetry, I liked action. He drove dangerously slowly, I liked to put the hammer down. He hated sports; I loved all forms of sports. He was the quintessential nerd, and I was the jock. He was the passive one and Ruth ruled the roost. I was a born leader and Michelle my strength. Yet, what Nelson and I did have in common, outweighed all our differences. We both had a deep love for God. We were kindred spirits, in all things important.

After he and I spoke, the girls came in and the four of us discuss all our options. It was agreed the wedding would wait till August. This would give Nelson time to finish teaching his summer classes, and give them both, one more summer with Michelle.

That evening, Michelle and I went for a walk and I got down on my knee and asked her to marry me. I put the ring on her finger, and this time I knew with absolute certainty, we would be wed.

Devastating Accident

The next day, Michelle went in for surgery. She had both feet done and both were in casts. She was now in a wheelchair. I was lifting her in and out of the car, and pushing her wheelchair everywhere.

One day, just a few days before we flew back to Boise, I was driving her father's car on the highway. The car in front of me was driven by an older gentleman. We were traveling at highway speeds; I would guess around 60 miles per hour. His car drifted to the right and caught the curb. It jumped up on the sidewalk and struck two teenage girls who happened to be running for P.E. classes.

It was a horrible thing to watch. I saw girls fly like rag dolls. One girl had been thrown into the trees, and the other went over the top of the car, and her body came to rest in the Highway gutter. I slammed on my brakes and skidded to a stop without hitting the girl at the side of the highway.

With her feet in casts, Michelle was horrified to realize she could do nothing.

I jumped out to help, but the old man just kept going.

I raced back to the young girl on the Highway, and she was moaning, so I knew that for the moment she was alive. I ran to the other girl, who had been thrown out into the trees, and when I looked down at her, I was sick to my stomach. Her face had gone through the windshield. The windshield wiper had split her face in two. The upper part of her skull had been deskinned, and her eyeball was hanging out of the socket. I assumed she was dead, so I ran back to the first girl, who was still alive, to see what I

114

could do. I took her hand and told her she was not alone. I told her, help was on the way. This was before cell phones, so I yelled at one of the other cars that had stopped, to go call for an ambulance.

Just as I did that, I noticed a firetruck and paramedic unit, coming in the opposite lanes, so I jumped up and started waving my hands wildly. They saw me and drove over the median straight to us. I learned later, that they had just left the hospital. They had just restocked their paramedic gear for a new shift. Within two minutes of the girls getting hit, they were both being attended to. They were put into plastic blowup body casts and transported to the hospital.

I had stayed by the one girl's side, holding her hand as they worked to save her life.

The older man that had hit them, returned. He was in a state of shock and had driven up the road, where he could turn around, and had come back. The police arrived and were doing their investigation. One of the investigators discovered that the girls had been hit at such a high rate of speed, that they were jerked out of their running shoes. The running shoes were still on the sidewalk, where they were originally hit.

They were students at Patrick Henry High School, the very school where Michelle had graduated. Michelle's younger sister and brother were both still attending there. We later learned, that both girls survived, but did not return to school, until the next year. The miracle of that day was the fact that just seconds after they were hit, the paramedics came driving by. I have often wondered how those girls' lives turned out.

One other time, I had seen someone get hit by a car. When I was in third grade, a young boy got off the bus and his mom was waiting, on the other side of the highway, for him. When he realized he had forgotten his trumpet case, he ran back on the bus and as he exited the second time, he just ran across the highway. He didn't look and ran out into the traffic lane and was hit.

All I remember is him flying and he was spinning so fast that his arm and legs were fully extended, so he must have been knocked unconscious. I can vividly see him spinning to a stop on the grass. I also remember that his trumpet case took the brunt of the impact and that a fence, kind of caught him. He was actually back in school several weeks later. I don't remember the seriousness of his injuries. I only mention it because I have seen several instances of people being struck by a vehicle. It is truly a gruesome experience.

Life is so utterly fragile. In an instant, it can change forever. These two girls experienced an accident that took less than a second to happen. Yet their lives were changed forever.

I drove back to the house, and my life was also deeply impacted by the day's events. Michelle and I flew back to college one last time. I was finishing up my last term of college.

Dr. Please!

During the last term of school, I took three classes that were all upper division and I needed to pass them to graduate. All three classes required **extensive** term papers. So, I decided to combine a subject matter, that would work for all three classes if that were at all possible. This was totally acceptable in academia, as long as it was completely your own work. Of course, you have to be sure that it meets every requirement, specific to each class. Some professors are looking for certain criteria for a specific paper.

Having looked over each syllabus, I found that the hardest class was Dr. Blue's class. (For reasons that will become clear, I have to change his name, it is not my intention to put a black eye on a long and illustrious career). He was a difficult professor, but from past experience, I had already learned about these professors, and what they were looking for. Yet I knew this particular professor was a bit more demanding. The other two classes were taught by two of my favorite professors and I knew them well. I was well aware of what they expected. I also knew they were flexible.

So, all three papers were almost identical, except for the small incidentals. I tweaked them to bring out the best in each class. At the end of the term, I received my grades. In one class, I received an outstanding 98 out of a possible 100 points, or essentially an A plus. In the other class, I received a letter grade of (A+). Yet in Dr. Blue's class, I received an F! I was shocked and immediately went to his office to challenge the grade.

Dr. Blue was curt with me and had a bitterness that was totally perplexing. I asked him, why I had received an F.

He told me flatly, "That is what you deserve."

Deserve? "What do you mean deserve?" I asked in all seriousness!

"That's what all you baseball players deserve!" He yells at me. "You shouldn't even be allowed on this campus!"

What??? I ask myself. Baseball players? He must think I'm a baseball player? He is making no sense at all.

When I ask him to be specific, he jumps up and points to the door. I protested, and asked again, "Are you kicking me out of your office without an explanation?" WOW!

I was so baffled I didn't know what to do at first. I found myself walking across campus, and saw the administration building and I decided to see Dr. Ford, the academic dean. He graciously accepted my unscheduled appointment. I quickly explain the situation, and he asked to see the other two papers. I quickly run over to my apartment, retrieve the other two papers and return to his office. I sit quietly in his office, as he reads all three papers.

He tells me he is impressed with my paper. The papers were exceptionally constructed and well thought through. He agrees, it is inexplicable that Dr. Blue would give me an F! Dr. Ford also agreed, the footnotes were spot on, the bibliography was perfect, and he admitted this made no sense to him, at all.

He asked me to accompany him.

So armed with all three papers, we walk back over to Dr. Blue's office.

Dr. Ford asks me to remain quiet, and he will do the talking.

We are ushered into Dr. Blue's office and Dr. Ford greets him warmly and in gentle tones. He is walking a fine line, and I notice he is almost treating Dr. Blue like a child. Yet when the issue of the paper comes up, Dr. Blue becomes enraged again. He spews the same unintelligible gibberish as before. Dr. Ford never loses his temper and excuses us and we leave.

As we get out of earshot, he stops me and puts his hand on my shoulder. "Mr. Arbogast, you are absolutely correct, and you have every right to bring Dr. Blue before the academic senate. If you do, I will back you the entire way, you will certainly win. But I would like to ask you to reconsider. You see this is Dr. Blues' last term teaching. He is retiring. He has been battling dementia. The entire staff has been heartbroken over his diminished capacity. We have had to endure the progression, and it has broken our hearts. He has had a long and spotless tenure here, and we want to honor him at graduation."

"You have every right to take him before the board, but if you do, it will get ugly, and tarnish his stature forever. We had desperately hoped we could get through this one last term, without incident, but you are unfortunately the innocent victim of his diminished capacity."

"When you were retrieving these other two papers, I took the opportunity to look over your academic standing. Because you received an A on midterms and another A on your final, this F, will give you a C in this class. You will pass. Your Grade point average will not be affected at all."

"I know I have no right to ask this of you, but would you consider letting this injustice stand, for Dr. Blues' sake? I will leave it up to you."

He reiterated, "If you do decide to take this further, I will defend you all the way. This is an utter miscarriage of justice, you deserve an A. You know that, and I know that. I am just thrilled you had these other two papers. What a perfect time to use your prerogative to write virtually the exact same paper for all three classes. That is divinely poetic."

Standing right there, I told him I would **not** pursue this any further.

I would see Dr. Ford one more time at school, just a few days before graduation. He called me into his office, and with the biggest grin on his face he says;

"Mr. Arbogast it would seem, that you are one Physical Education class short of graduation! I did a little digging and found that you have eight P.E. credit hours, at Blue Mountain Community College, that we did not accept as accredited when you entered NNC. I believe Mr. Arbogast, that you have shown that, to overlook a miscarriage of justice, is an honorable trait. I believe I too, will overlook your lack of credits, and prepare your diploma."

Would he have overlooked that one credit hour anyway? Probably? But it was his way of letting me know he appreciated my grace towards Dr. Blue!

I graduated a few days later and immediately drove to my first assignment. I had been hired as youth pastor of the Yreka California church of the Nazarene.

Yreka

The Nazarene church in Yreka, was in the middle of a building program when I arrived. So, my duties varied. Youth pastor and construction worker. I had helped my uncle build a house in high school, and the experience I gained working construction at Yreka, paid dividends throughout my (40-plus years) of ministry. God used that time in Yreka to prepare me for all the times I would need it, in later years.

Assent of Mt. Shasta

That summer, I planned an adventure, with the young men in the youth group. We wanted to conquer climbing Mt Shasta. It is a two-day climb. We would climb up to base camp on the first day, and then leave at 4 am the next morning and attempt the summit. It was July, so it was difficult and dangerous to climb if the snow got too soft. If we left early enough in the morning, we could make it, up and back, on hard-packed ice and snow. We were prepared with ice picks and crampons. (Crampons are spikes you attach to your climbing shoes.)

It took all day to hike to base camp. The adrenalin was running fast through my body.

It was so bitterly cold that night, that I could not sleep. I had been a poor struggling student and couldn't afford a decent sleeping bag or coat. The temperatures, were well below freezing that night, and my body shook with shivering. Fortunately, the sky was crystal clear and the moon and stars glistened off the snow. It seemed almost light. We were at such a high altitude, I could see the glow of yellowish lights, from the San Francisco Bay area. Nearly 240 miles away. From that high, you could see the curvature of the earth.

Eventually, I gave up on sleep, got up, and walked around to keep warm.

When we started the climb the next morning, there were a number of us. Unfortunately, half of them succumbed to altitude sickness and had to return down the mountain.

You really must have a great desire, if you want to climb a mountain of this size. Mt. Shasta was 14,180 feet high, just 300 feet shorter than Mt. Whitney, the tallest mountain in the lower 48 states. Mt. Shasta is the sentinel of Northern California, while Mt Whitney is the Sentinel of Southern California.

Some of the young men, simply could not handle the extreme harshness of the climb. They turned back. Yet there were a few of us, that were utterly determined to make it. We kept encouraging each other, to keep going.

The winds at that altitude were very high and you needed to be right next to someone to hear them yell. The wind chill was probably dangerous, but I wasn't going to let anything keep me from the top. The cruel part of climbing Mt. Shasta is the secret it hides at the top.

The last 300 feet are almost totally vertical. Every step is agonizing and you feel like you're gasping for breath.

I had run the mile in track when I was in High School. I remember the taste of blood, you can get in your mouth, and Climbing at this altitude, was no different. On that last 300 feet of the climb, you could only take one step, pull yourself up, then rest, trying desperately to catch your breath. Then another and rest. It was hand-over-hand climbing. Slamming your ice pick into the snow to get a grip and making sure your crampons were secure and then you would hoist up one step. It took well over an hour for me to navigate the last 300 feet. It seems comical, because that is the distance of a football field, yet at that altitude every breath is excruciating. I could jog a hundred-yard dash in under 20 seconds, but up at the top of this mountain, I couldn't seem to catch my breath after a single step.

When I finally made it to the peak, the wind was so hard, we had to stay on our hands and knees. We crawled around and then were forced to remain seated, for fear we could be blown over the side.

On the peak, there is a metal box, chained to a metal post. Inside the metal box, is a notebook. Everyone who makes it to the peak leaves a note and signs the book. I still remember what I wrote, "Never, ever again!" This was my last climb to the top of Mt. Shasta. Later in life, I climbed other mountains, but not this monster.

They say when you conquer a mountain, you like to stay on top and enjoy the view. Not true. All I could think of was getting out of the wind, and back down to safety. Perhaps if I had been dressed more appropriately for the climb, I would have felt differently, but all I could afford was an old coat, that was threadbare. I look back on it now and marvel at my reckless stupidity. But I also accomplished something, most in the human race, will never even attempt.

Counselor Search

The highlight of every year for any youth group is summer camp. A week of amazing activities. As the week starts, the camp is divided into teams. Throughout the week, they participate in countless challenges, to earn points for their teams. At the end of the week, there is the grand finale. Campers and Counselors alike, look forward to this event.

Throughout the week teams earn a thousand points here or there. Yet in the Grand Finale, the object is to locate Counselors, who have hidden themselves. Basically, a combination easter egg hunt, and a massive hide and seek. Needless to say, it is a point of pride for the counselors not to be found, and they take hiding, very seriously.

If a camper finds a counselor, then it is worth 5,000 points for their team. Campers, therefore, hunt with extreme due diligence. If they can find even one counselor, they are celebrities on their teams. With the coup-de-grace to find the last counselor. The last counselor is worth a staggering 25,000 points. So, for the pride of the week, counselors, every year, try to hide so well, that they get the honored distinction of "last Counselor". It's like the movie "The Hunger Games", in that you hear over the loud pa system, across the entire camp, as each counselor is found, and how many are left.

Imagine 300-plus high school kids, searching with all their might, to find a limited number of places to find counselors. And one of the biggest challenges is to become the first epic counselor that cannot be found at all. That was my goal that year. I wanted to be the first counselor, that couldn't be found. Oh, and I should mention, that once a team finds a counselor then that counselor helps that team in the search. So, you never disclose to the other counselors where you are planning on hiding.

That year I had decided that I was going to do something amazing, I took a shovel and dug a shallow grave, put dirt over me, and then to cover the freshly dug dirt, I covered myself with pine needles. Including my face, so I breathed through the pine needles. I didn't want to have them step on me, so I found bushes and buried myself in them. That way I was fairly safe that they would not step on my face. For several hours I listened, as one by one, each counselor was located, but eventually, the entire camp was looking for me. I succeeded in the first part of my plan, the last counselor! Now I wanted to be the first that could not be found.

Eventually over the P.A. system, came the announcement, 10 more minutes, 5 more minutes, and then the countdown, 10-9-8-..... and then the words I had been waiting for all week. "Perry, we are unable to find you?"

There were a number of campers standing near the bush when I came up out of the ground through the pine needles. I startled them! I must have looked like the rising dead. I had done it. I was living large until that night.

I would later learn that I had inadvertently buried myself in Poison oak. To make matters worse the most toxic oils, are found in the root system. My body began to form little blisters, then it began to ravage my body until I ended up having to go to the hospital. The blisters began to break and form large lesions. At first, the doctors told me, that it would only last a week or so. I told them that was great because I was getting married on August 3rd. That was still three weeks away. I had a two-week cushion.

Unless you are allergic! Which I was. The rashes and blisters began to grow, and I was bleeding this putrid clear substance. Eventually, they were changing my dressings every half an hour. Not only did it not go away, but the doctor couldn't get it under control. When I finally arrived in San Diego, a week before my wedding, Michelle's mother, a nurse, took one look at me and called a specialist she knew.

When the Doctor found out I was getting married in a few days, he graciously asked me to come to see him that very day. He worked with me, and it began to improve, but not enough. I was married with Poison Oak rashes and blisters over my body.

NOT HOW I HAD PICTURED MY WEDDING!!!!!

The Perfect Wedding and Not-so-Perfect Honeymoon

Michelle and I were married in an idyllic setting. In a chapel on the Point Loma campus. It was a beautiful sunny day, and the birds were singing in the trees. Then we went to a marina, on Del Coronado Island, for our reception. We spent the first two days of our honeymoon, at the Del Coronado hotel. On the first day, Michelle got a horrible sunburn. Her shoulders were so badly blistered that you could see the scars from them, for the rest of her life.

The Honeymoon went from bad to worse. We had borrowed a car from the pastor's family, because my car, was an old brown Plymouth Valiant. Not only ugly but completely unreliable. We received a phone call from the pastor, and were asked to cut our honeymoon short, and return their car.

Our pastor and his wife, Alvin and Celia Jolly, had a family emergency and needed the car. This is what we learned. At a reunion in the Seattle area, six members of Alvin's family had jumped into a car and were driving down to the local 7-11. On the way, they were hit by a drunk driver and killed all six of pastor Jolly's family. Pastor Jolly, needed the car to drive up to Seattle, to be there for the rest of his family.

It was just as well. Our game plan was to drive up the coastal highway for our honeymoon. But Michelle got car sick, after just a few miles. I am itching and bleeding, and Michelle is desperately trying not to vomit. To make matters worse it was extremely hot in southern California in August. We jumped on Interstate 5, and that was the end of a not-so-perfect honeymoon.

Poverty

When we were married, the only housing we could afford, was an old camp trailer. It had not been used for years, so it smelled musty and moldy. We couldn't afford to park it in a trailer court. An old couple from the church, allowed us to park it out on their property. The placement was a disaster. We were sandwiched between the railroad tracks and the Highway. All day long, and all night long, the trains would scream by us, at full speed. It was so loud, it sounded like it was coming right through the front door.

On the other side of the trailer, was the constant noise of trucks and cars rushing by on the main highway.

The trailer was also several miles from town, so we were somewhat isolated. Yet, it was all we could afford.

I was a youth pastor, and the church could only afford to pay us $500 a month. Out of those five hundred dollars, we had to pay Taxes, Social Security, Rent, Fuel, Food, and everything else. We couldn't really afford food, so we bought Top Ramen noodles in bulk. We couldn't afford a bed, so we slept on the floor.

On the first night, after we turned out the lights, Michelle felt something like raindrops on her face, so I got up and turned on the lights. To our horror, it was swarms of earwigs dropping from the ceiling. Tens of Thousands of earwigs came out of the walls. The ceiling was teaming with them, and they were dropping on the floor. It turned out, the trailer was completely infested, with the little creatures.

We didn't get much sleep that first night. The bugs were crawling all over the ceiling, walls, and floors. As soon as we turned out the light, they came streaming out of the cracks in the paneling, light fixtures, and outlets.

When you are poor, there are many indignities that you have to live with. You can't afford anything new, so you buy used. Someone else's cast-offs. Many times, it is broken, worn out, dented, or damaged. It is exasperating, to continually be fixing things when they break. You can't afford to replace them, so you are constantly patching them back together. It is embarrassing and humbling.

Poverty isolates you. You don't dare invite friends over. You can't afford to feed them, or even offer them something to drink, but water. You can't afford snacks; those are a luxury. You are too embarrassed to show them, that you can only afford two chairs around the table, and those two chairs, are patched up chairs. You must keep someone from sitting on them because they could collapse.

You are ashamed to have someone over, or they would discover you can't afford heat. Michelle and I had to endure the indignity of dressing in winter clothing, with gloves, in our trailer. We could see our breath. And ice formed on the inside of the windows. The baseboard heating was simply too expensive. There is no fireplace in a camp trailer. So, we were forced to endure the freezing temperatures!

Yet it was those embarrassing indignities, that God used to encourage Michelle and I to change our financial futures. We didn't want to live the rest of our lives in poverty, like our parents. Our parents had always lived in oppressive debt. They had always lived, paycheck to paycheck. Neither Michelle nor I enjoyed wonderful vacations as children because our parents couldn't afford vacations. Our parents never had savings accounts. They simply accepted their debt, as a natural way of living. Michelle and I wanted to change that paradigm. We didn't want to live that way. We were prompted, to change our financial course and direction.

We lived our lives, debt free, and never bought anything on credit. We had watched our parents paying 15 to 30% interest on credit cards. That seemed like a great waste of money. I have often wondered how many hundreds of thousands of dollars, our parents shelled out in interest over their lifetimes. Michelle and I were determined to change that in our marriage. We hated the indignities of poverty, so we started the long climb out of the pit of debt.

It turned out to be one of the best decisions in our lives. Yet in the first year of our marriage, we had to endure living in a camp trailer.

Burglar

We had some pretty scary things happen in that old camp trailer. One night while we were sleeping, we were awakened by the front door squeaking open. My hair stood up on end. A burglar had entered the trailer, in the middle of the night. We could hear him rummaging through the kitchen.

We were next to the highway, so I assumed he had seen, what must have looked like an old abandoned camp trailer. He wasn't trying to be quiet at all.

It was somewhat dark, so I stealthily stood up and ventured towards the bedroom door to look down the hallway, into the kitchen. Unfortunately, as I peered around the corner, I came face to face with the Burglar. He was standing inches from my face. I screamed like a third-grade girl and jumped back, fists at the ready. Michelle started laughing.

That confused me…. here I was, more terrified than I had ever been, and she was laughing? It was surreal, and for that nanosecond, I rationalized she was so scared, all she could do was laugh.

Then it hit me that the burglar was stark naked and in the same pose I was in. That's when I realized that I was looking at myself, in the full-length mirror, on the back of the bedroom door. It was still closed!

Turns out, our burglar was a cat, that had nudged the front door open, and was looking for something to eat.

Soap

Living at this level of poverty, was the hardest for Michelle. I, personally, had been struggling with poverty, as a college student, for years. I was well aquatinted with being poor. I grew up in poverty. She had grown up middle class. I had lived all my life, as trailer trash. She had grown up, in a beautiful, middle-class neighborhood.

One day, when she returned from buying groceries for the week, I could see, she had been crying. When I asked her why she had been crying, she explained to me, that we could only afford one type of soap.

"What?" I asked.

She realized at the store, that instead of being able to purchase Shampoo, Dish soap, Hand soap, laundry soap, and something to clean her glasses, she could only purchase one soap. It would have to do, for all our cleaning needs. We washed our hair with the same soap we used to wash the dishes.

In the study of human relationships, they discovered that shared trauma bonds people together. In battle, soldiers that survive a near-death experience together, form a tight bond. When we live through a devastating experience with someone else, we form deep attachments with them.

This happens in marriages as well. When two people pull together and work through a devastating experience with each other, their relationships are strengthened. What we later learned was God was using these early years to bond us together. We had to work together to survive, and it actually worked in our favor.

Struggling is not all bad. When a butterfly is in the cocoon, it has to struggle for days to escape. But that struggle strengthens its wing muscles, so when it does, finally work its way out, its muscles are strong enough to fly away. If someone tries to help the butterfly and opens the cocoon prematurely, it will lead to the butterfly's death. Its wing muscles don't develop and it won't be able to fly. It is then helpless and becomes easy prey for the birds.

It's one of the ironies of life. Hardships, and struggles, develop strength and character. It teaches life lessons, that will prove to be beneficial throughout life. There are disciplines in life that are only developed in difficult struggles. If we jump in prematurely and try to save the day, we may actually be doing grave damage in the long term. Children, who are constantly saved from negative consequences, grow up to become soft. Life, in the long run, becomes more difficult to survive. It is not all bad, to

124

allow someone to fight their way through difficult circumstances, because that struggle, is invaluable as a teaching tool.

Our struggles in poverty, and having to endure maddening experiences, strengthened our resolve to escape. It worked to inspire us. It gave us the passion to change.

It worked as a deterrent. Consequences can do that. They are so nasty, that we never wanted to experience them again. So, it inspired us to change behaviors, and practices, that led to those horrible consequences.

Part of the reason our prison system isn't working, is that we've made it too comfortable. Why stop illegal behavior, when the consequences are so soft? Prison only works, if it is a deterrent. For punishment to work, it must cause the perpetrator to want to change their behavior. Why should they want to change their behavior, when life in jail, is made so delightful? Gyms to work out in, watching T.V. all day, Recreational sports, computer rooms, and three meals a day, that they don't have to work for. What's not to like? Why change behaviors on the streets, if this is what awaits in jail?

Part of the reason the murder rate is so high in the United States is that the perpetrator doesn't fear any real consequences. What's the worst that can happen? To keep someone from pulling the trigger, there has to be something, so horrible awaiting them, that they fear pulling the trigger. There has to be a deterrent, so horrific, that it would keep them from even considering murder. This is the very reason, most countries around the world, have a public death penalty. Others, who witness the hanging, or execution, say to themselves, "I don't **ever** want that to be me!"

Unfortunately, we have taken the consequences for murder, softened them, and made them so sterile, that they no longer work as a deterrent. We have taken the fear of the death penalty off the table. Somehow, in an effort to come across as compassionate, we have taken the sting, out of punishment. This has led to an unanticipated consequence. What we have inadvertently done, is causing the death of millions of other innocent people, who perhaps wouldn't have been murdered, if there had been the death penalty awaiting the perpetrator. Since we have taken away the deterrent, it has unintentionally led to more deaths.

Consequences are actually a good thing. They cause us to pause and consider. If the consequences are severe enough, we will choose to forgo the instant gratification we could experience now, rather than risk the horrific consequences. This is why God put severe consequences in the bible. He is wise enough to see that without punishment, without deterrent, even more harm is done in the long run. In the long run, our softness on punishment has caused even more pain and anguish. Because we were trying to show compassion for the criminal, we have caused more, literally millions more innocent victims. That's the irony of being compassionate, we must balance all the consequences, short-term and long. With all parties, the perpetrators and potential future victims.

We see this same principle at work in our failed welfare system. The reason welfare is so destructive is it makes living as a dependent, too easy. Why struggle to find a job and work, when the government makes it so easy not to? The welfare system rushes in and saves the day, but unintentionally breeds a level of apathy, which develops a dependent. If someone has to experience the full weight of consequences, it works as a deterrent. This will cause them to change their behavior to escape the consequences. Only harsh consequences motivate! Our welfare system does nothing to motivate. Quite the opposite, it encourages dependence.

Humans naturally gravitate towards ease. The way of least resistance. But in the long run, it may cause a softness, the is detrimental. The evidence is all around us, in the United States, if we are brave enough to genuinely examine it.

It may seem contradictory to hear this, but in many ways, I am glad God allowed Michelle and I to struggle in those early years. Those struggles have bonded our marriage into an unshakable fortress. They produced a strength, that has helped us endure the long haul.
Sometimes it even led to some comical experiences.

Secret Shoppers
Fast food corporations, have a program, to keep tabs on the quality, of their restaurants. We were approached by someone about being secret shoppers for Burger King. Since we couldn't afford to eat out, we jumped at the opportunity. What a treat, to have a date night, with a free meal, provided each week, by Burger King.

Once a week, the corporate office would send us enough money to purchase a predetermined meal. In addition, they paid us a small salary for our time and effort. We looked forward to going into town, and having a sit-down date, at Burger King. Secretly, we would start a stopwatch and time how long we waited. We would take the temperature of our food. We would report on the cleanliness of the restrooms. Sometimes we were asked to use the drive-through and share our experience. It was one of the simple pleasures of our young married lives. Of course, it gives us something to laugh at now.

The Dump
Michelle and I couldn't afford garbage pickup, so we would go to the dump, once a month, to take all our garbage. It was free back then.

On one such trip, we were grabbing bags of trash out of the trunk, when this homeless-looking old man next to us, started whooping it up. He rushed over to show us his find. He had been rummaging through the garbage and came across an old military binocular case. When he opened it up, to his shock it was filled with gold coins. Evidently, someone had cleaned out the attic of their grandparent's home, and tossed everything, without carefully checking what they were throwing away. They had thrown away, tens of thousands of dollars, in pure gold coins.

The number of coins, in that case, represented years of our wages. I have always had an aching in my heart, that I had not found, that old case. Yet God knew what he was doing.

Our poverty represented a shared crisis! Like I said before, there Is a bond between people who endure and survive a traumatic event. Michelle and I shared the harshness of poverty, and it bonded us together like glue. Perhaps God knew that if we had found that case, it would have been detrimental to what He was teaching us.

We have often laughed; at how little you can live on. It also taught us, what is really important in life. Each other! Circumstances didn't determine the depth of our love; we determined that, and we chose honoring love. We didn't have anything, but we had each other. Bless that old man, perhaps those riches changed his life for the better, I have always hoped so.

Food Pounding

During Christmas, the largest churches on the district, adopt a smaller church and give them a food pounding. The Church members from the big churches are asked to bring in food, and it will be given to the poorest pastors. On the surface, this sounds like people care for the pastors of smaller churches. Yet, the truth is, it soon becomes obvious their hearts are not in it. Many in the church, just throw away their trash food, from their cupboards. On Christmas Michelle and I had to live through the indignity of a "pounding!"

We were unpacking the sack of groceries, and we noticed a can of Wieners, that was bulging. They were years old and rotted. The smell was atrocious. We came across a can of evaporated milk that had rusted out the bottom of the can, and the milk had actually, "evaporated." Pun intended!

There was a can of sauerkraut. Obviously, someone saw the can and threw it away to a pastor. Michelle showed me a box of cake mix and we were actually excited until she noticed that the promotional coupon, for silverware had expired in the early 1960s. The cake mix itself had expired years earlier than that. That box of cake mix must have been thirty or forty years old.

It was obvious, that very little care had been taken in the preparations or any sort of vetting to make sure the food was safe. Almost all the food was expired or rotted. We were sharing our story and someone else received, already used tea bags. What heartless individual, cares so little about honoring a pastor, that they would put something like that, in a sack of groceries? I hated being poor.

Debt-free

Michelle and I made two very important decisions, in the first few weeks of our marriage. The first was, we decided that we would go a full year, without T.V. That way, we could spend our time, truly getting to know each other. We played card games, went for walks, worked together, and did puzzles. We did all kinds of creative things together.

We wanted to love deeply. We devoted ourselves to one another. We made a conscious effort, to avoid any distractions, that might draw us apart.

When we came up with the idea of no television, we had no idea how good it would be for us. It forced us to be creative. It also meant, we talked for hours, every day. At the end of that first year, the experience was so amazing, that we decided to go another year. We never planned it, but as it turned out it was nearly 20 years before we finally got a television. Not because we were opposed to Television, but because we didn't want to lose the amazing closeness we had developed. We were concerned that Television could, over time, distract us from one another. We could see that it was immensely good for us.

The second decision was to live debt free. We had seen what debt could do to marriages. We learned, that two out of three marriages, end due to financial fights. We wanted to have the best marriage possible, so we purposely avoided anything, we felt, might put our relationship at risk. The only big fights we saw our parents engage in, were almost always because of bills. Financial strain puts the whole marriage under stress.... yuck! We wanted our marriage to have joy!

We knew that the bible taught about money, so we studied all it had to say about finances. God showed us, that his children were not to be in debt, to anyone. We were to be servants of Him alone, and if we borrow from someone, at some level we were obligated to them. We put ourselves in bondage, to pay them back. We would have to serve them until we could pay them off. Only then, could we get them off our backs!

We didn't want to be servants to anyone but God alone. Wow, did that turn out to be a good decision! Imagine being married forty years, and never paying interest to anyone.

My parents and Michelle's parents were paying out a fortune in interest, all their lives. Common sense told us, if our parents, had saved all the money they threw away on interest, it would have been hundreds of thousands.

If they had earned interest on that money???? Wow, they would have been wealthy! They opted instead, to live their entire lives, in bondage to debt. We decided: "Not us, thank you very much!"

We just felt it was stupid to pay interest, when interest, is a self-imposed tax. We paid enough taxes to the government. Why would I voluntarily choose, to give my hard-earned money, away? For instant gratification? That's juvenile! Why not take a few extra days longer, and buy it out right?

The hundreds of thousands of dollars my parents paid out in interest, could have paid for my college, instead, it paid for the bankers' children to go to college. Instead of taking vacations themselves, they paid out interest and sent the banker's families on vacations. One way of life seemed foolish, and the other seemed wise we decided, that we would err on the side of wisdom.

We hated poverty, why would we want to prolong it?

We began to daydream of better days. We just imagined coming to the end of the month, and instead of being broke, we had extra money.

If you're reading this and believe it's impossible, then consider this. We did it earning only 500 dollars a month. When you are completely debt free, all you have is utilities at the end of the month. Just imagine what life would be like, with no bills. Truly dream of what that might feel like.

Michelle and I have never been sorry for that decision. Not one time have we regretted it. Truly one of the best decisions we ever made!

The Kiss of Death

That first Christmas at the Yreka church, our church choir was practicing the Christmas musical. I was sitting in the back of the choir, because of my height. I bent forward and whispered something into the ear of Mark York. Mark was a cowboy and rancher. He was a big part of that church. He was also one of the funniest men, I have ever met. What happened next has gone down in lore, at the Yreka church. In large part, because of Mark. In fact, at my retirement, this incident came up.

When I bent forward and whispered in Mark's ear, I inexplicably kissed his neck, as I was used to doing with Michelle. The instant I did it, I thought; "What did I just do?" Mark jolted out of his chair like he had been shot, and screamed "Get away from me you pervert!" I was mortified!

The roar of laughter drowned out all that Mark said in those few moments, and that is probably a good thing for him. I knew it was futile to try and explain. It was habit. I was in the habit of whispering something to Michelle and kissing her neck.

Mark demanded that the choir director sit him "as far away from that "Sexual deviate" as he possibly could. When he said that, there was a roar of laughter that erupted from the choir. It was pure pandemonium.

Mark wouldn't let it go. Every comment he made, just set the choir laughing again. Now it just so happened, I was playing the part of Judas in the cantata. Mark, seizing the opportunity, commented on how appropriate that was. Every time the choir director would try to restore order, Mark would make another comment, and chaos would reign.

Mark asked for disinfectant wipes and demanded that from that time forward, I will be forced to wear rubber gloves.

On and on it went. He warned all the other men sitting next to me, "Watch him closely, if he wants to pray for you, don't let him hold your hand!"

For the rest of my ministry in Yreka, Mark never let it go. I would walk into the church and he would run away, making hilarious comments about saving the woman and children first. I will never live that faux pas down. To Mark York, 'Perry the pervert' will live in infamy. It is one of the many times in my life, I wished we could push rewind, and have do-overs.

Unfortunately, Life is a one-time event. No do-overs! We have one shot at this life. We have one shot to get it right. If we get it wrong, we will pay for it eternally. I often think of those who die and come to realize too late, that there was a God.

A very wise man once stated that life is a gamble. He went on to say, that since life is a gamble, we should play the odds. His argument went like this: If you gamble that there is no God, and you are right, you gain nothing. But if you gamble that there is no God, and there is a God.... you lose everything. On the other hand, if I gamble that there is a God, and there isn't a God, I lose nothing. But if I gamble that there is a God, and there is a God, then I gain everything. The conclusion is this: you have nothing to gain and everything to lose, versus I have nothing to lose and everything to gain. Go with the odds, or you may regret it for eternity.

We have no idea when we might enter eternity. I have been very close many times.

Van Gas

One day, I was driving in the Humboldt Mountains, visiting one of the teenagers who attended our youth group. I had two other teenagers with me at the time, and we were driving on dirt roads, making our way up the mountain. Suddenly, coming around the corner, straight at me, was a propane truck. I slammed on my brakes and looked into the windshield, no driver. On the right side of the road was a sheer bluff, going straight up. On the left side of the road, was a cliff, hundreds of feet down. I had nowhere to go.

I could only wait for the impact. I had almost slid to a complete stop, but the truck was traveling about 20 miles an hour and hit me head-on. It was a violent collision, but we were all wearing seatbelts. The driver suddenly pops up in the windshield. It was a slow-impact accident; thankfully we are all ok.

The driver of the truck jumped out and came running up to us, explaining that he had dropped his calculator, on the passenger floor, and had bent down to pick it up. He apologized and accepted full responsibility.

Since we were in the mountains, there was nothing to do, but try to make our way back to town. We didn't have cell phones back then, and it could have been hours before someone came driving by. My car was still drivable, so we both drove to the Van Gas terminal, and chatted with his boss.

I expected their insurance to accept responsibility and the repairs to be a slam dunk. Yet, later that night I received a phone call from the Manager. He informed me that the insurance company was refusing to pay. What he told me next, I have shared with as many people as I can.

Insurance companies know that if they refuse to pay, even if they know, they are in the wrong, a certain percentage of people, will drop their claim. The insurance company saves money. They also know if they refuse a second time, that another percentage of people will give up. The insurance company saves even more money. Then the insurance company may send out a legal-looking letter, with empty threats of a countersuit, but it is a percentage game with them. The insurance company saves billions of dollars a year this way. By simply denying a claim three times and delaying or bluffing, they know that half the claims will be dropped. They know that the percentages are in their favor, perhaps 60 to 70 percent of the people are intimidated, and will not pursue justice.

Most insurance companies will deny payment three times. Regardless of the excuses they give, they are simply playing a mathematical game. If you submit the same claim four times, that is normally when they will pay.

The manager, bless his soul, gave me these words of advice, the conversation went something like this; *"Perry, I am going to tell you something, keep it between us for a while, or it could cost me my job. What I am about to tell you, is off the record, and I will deny telling you this if I am questioned.*

Our insurance company is playing a game of percentages. They told me, you look too young to pursue this. They are going to play the odds, and see if they can intimidate you into dropping this case.

They know you are a youth pastor, and probably can't afford to hire an attorney. They know we are totally in the wrong, but they are going to bluff anyway.

What they are doing is despicable! It galls me, but to keep my job, I have to play along. Understand this, Perry; If I am ever questioned, I will deny ever telling you this, but I want you to go the distance with this. Don't let them win. Just hang in there and in the end, you will get what is rightfully due you. I have to represent the company in court. I will be forced to play along. I will act as if we have a case, but we don't. Please don't let on that we talked, and that I told you this. Know this, no matter how I act in court, I want you to win."

We did go to court, and when the judge found out that the driver dropped the calculator on the floor, and was reaching for it, he exploded in anger. "What are we doing here? Why are you wasting my time? This is an obvious case of inattentive driving, pay for the man's car and let's move on."

The Judge went on to chastise the driver, and told the manager, that it was only by the grace of God, that the truck didn't blow up, and take half the mountain with it.

The manager winked at me, with a grin. He couldn't come over and say anything to me, but we both knew, that justice had been served. I thank God for watching out for me and sending an honest man. I also thank God for teaching me about the game of percentages, insurance companies play. That has saved me tens of thousands of dollars in my lifetime.

Most people are too intimidated to keep the pressure on insurance companies, and the insurance companies are counting on that.

Sammy

One day I was in my office when the door opens and the craziest guy the world has to offer came running in. He is high on drugs and tweaking. (Tweaking is a term describing a drug-induced trip) He jumps up on my desk and starts this gibberish yelling. I am so startled; I scoot my office chair back to the wall, behind me. I try to talk him down, but he is acting like a wild animal. I somewhat fear for my life. This guy of completely out of his mind. I knew that at any moment he could get violent. At that moment, he is more animal than human.

I continue to try and talk him down, and eventually, he jumps down off my desk. This is my first encounter with Sammy. He is homeless and a drifter. He is living near Yreka because drugs are so prevalent.

Sammy is utterly messed up. I will learn over time Sammy's story; He had received an inheritance settlement and because of his young age, he had spent it on drugs and alcohol. When the money ran out, he did anything he could, to get drugs. He would have sex with anyone, at any time. He had no sense of right and wrong. His mind was damaged by meth and Heroin. When he couldn't find drugs, he told me, he slammed rat poison, to end it all. ("Slammed" is drug culture slang, for injecting it with a needle.)

His eyes were wild and full of fear. Yet even a wild animal can sometimes sense when someone is trying to help. All I could do was listen to his wild rantings. I felt compelled to listen. Sammy told me later, that even in his wild drug-induced hallucination, as he walked by the church, he knew he could find help inside that building, (our church).

132

Sammy and I became friends. He sensed a genuine love from the church, and eventually, he accepted the love that God had for him. Of all the people I have known, who had a relationship with Jesus, Sammy's transformation, was the most dramatic. With God's help, he was able to quit drugs and drinking. Eventually, he came to me and confessed that he was wanted by the police, and asked what he should do. He told me he felt like he should turn himself in. He wanted to face his actions, take the consequences, and put them behind him.

When God's spirit comes into us, that spirit is pure, holy, and honest. Lies become detestable to us. This is what happens to someone, who becomes filled with the spirit of God.

I told him, he was a man of honor now. He was a man of integrity. He was an honest man, with nothing to hide. The sense of justice is a hallmark of the Holy Spirit. An honest man, that has truly been transformed, faces every aspect of his life, in pure truth.

When he walked into the police station, at first, they didn't even recognize him. He was well dressed. Wearing clean and respectable clothes. He looked years younger, and in his right mind. He told them God had completely transformed his life, and that he was no longer going to run. He shared that it was God, that had told him to turn himself in. Sammy told them he could no longer live a lie. He could not move forward in his life until he dealt with his past.

His transformation was so amazing, that he made an impact in the jail. When he stood before the judge, he told the judge he was guilty. He respected their time and didn't want to waste it with a trial. He said "I regretfully did all the things I am accused of, and so much more. I am ready to accept whatever you deem is my due punishment." Sammy was so humble and honest, that it took the judge by surprise.

The judge told the court that the purpose of punishment is to ultimately change behavior. We inflict punishment as a deterrent for future conduct. Part of the jail time is so that the defendant will reflect on their life, and desire to make changes. Yet Sammy was miles down the road from there, so the judge could see no benefit in giving him more time. God had worked it out!

Why do I tell that story? Thousands upon thousands of lives have been transformed by God. That is not unusual at all. What happens next though, really impacted my ministry and theology. It really explains why Jesus became so angry with the hard-core religious men of his day. Those letter-of-the-law, holier-than-thou, hypocrites.

About six months later, I was exiting the back door of the church, following the morning service. I distinctly heard someone crying. I ventured out behind the building and found Sammy just sobbing. I came over to him and put my arm around him, "What's wrong my friend?" I asked.

What he told me made my blood boil. "I have given up so much in my life", he said. "I gave up all my drugs, including weed. I've given up drinking, and not just hard liquor, but even beer. Even one beer leads me to places I don't want to go. I've given up selling drugs and selling myself. I got a job. I've given up so many things. But I don't know, I guess I'm not really saved. I'm not a real Christian yet."

"What are you talking about, Sammy?" I asked incredulously.

"Well Mrs. McGillicuddy....", (a name pastors use to describe dissension-raising busybodies, not unlike the "church lady" made famous by the comedian Dana Carvey), Sammy continued, Mrs. McGillicuddy, ".... just confronted me, and asked me, what made me think I was a Christian? She told me 'No honest upstanding Christian, would do what I still do! "

I thought to myself, what in the world could he still be doing, that is so egregious? Stealing? Fraud? Child molester? What horrible crime was he involved in?

What he told me next, stopped me cold! "I still smoke a cigarette once in a while." He said.

I sat there staring at him, speechless. This was the big crime? He smoked a cigarette?

I almost shouted, "Stop right there!" "Are you telling me some crotchety old woman, told you, that if you smoke a cigarette, you can't be a Christian?"

I was livid! How dare she inflict such drivel, upon one of God's beloved children. She was wrong on so many levels, I didn't know where to start.

I told him, first of all, smoking a cigarette has zero impact on your salvation, any more than drinking Pepsi or chewing gum. Secondly, your salvation is based on trusting in Jesus' righteousness, not your own.

I understood why Jesus became furious with the teachers of the law. They are extremely harmful to God's kingdom! Perhaps that is why Jesus pleaded with us to show mercy, rather than petty judgementalism. How dare she!

Sammy eventually got married and had children. His life, like so many others, was so dramatically changed. This is what happens when someone follows God. He became a wonderfully productive member of society. God had reparented him. Just as, He was reparenting mine.

Sammy and I were utterly convinced that there was a loving God. We could see the contrast, between our lives before Jesus, and after.

Circumstances

Later that year, I was driving a bus full of teenagers to the coast for a retreat. I was working in concert with another youth pastor, and we planned to combine our youth groups and hit the beach. To save money, we planned on camping at their church. We were on our way and having a great time together on the bus.

I love to engage the young people and came up with a bunch of games we could play as we traveled.

One of the activities was voice imitations of characters. I had a few cartoon characters that I could do very well. My favorites were Hannah Barbara and Warner brothers' characters like Snagglepuss, Yogi bear, Booboo, Sylvester, Tweedy bird, and a few more. Some of the kids did great impressions of movie stars like John Wayne, Jimmy Stewart, May West, and several others.

That progressed into animal sounds. Dogs barking, Cats fighting, Elephants, and every animal I could think of. Some of the impressions were incredibly accurate. As we entered the church parking lot, the entire bus sounded like a farmyard. We were imitating a Pig at the time.

Picture the scene: fifty teenagers making the sound of a wallowing pig, when an extremely obese teenager walks out of their church. She was well over 300 pounds. She looks up at our bus and assumes we are directing it at her. In that nanosecond of sheer panic, all I could think of was; "Quickly another animal!!!, and I shouted out the first animal I could think of, COW! Now the entire bus is mooing. The poor girl bursts into tears and runs back into the church.

I was mortified. It took me a minute to pull the bus to a stop, and I made my way inside the church, to find this poor young lady. I walked into the teen room and found her sobbing. The youth pastor, and several girls from their group, were trying to comfort her. They glared up at me.

The youth pastor angrily shouts at me: "Seriously, how could you?"

I tried to explain, but they were not buying what I was selling. It wasn't until my wife came in, and confirmed my story, that things began to calm down.

I don't know if we ever convinced the young lady though!

This was another time in life, I wished I could just push rewind!

Men's Fast Pitch Softball

That year I played in the fall softball league. Just like in most communities, they had co-ed leagues, woman's leagues, and men's leagues. I liked competition, and men's fast-pitch softball was right up my alley. When I had been in college, I played in very competitive collegiate leagues. I liked playing at a high level. Slow-pitch softball just wasn't intense enough for me.

We were one of the better teams in the league that year. One evening we were in a tight one-run game with another top team. It was the last inning and they had us by one run, but we had the last at-bat. The pitcher had allowed two on base and no outs, so it looked like we had the victory in hand. I came up to bat. My thought was, all I needed was a base hit, and we would score the tying run, or even score both runs and win the game.

Just as I was walking to the plate, the captain on the other team calls a timeout and substitutes a woman in as a pitcher. This causes pandemonium. She is not eligible to play in an all-men's league. The captains are in each other's faces. The dugouts empty and the arguing is intense. Men are yelling and screaming at each other.

Their team is accusing us of being afraid of a woman. They are mocking us "What's the matter, you afraid of a girl? You afraid she might be better than you?" Our men were adamant that it's not allowed, in an all-men's league. If she wants to play, there are other leagues for her to play in.

Our team is arguing that what they are doing was specifically designed to take the satisfaction out of our win. It would steal our, Mano a mano, victory. They were trying to steal our thunder.

One of our men shouted, "Take your beating like a man, don't hide behind a woman's skirt!" It got ugly, and I was afraid a fight was going to erupt. To imply that tensions were running high, would be an understatement. Some of the wives finally get involved and tried to reason with their husbands. They just wanted to get the game over, so our captain relented and let her pitch.

She is obviously a college player, a ringer! In her warm-up pitches, she can put the heat on. Now I'm fearful of being humiliated. I had one thing on my mind. Just make contact! As hard as she was throwing, if I just made contact, the ball would be sizzling off the bat. What was running through my mind was; shorten up the swing, or she will put it right by you. They were probably counting on me swinging a haymaker, to hit it out of the park, against a woman. That would put me behind the fastball, and she would strike me out.

All this is going through my mind as I let the first ball go by. I am watching to see if I can "see" the ball. I'm pretty amped up and my concentration is at a high level. Sometimes if you think of it coming in extremely fast, it slows the ball down in your mind, and you are able to get a read on it. On the next pitch, I smash it straight out to the pitcher and it hits her so hard, she is knocked down. It was bang, bang. It happened so fast I couldn't wrap my head around what had just happened.

Of all the things, I had running through my mind, hitting her was the last thing I would ever do. It was not even something I would ever think of. But here I had done it. I had made such good contact, she hadn't had time to respond, and she was seriously hurt. She let out a scream and was writhing in pain. The benches emptied and the fight was on. It was the worst possible outcome. To this day I'm sure people at that game were convinced, I had done that on purpose.

Feminists don't want to hear this, because it doesn't fit into their prejudice, but men want to save maid Marion, not hurt her. We want to rescue, not injure. We want to care for woman, not wound. It's a false narrative to keep pushing the agenda that every man, just wants to subjugate a woman. That is simply not true.

It affects men to witness the wounding of a woman.

One of the many studies that have investigated this issue, determined that when in combat, while it is true that a man is adversely affected when a buddy is killed. It has been proven that the psychological impact is magnified when they see a woman killed. The military has known that for years. That is why they have hesitated to put a woman in combat roles. If a man is held prisoner, and they hear what they believe is another male prisoner being tortured, it is very destructive. Yet if they hear a woman being tortured, the male will divulge almost anything to save her.

Studies prove that first responders are more likely to struggle at an accident scene, where the victims are women and children.

If you have a basketball game, and it's all men playing, and you add just one woman, the play becomes noticeably more docile. The chemistry changes.

Just as women (as a whole) protect children with fierce determination. Men protect a woman. Throughout human history, and in most cultures, it's women and children first, that are saved. It has always been reprehensible, to see a man try to save himself, before his children or wife.

This was another time in my life, I wished I could push the rewind button. I am not the only one that has this desire to push rewind. As this next story will illustrate.

Movie night

As pastor and wife, on occasion, we were invited to someone's home for a meal. On this particular occasion, we were invited by a couple, to join them at their home for a meal and movie. This couple just happened to struggle with Multiple sclerosis which, affected their muscle coordination. It is often accompanied by involuntary tremors. The effects are magnified in a stressful situation. Both of them were battling the disorder. Yet they were living as normal a life as possible.

The meal she prepared was truly a masterpiece of culinary art. She was an amazing chef. The house was immaculate, and the table was beautifully set. I was so impressed at all the work they had gone through, to make this a special night.

After the meal, we retired to the living room, for a wonderful Walt Disney movie. They had rented it from one of the movie rental houses, in Yreka. He grabbed the VCR movie out of the box and slid it into the player. When he returned to the couch, the movie began to play. To their horror, it

137

was an XXX-rated, pornography movie. Someone had played a practical joke at the store and switched movies.

Our host, who was obviously horrified, was desperately trying to get to his feet, but he was so stressed, he lost most of his motor skills. I could have done it, but I was afraid of offending him.

When he finally made it to the VCR, he tried to push the eject button but was tremoring so badly, he couldn't hit the button. In utter frustration, he eventually, just threw himself over the TV. I didn't want to insult him by interfering with him, so I remained seated. Eventually, it became obvious, I needed to get up and turn everything off.

They were horribly embarrassed, and reiterated over and over, that it was not their movie. We laughed about it later, but that night they were both almost inconsolable.

In life, since we don't have a rewind button, it helps if you have a sense of humor. It also helps, if you don't take yourself too seriously.

Blowout in L.A.

The day came when we realized that we could not make it financially, on only $500 dollars a month. At about the same time, the church board came to us and shared that they were in financial trouble. They begged us to stay and find jobs in town until they could afford to pay us again.

God was already working ahead of us, and we received a call from a church in Bellflower California, a suburb of L.A. It was an easy decision, the church in Bellflower was offering us four times the pay, and a parsonage to live in.

During the interview, the pastor asked me if I was a team player. I assured him I was. He then asked an odd question; Will you have my back? If someone comes to you and starts complaining, will you stand by me? He then looks at both Michelle and I and makes a strong statement. "I believe in standing together, as a team, in ministry. We defend each other, and we protect each other. I need your assurance, that if I hire you, you will have my back!" I assured him again, that I was a team player. We were offered the job.

We packed all our earthly belongings onto a little flatbed trailer. We then took ropes and tied the load down. The little trailer was so small, I could tip it up against the house to get it out of the way. The trailer tires were the same size as you would see on a wheel borrow. They were tiny. We were pulling it with a little Honda Civic.

When we arrived in L.A. it was late evening. We were on the I-5 freeway. Suddenly the right tire blew out on the trailer. I pulled over as the traffic raced by. I didn't have a spare tire, so I unhooked the trailer, removed the tire, and threw it in the trunk. I drove off, leaving the trailer on the side of the freeway.

I was desperate to find a service station, that might have a little tire. No such luck. As the evening turned into night, more places were closed. I decided to just return to the trailer and sleep in the car. We couldn't afford a hotel room. The problem was, I had no idea where I had left it. All I knew was it was on I-5 somewhere. So, I asked for directions to I-5.

I drove for hours trying to find the I-5 freeway. I was tired, stressed, and I could not find the stupid I-5 freeway, and I was getting angry.

I would stop and ask someone, "Where I could find the I-5 freeway?" They would give directions, but when I would follow the directions, I could never find it. Finally, in utter frustration, I found a phone booth and called the police.

The officer asked me where I was, and I told him I had no idea. I gave him the name of a side street, and he asked me what color I was. I told him I was white. He told me to, "Hang up immediately, drive ten miles and call him back", He gave me his direct number. He was firm, "Make sure you call me right back, I want to make sure you're ok."

Evidently, I had gotten so lost, I was in Watts. When I called him back, I remember him saying "Son you must have God on your side, because your life was truly in danger."

I explained that I couldn't find the I-5 freeway. That's when he told me that it's called the Golden State freeway. Something I had seen all night long but assumed it was the wrong freeway. So, I had wasted hours, looking for a freeway that I knew as I-5, and that all the people in L.A. knew, as the Golden State freeway. Oooh, I was so frustrated.

The officer wanted to help me find my trailer, so he asked me how long I thought I had been driving in the city before I had the blowout. I told him I had just entered the city. I also remembered some place called Magic Mountain, just before the tire blowout. I could hear the anguish in his voice, "Are you telling me your trailer is near Magic Mountain." "My goodness son, how in the world did you get that lost, do you realize your hours from Magic Mountain!" (Not the exact expletives he actually used)

After this, he could see that this young couple needed help. He took a genuine concern for my predicament. By this time, it was near morning. So, he kept me on the line, and he made some calls and found a place that had the tire. He found a place that was willing to take it off their portable cement mixer. I'm sure the police are still talking about the "truly lost!!!"

I was given very explicit directions to the place that was willing to give me the tire. Then they were extremely careful, to tell me how to find my way back to my trailer. I eventually found my trailer, and to my surprise, they hadn't stripped it clean. I replaced the tire and drove the few hours to Bellflower. By this time, I had been up thirty-some hours.

Unfortunately for Michelle and I, our parsonage was being renovated, and we had to stay with an elderly couple from the church. That would turn into a disaster.

Kidnapping and the Turtle

The old couple owned a sixty-year-old Turtle, that had been in their family since their kids were babies. The children had all grown up with this Tortoise. Of course, the kids were adults now and had families of their own. But this turtle was now the center of this old couple's lives. The family album was filled with pictures of their beloved pet. It would eat Lettice right out of our hands.

Now the old couple had purposely planned a vacation, to correspond with the two weeks we would be there. That way, there would be someone, to watch their prized turtle. Since our house wasn't finished being refurbished, we were glad to do it.

They gave us very explicit instructions about this turtle. How to feed it, how to tend it, how to care for its every need. They also had a warning, don't, under any circumstance, leave the back gate open, because the turtle might get out.

They had been gone, maybe a couple of days when early one morning, I hear squealing breaks, and a woman screaming at the top of her lungs. I run out the back door, and see a red pickup truck with two men, trying to grab an attractive woman. They were trying to kidnap her off the sidewalk. She was putting up a bitter fight.

I screamed for Michelle to call 911, and I ran out the back gate to join the fight. As I got near the perpetrators, they jumped in the truck and raced away. The woman was naturally hysterical. She had simply been out for her morning jog, and these two saw an opportunity and tried to abduct her.

I stayed with her until the police finished their reports. Michelle had also come out and was comforting this poor woman. After we were through, Michelle and I walked back to the house. We were shaken by this incident as well. We had been in L.A. for less than a week and we had already had two harrowing experiences.

That evening we started looking for the turtle, but he was nowhere to be found. We looked everywhere in the yard, but no turtle. Then I remembered the incident that morning. I wondered if I had left the gate open when I ran to help the woman. The gate was of no consequence to me, all I was thinking about was saving that poor woman. The gate hadn't even been a consideration.

We began to hunt and search all around the house. Then expanded our search to the neighbors' yards. We knocked on doors, we pleaded for people to keep an eye out, for a large tortoise. We searched every house within blocks, and then it got dark. Our hearts were sick with worry. That family loved that old tortoise. They would be devastated.

Every day we went out looking for that Turtle. How could a slow-moving tortoise just disappear? We began to assume, it was such a rare find, that someone had seen it on the street, and absconded with it. We kept knocking on doors, but we had no luck.

We were so upset, that we didn't sleep. I couldn't concentrate. All we could think about was that turtle. We had no way of getting word to the couple, to let them know that their family member had vanished. A couple of days before they returned, we were told that our house was ready. Since the turtle was gone, we had no reason to stay, so we moved all our stuff into our new home.

While we were moving, we wanted to notify the entire neighborhood, of our new address and phone number, in the unlikely case the turtle showed up. We were walking to the next-door neighbors, when to our delight, they informed us, that they had found the turtle in their flower garden. What a relief. It had been right next door the whole time.

We took the turtle into the backyard and secured the gate. We finished our move that day, and since the couple would be back in just two days, we decided to stay in our new place.

That evening we dove over to their home and made our way into their backyard. We made sure to spend some time with the turtle and made sure it was well-fed and had water.

We did this for a couple of days. On Saturday, the couple was due back from their vacation.

When we went over that Saturday evening, to meet the old couple, and return their keys, we were met with disastrous news. The couple had returned home, to find that a pipe had burst, and their home was completely flooded. They were furious with us for not being there. The decision to stay at our new house cost us!

Their house had wood floors throughout, and it cost them, tens of thousands of dollars to replace the flooring. That couple pretty much hated the sight of us, after that. Even the pastor chewed me out, for the irresponsible decision, to stay at our new place. Michelle and I could only imagine what they would have done if they had found out about the turtle??? We decided "That would be our little secret."

We made a few more decisions we regretted the first few months in L.A.

At Gunpoint

My new title was Associate Pastor of Youth Ministry. I was responsible for the Jr. High, High School, and College age ministries. Each age group had voluntary staff, that made up our leadership team.

I wanted to make personal contact with everyone on my leadership teams. These were key people helping in the youth program, and I felt it was important to make personal contact.

During the first few weeks, I took the time to drive, one by one to each of their homes. I drove to the addresses listed in the church directory. I had one black lady that was especially helpful and decided to drop in on her. When I found her address, it turned out to be a dirty apartment building. I was still pretty naïve, about the inner city.

I parked the car and walked up to the apartment. There were large groups of people outside, and it seemed that everyone was watching me. It made me feel somewhat uneasy. I knocked on the door, and when the door opened, I had a gun pointed at my gut. It was my youth leader, but she had a furious look on her face. She reached out, grabbed my shirt, and jerked me into the room. She slammed the door behind me. She was obviously very angry.

She began verbally assailing me. "What in the world are you doing? Get out of here and don't you ever come back! Are you trying to get yourself killed? How dare you just show up uninvited! Are you trying to get me in trouble? You idiot!" She opened the door and shoved me out and slammed the door behind me. I was in a state of shock. What had I done?

It turns out, I was in the Watts projects, and whites were hated in that part of L.A.

The next Sunday morning, this lady came to my office and explained she was not angry, as much as concerned for my safety. If I had stayed even a few minutes longer, the gangs would have come to her door. She told me, that I had put her, in an awkward and unsafe situation.

In the 1960s, right there, where she lived, they had the famous Watts riots. In the years to come, this place would burn, in the Rodney King riots. This is a lawless place, that is run by gangs. There have been times when the police, wouldn't even respond to a call in Watts.

I can see now, that once again, God had protected me.

On-ramp

We lived next to the onramp of the I-71 freeway. Unfortunately, the noise was frustrating, as the cars were racing up the onramp 24/7. I got used to the noise, but it was always in the background.

It was raining and a car broke down on the freeway. The elderly couple was stranded and a policewoman came to their aid. Her lights were flashing, and when a semi came near and saw the flashing lights, he put on his brakes and the truck slid out of control. Tragically he struck the policewoman and the elderly woman and knocked their bodies into the brush in our backyard.

That incident was on my mind one afternoon, when I heard a woman screaming, "Help me, someone please help me, he is trying to kill me." I ran out the back door to see a man trying to toss a woman into the traffic lanes. I rushed up the embankment, I was yelling at him to let her go. When he saw me, he stopped.

We were probably a hundred feet from each other, and he started cursing and threatening me. Telling me to mind my own business. I started walking closer and he threatened me. I was a much bigger man than he was and I yelled back, in an effort to intimidate him. As I got near him, he could see how big I was and he ran back to his car.

At this point, I began to worry that he might pull a gun on me. I just stood there, next to his girlfriend. Then the strangest thing happens. The girlfriend starts yelling at me! "Leave him alone!" "What are you doing?"

I am incredulous, "Listen lady, you're the one who called for help!" She started defending this guy, that just minutes earlier, he was trying to kill her. Go figure!

She then begins cussing me out and telling me to go back where I came from. I am utterly confused. They eventually jumped in their car and took off. I found myself standing alone, on the onramp, wondering what had just happened!?

Pastors and law enforcement have always worked together. A number of officers have told me, that the most dangerous call to respond to, for law enforcement, is domestic violence calls. I understood why. The victim can flip on a dime!

I also understood at a much deeper level, the teaching in scripture, that warns that "Entering into a quarrel that has nothing to do with you, is as dangerous as grabbing a dog with rabies by the ears." Proverbs 26:17 Not only will you get bit, it could cost you, your life.

Air Mexico Disaster

Michelle received her RDA (Registered Dental Assistant) license, at Bryman Dental school, while we lived in Bellflower. She worked for a dentist in Cerritos. Her office, just happened to be below, the devastating collision of the Air Mexico airliner and a small plane. The midair collision ripped apart the airliner, and human body parts were scattered over the area. This included the offices, where she worked. The police closed entire streets, and used cadaver dogs, to comb for human remains. For nearly a week she did not return to work.

I thought of those poor people. They were sitting in their seats, excited to be on a trip, one second later, even before they were actually aware, their bodies have been ripped apart and floating towards earth. They never knew what hit them.

The lesson is this, life is utterly unpredictable. We put off decisions, thinking we have a lifetime to decide. It has been my experience, that this is not at all the case.

Chrystal Lewis

At camp that summer, we were divided into small groups, for personal devotional times. One of the girls in my group was Chrystal Lewis. As the week went on, the small group grew close, as we shared our lives with each other. At the end of the week, we were in the group when I was handed a note. "Come to the office, Emergency."

When I arrived, I was told that I had received a call from our Bellflower church and I was to call this number. I was confused because the number had a Washington area code.

To my surprise, it turned out to be one of the young women, who had been in the Enumclaw youth group. She was engaged to be married to my good friend, Steve Rashic. One of the boys I had climbed Mt. Rainier with. We had faced death and survived.

She was crying. I asked her, what was happening? She told me that Kurt and Steve along with some others, had hired a guide to climb another mountain, and they had been hit by an avalanche. Steve and the guide were killed! Kurt was hospitalized. My heart stopped beating, and my ears were ringing. I was in a state of deep sorrow. I didn't know how to respond or what to say. I felt my face flush and my eyes started to burn, as the tears began to flow. These two were, the very two, that had been on the mountain with me, when God helped us off the cliff. Now Steve was dead.

I slowly made my way back to the group and shared the tragic news. The group was reverently silent, and we all began to pray. At the chapel, Chrystal shared with the entire camp the news, and then sang Amazing Grace, a cappella. There wasn't a sound in the room. It is still the most beautiful rendition, I have ever heard, of Amazing Grace. The spirit of God descended upon that chapel, and all over the room kids were deeply moved. Chrystal spoke softly and told them that Steve was experiencing eternity. She warned them, that Steve had no idea that morning, that his life would be taken that morning. She then paused and asked: Steve had been ready for eternity, were they? It was a powerful chapel service.

This incident makes the point though. We never know our last day. Life is utterly unpredictable.

We couldn't have known it then, but Chrystal Lewis went on to became a famous singer. She became a well-known Christian music artist. Now Chrystal's daughter is a singer as well.

The Accused

True to form, when I arrived in Bellflower, I played Softball and basketball. They had a Christian Basketball league, so I joined a team. Our church was so large, we had multiple teams. Every Saturday Michelle and I would travel to a church gym somewhere, and I would play a league game.

One particular Sunday, I entered my office early and found a letter on my desk. I picked it up and began reading.

Mr. Arbogast,

"I am accepting your resignation, effective immediately, for behavior detrimental to the church. Your conduct was so reprehensible, that it is incumbent upon me to release you from ministry…."

It went on and described how I had punched a referee in the face, and embarrassed the Bellflower church. It had a list of people who had witnessed the incident. At the bottom, it was signed by my Senior Pastor.

It was so outrageous, I naturally assumed, it was a practical joke. I made my way over to his office and knocked on the door. When he opened the door, I had a big grin on my face, and said "This is hilarious, you had me for a second."

"I don't find it funny at all," he scowled. Then promptly closed the door in my face.

I stood there for a second, almost waiting for him to open the door and start laughing, "Gotcha!"

As the seconds ticked away, it began to sink in that perhaps this wasn't a joke. I knew there had to be some mistake, so I kind of blew it off. I really couldn't take it seriously, because no such thing had happened. I walked back over to my office, and reasoned that I would clear it up after service.

After the morning service, I made my way back to the pastor's office, to straighten this mess out. What I didn't know, was the Pastor had left directly after the service, to Attend PALCON. (Pastors and Leaders Conclave)

It was a large gathering of Nazarene pastors, from all over the western United States. It is held on the campus of Point Loma Nazarene University. It only happens, once every four years, so it is well attended, by almost every pastor, and their staff. It lasts nearly a week, so I was going to have to wait a full week, to clear this up.

When I got home, I was naturally perplexed. What was this all about? I decided to call the head of the basketball league, Mark Hamilton. Mark had been a friend, and we served on the same southern California NYI counsel together. (Nazarene Youth International). Mark was the youth pastor at the Long Beach first church. I figured he would be able to give me some idea what this was all about.

When I called him, he sounded curt and short! "What do you want?" He asks.

145

"Hey, Mark have you heard about a fight?" I asked politely.

"Heard about it?" He mocked, "I'm the one who filed the letter of complaint, with your pastor yesterday. I hope he fired you!"

"What are you talking about?" I protested! "If this is your idea of a practical joke, it isn't funny anymore!"

He hung up on me. Now I was getting angry. I decide to drive down to the Long Beach church, before Mark left for PALCON. I wanted to talk to him, face to face. I needed to get to the bottom of this.

When I drove up, I could see him walking to his car. I pulled up to him and stopped. I jumped out of my car and began walking towards him. He backed up, with his hands in the air, like I was going to have an altercation with him, or something.

"What is your problem, Mark?" I asked incredulously.

"You here to beat me up now. You ought to be ashamed?" He says with a tone of condescension.

"I have done nothing wrong, Mark, and I am trying to be patient!" I tell him. "I am simply trying to get to the bottom of this." I protest.

"You're a real piece of work, Arbogast!" He says in a sarcastic tone. "You're actually going to stand there and try to deny this? You're pathetic!"

"Of course, I deny it Mark!" By this time, I am actually shouting.

He then informs me that, "We have twenty or thirty witnesses, who saw you. Many of them are respected members of our church. The whole crowd saw you!"

"That's impossible!" I protest.

"The referee personally identified you, Perry. So just accept it like a man and stop this pathetic charade!"

I was so frustrated at this point; I was out of ideas. So, I asked him for the phone number of the referee. I figured, perhaps he would have some answers.

Mark flatly refused to give me the referee's phone number. I asked Mark, to give the referee my phone number, and have him call me.

"This is my life you're playing with Mark, it's the least you can do." I pleaded with him and reminded him, that I would never be able to stay in ministry, if I didn't get this cleared up.

Michelle walked over, and calmly told Mark, she had been with me the whole day. She told him, she was at the game, and that I had never done any such thing.

We then returned to our car, and drove home. But our hearts were heavy.

I asked Michelle to help me understand. Even if it had been true! I pleaded, "Why hadn't the pastor given me the benefit of the doubt? Why was Mark so quick to accuse me?" He knew me! I had never given him a reason to believe such a thing. Even if a staff member did have anger

146

problems! Why wouldn't the pastor, take him under his wings, and help him work out his issues? Shouldn't the pastor have shown some grace? Offered counseling, or something?

When I first interviewed at Bellflower, the pastor stressed a number of times, that as loyal staff, I needed to have his back. Why hadn't he had mine? He jumped on the bandwagon, without so much as a phone call. Why hadn't he done, even an elementary questioning? He hadn't done any due diligence. He hadn't even spoken to me! I felt that it was cowardly of him, to leave without first having a talk with me.

Throughout the next week, I received phone calls from all over the United States. I heard things like:

"I heard you got in a fight and were terminated from ministry? What happened?"

"Sorry to hear this about you Perry, you should get some counseling."

"It breaks my heart to hear how you've fallen, you need to get back on your feet, and overcome this struggle in your life."

Even College professors were calling to offer their disappointment in me. I would ask how they had heard? "Well, our pastor overheard your pastor explaining how he had taken immediate action and would not tolerate having anyone like you on his staff."

My reputation was being smeared all over the country. I knew instinctively that gossip like this, was like trying to collect the feathers from a down pillow, after it has been opened in a hurricane. Once it's in the wind, there is no recovering all the feathers. Even if you prove your innocence, most people will never get the memo. The rest of their lives they will believe what they heard.

It was hard to endure. I fully understand, what it must feel like, when a newspaper smears your reputation. Or when gossip rags repeat utter lies about someone, quoting "sources!" Yeah right, it's all fun and games till it's you…"sheeple" want to believe the worst.

Late that week, I finally received a phone call from the referee.

I asked him, "If he knew who I was? How did he get my name? Why had he identified me?"

"I know exactly who you are," he said smugly! "You're the youth pastor at Bellflower."

"I'll tell you how I got your name," He brags. "It was easy!" "When you ran out of the gym, we all saw your jersey number, and simply looked up your name in the scorebook." I already knew who you were. I've been dealing with you for years." He stated with confidence.

"STOP!" I jumped on what he had just said. "Years?" "I just moved here" I informed him. "This is my first season in this league."

I asked him to describe the person who hit him…and the description floored me!"

"Your 6 foot 8. Blond hair. Early 20s." He said with an air of confidence.

Then it was like a bomb went off in my head. He was describing Steve our Jr. High director. Then I remembered! Just after the game that Saturday, Steve had asked to borrow my jersey, because he claimed he had left his home.

I was finally putting the pieces of the puzzle together. The witnesses **didn't** identify **me**. They had identified my **jersey**! They had gone to the scorebook and found, where Steve had printed my name, instead of his own.

In just a few seconds, most of it was making sense. But why had Steve used my name? Why had he punched a referee? Why had he remained silent all week? Why hadn't he come forward and cleared this up? Why was he letting me fry?

I explained to the referee my suspicions, and told him I had dark hair, and only wished, I was six feet, eight. I shared with him everything that I now understood. I assured him, I would be getting to the bottom of it. He apologized for the mistake and we hung up.

I jumped in my car, and drove over to Steve's house. I wanted to get the rest of the story.

Steve answered the door, and he let me in. He was very sheepish, but he confessed the entire plan.

Steve said, "He had assumed that he would be the next youth pastor." He was angry and hurt, that the church had overlooked him. He explained that he felt that it had been unfair, of the pastor, to hire a new youth pastor, without asking him.

Steve confessed that he had become vindictive, and felt that if he could get me fired, he would be more aggressive in getting the position the next time.

He told me, that he had recruited some others to help him. They also felt it was unfair. They had counted on Steve being the next youth pastor. So, they joined Steve in his plan to set me up.

Two sisters, had gone to see the pastor several weeks prior, and complained to him, that they were fearful of my "Anger issues." Another young man, told him that I had purposely hurt him, playing a basketball game, and that I was an "Angry person." Steve said, "We set you up!"

Steve went on to explain; "I purposely borrowed your jersey because I wanted to frame you. He also admitted that he had never liked that referee. Steve confessed: "That referee has always had it in for me, so I looked forward to punching him in the face."

Steve went on to say, "I really don't have anything against you personally, I just felt that I deserved to be the next youth pastor. It was completely unfair of them, to have brought you in, without asking me first."

It was all making sense now. Steve agreed to accompany me, when the pastor returned, and confess everything he had shared with me.

The following Saturday, I saw that the pastor was down at the church, so I called Steve and we met in the parking lot. Steve and I, walked together into the church and knocked on the pastor's door.

When the pastor opened the door and saw me standing there, he sarcastically asked; "What are you still doing here?"

"I wanted to clear my name," I told him.

He rolled his eyes and started to close the door on me, so I stuck my foot in the door. I forcefully pushed it back open, not hard, but firmly. He backed away with fear in his eyes. He had not seen Steve standing outside, so he was surprised, when we both walked in.

"I think Steve has something he wants to share with you," I said with an authoritative tone.

So, as we all stood there in the pastor's office, Steve spilled the whole story.

When Steve finished explaining, I expected the pastor to humbly apologize for what he had done to me. Instead, he angrily shouts, and I quote: "Both of you, get out of my office, I don't want to hear any more about this."

I was stunned.... again!!!!

I walked alone back to my house, which was just a few doors down from the church. Now that I had cleared my name, I decided I would resign on my own terms. I could no longer work for this man.

I spent the afternoon writing my resignation letter. Sunday morning, I handed it to him. He accepted it and told me, "I've already hired another youth pastor, while I was at PALCON! He can't move here for another couple months, can you stay on till he gets here?"

How insulting! This pastor was unbelievable!

What I learned through this incident, is that most attacks against us in ministry, are from inside the church. They come from those we would expect better from.

There is an evil spirit, that is active on this planet, and it knows the most effective way to wound us. The wounds are deeper, and more disastrous, if it is someone, we feel loves us.

I believe the Bible. It tells us that there is a being, a force, a spirit that is utterly evil. God calls it by the name, Satan.

Of course, it is not some creature dressed in red tights with pointy horns. That is a cartoon character, designed to keep us from taking Satan seriously. But the spirit of **evil** is real. It exists! Call it what you want, but it is real. Those who dabble in the black arts, know it's real. Every culture has acknowledged, that there is an evil presence, that exists. They have called it by a hundred different names, but we intuitively know, that something around us, is evil.

God acknowledged that it's real. Is God a liar? If there is no Satan, then God is a liar! God not only tells us all about this evil creature, He teaches us all Satan's, tricks of the trade. God didn't want us to be caught off guard, so he tells us, be aware of Satan and his tactics. Don't fall for his eye candy! Satan is setting traps continuously for you. If you recognize them, you can avoid them.

The second half of this equation is, God encourages us to trust Him, and He will turn the tables on Satan's schemes. What Satan plans to use to destroy us, God will take those plans, and miraculously make it work out to our benefit. I've seen this in action, all throughout my life. Satan uses someone to trap me, then God uses that trap to bless me. Satan sets up circumstances to destroy me, and God takes those circumstances and I come out smelling like a rose. I've seen it happen so many times, that now I just expect it. Ok God, I'm waiting to see how You're going to work this out, I know you will. I just stand back and marvel at how God always works it to my favor.

There are two specific teachings that work in concert in the Bible. First God says I will work all things together for the good of those who love Me! I really like how one translation puts it..." We know that our Father is always at work for the good of everyone who loves Him..."

The second teaching is God's warning, "Don't take vengeance yourself or you'll mess up My plan." God sees everything that Satan is setting up. He sees all the possible scenarios. He actively organizes it to benefit me. The problem is, if I rush in, and intervene in anger, I sabotage what God was doing. Now I have made a mess. God encourages me to keep calm, He tells me, "I got this!"

There is a really funny story of Moses. God told him, "I know it looks bleak, but stand back and watch what I will do!" That cracks me up. I hear God telling me that, on a daily basis; "Perry stand back, my boy, and watch what I will do!" If I trust that God will work it out, and if I don't get in Gods way, God always works it out. He doesn't need my help. I only get in the way.

When Satan used Steve to destroy me, God was already setting in motion a plan, to use it to bless me. I had no plans to continue any more schooling. Yet when I left Bellflower, I decided to return to graduate school, in Kansas City and get my Master's degree. That decision, turned out to be one of the top ten best things I ever did. God used Steve's vindictive plan, to prod me back to school.

I would never have returned to school, if I hadn't been forced to. God used our time in Kansas City, to bless Michelle and I, throughout our lives, in a hundred little ways.

Move to Kansas City

We loaded up the tiny trailer again and headed east. We struck out across the vast expanse of the United States, headed to Kansas City. We had no money. We had no jobs. We only had enough money to pay for the fuel and some food. We slept in the car at night.

The little car we were towing with, was utterly insufficient to be towing. It didn't weigh as much as the trailer, so it would start fishtailing if we got much over 55 miles an hour. The front of the car was pointing up in the air. I knew it wasn't safe or optimal, but we didn't have an alternate plan B. On the third day out, we were driving through Oklahoma, I was tired, and decided to stop on the side of the freeway.

Just as we were coming to a stop, the tongue on the trailer snapped in half, and like a spear impaled into the soft asphalt. The safety chains held and they jerked the car to a halt. God had saved us yet again. If that had snapped even ten seconds earlier, we surely would have jackknifed and rolled. We were also traveling slow enough when it broke, that the load was not thrown off the trailer.

I unhooked the chains, and removed the receiver, that was still attached to the ball. I drove into the next town. It was around six o'clock, dinner time. I stopped at the only gas station in the tiny town. I asked them, if they knew of anyone that might be able to help me. They suggested that I walk over to see Travis. I walked over to this small home, just across the street. I could see through the screen door, a family was sitting at the table, enjoying an evening meal.

I hated to be interrupting such a Norman Rockwell scene. I hesitantly knocked and I heard a hearty "Come in!" I walked through the living room, and out into the kitchen, where they were sitting at the table.

I felt like an intruder, and I apologized for bothering him, at dinner time. He reached out to shake my hand, his grip was solid and firm. He cheerfully told me, it was no problem, and asked what he could do for me? I explained that I was traveling and my trailer hitch had snapped in half. He immediately stood and grabbed some keys, that were hanging on a hook.

I quickly implored him, "Please sir, finish your meal, I feel horrible interrupting your family time. I can wait."

"Nonsense" he belted out, "let's go see this trailer of yours."

Now in my mind, I expected this guy to jump into a pickup. I assumed he was going to follow me out to evaluate the situation. I had told him I was parked at the service station across the street and that I would wait for him there.

I ran across the street and jumped in my little car. Suddenly this big Diesel Kenworth utility service truck pulls up beside me. It even has a crane attached. It is fully self-contained with a very large Miller Electric welder, incorporated into the chassis. He obviously services the farmers in the Western Oklahoma area.

I am now worried at how much this is going to cost. I just thought he was a farmer. I had assumed he was just going to look over the situation. Then figure out how we might get this fixed. I had no idea he did this for a living and owned a big old semi service truck. I'm feeling awkward, because it hadn't even occurred to me, he was coming out to fix it right then! If I had known that, I would have asked him what a service call would cost.

I am terrified he is going to get out there to the trailer, and become angry that I hadn't told him I couldn't afford this. I assumed he was a farmer. He probably thought I knew; he did this for a living.

As soon as we arrive at the trailer, I jumped out and approached him, I felt I had to be upfront with him. I wanted to let him down easy, and so I shared my surprise, that he had this big old truck. I hadn't realized he owned something so nice. I apologized for not asking earlier, but how much does he need for a service call?

He just ignored my plea, and told me, "We will settle up at the end!" He marveled at my good fortune! "It's a good thing you were coming to a stop when this snapped." He said, "Because if you had been going highway speed, this would have been a bad accident."

He jumped back into the truck, and pulled it up alongside the trailer. He hooked the cable of his crane, to the trailer and hoisted the tongue out of the asphalt. He then grabbed metal plates he had on the truck, and welded a whole new tongue assembly. When he finished, he had a big grin on his face and announced, "Better than new!"

I ask him how much I owed him, and he looked me straight in the face. "It's free, I was glad to do it for you folks, just pass it on someday, when it's in your power to help someone in need!"

I hadn't realized how stressed I was and how much tension had built up in my body, because when he told me this, I felt like just breaking down. My eyes started to burn. He turned, hopped into the truck, and honked as he left.

The Bible says that many times we come across angels and don't realize it. I have often wondered if Travis was an angel. He is one of the people in my life, I wish I could see again, and let him know, just how much his small act meant to me. I wanted to honor him, by passing onto others, what he gave me. God has given me many opportunities to pass it on. Just like Travis, I was genuinely glad to do it.

Neal Napoleon

When we arrived in Kansas City, we stayed with Steve and Barbara Sheets, Michelle's brother and wife. We quickly found an apartment, and

Jobs. Michelle was a Registered Dental Assistant, so she had a job within just a few days. I found a Job driving armored trucks.

My partner was a big black man, named Neal Napoleon. We hit it off immediately. At first, I was the driver and he the Messenger. The Messenger is in charge, and they handle the money and paperwork. Over time though, I was given more responsibility. The manager informed Neal and I, that I had passed the FBI background check, and asked Neal to begin to train me as a messenger. We began to trade off, whenever he needed a break.

We spent every day just inches apart, separated by a steel wall. Even though we had a barrier between us, we still had the ability to chat. We could also see each other through the bulletproof glass. We became great friends. The weeks turned into months, and by the following year we decided to go hunting together.

One of our customers, gave us keys to their property in northern Missouri. The deer were so plentiful on the property, they were a nuisance. So, for hunting season, we were privileged to have, this customers private property, all to ourselves. The owner called it harvesting, not hunting.

The first morning of hunting season, Neal picked me up in his pickup, and we headed north. Just around daybreak we needed fuel, so we pulled into a small nondescript town. Neal hopped out and asked the attendant to "fill er up." The attendant told him to get back in his truck, and keep driving, he didn't serve niggers. I couldn't believe my ears. This was 1989, and we were in upper Missouri. Did he just call Neal a nigger?

The truth is I wasn't even cognizant of Neals color. He was just Neal, a buddy of mine.

Neal told the attendant, he wasn't looking for trouble, just a fill up. I jumped out of the truck and came walking up. The attendant turned to me and asked me to take my nigger and leave. He then turned and walked into the station. I started to follow, incensed at his treatment of my friend, but Neal called out to me to let it go and let's move on. I was not going to let this injustice stand, and I walked into the station. The attendant was just hanging up the phone. I tried to reason with him for a few minutes, and was getting no satisfaction.

Just then a number of pickups came driving into the station. All dressed in hunters' attire, some hopped out of the bed of trucks, carrying their rifles. One of them walked up to me and asked the attendant if I was the nigger lover. Obviously, this attendant had called some buddies of his.

It was a scene straight out of Mississippi Burning. I couldn't believe what was happening. The redneck told me to "Jump in your truck an git!" Neal was already behind the wheel, so I jumped in and we took off. The caravan of trucks followed us to the edge of town. As we drove on, they all did a U-turn on the highway behind us. A part of me was enraged, and a part of me was relieved. I truly thought, when they began following us, we were going to be shot at.

Did that just happen? My mind was racing. Neal was quiet. I didn't know what to say either. Sometime later, Neal broke the silence and said "That's why you don't see black people driving on vacations in the states." I wasn't even aware they didn't. I had never really been aware of that level of prejudice, until that day.

In a twist of irony, Neal apologized to me, for what had happened.

I was stupefied! "Are you kidding me?" I yelled back, "I'm the one who needs to apologize" I insisted!

We retraced our drive back to a previous station, and fueled up. We had both lost our desire to hunt and returned to KC. That incident put such a distaste in my mouth, that I didn't hunt again for almost 25 years.

Air Cover

After a couple years, working with Neal as my partner, Neal was moved to another route and I became the messenger of the route. My new driver, was a fellow Seminary student, and a great friend. I had encouraged Chuck to apply at the armored car company, never guessing they would let us work together. Chuck and I had a lot in common. Both Seminary students, same major, lived in the same apartment complex, and our wives were best friends as well. Now we both worked at same armored car company and were teammates on the same route.

One night I received a call around 3 am. It was the manager of the armored car company. He told me to arrive, at a predetermined location, in one hour. He told me to wear my uniform, but not to retrieve my sidearm, one would be supplied. That is all I was told. This had never happened before. So of course, my curiosity was naturally heightened.

When I arrived, a number of others were already there, including Chuck. No one knew anything. They had all received the same none descript call. The nervous tension was palpable. We all wanted to know how come we were meeting at this location. Where was the manager? What's the helicopter circling above us for?

The manager arrived in an unmarked car. Suddenly it got quiet. He told us not to ask questions, just do what we were told. Three identical-looking trucks from our terminal arrived and more men jumped out of these trucks. They had retrieved our side arms and passed them out. Then each of us were issued a shotgun and ammunition. This looked like a paramilitary mission.

The three drivers were taken aside and given orders that the rest of us were not allowed to hear. Then the manager called out names, and each of us were assigned a truck. We loaded into the back and all three trucks began to wind their way through the city.

Chuck and I were selected to load into the same truck. It just so happened to be the very same truck we used every day. We knew it well. It felt odd not having Chuck in the front seat. We quietly and excitedly talked about what this could possibly be all about. Why the shotguns? Where were we headed?

We were definitely headed north of Kansas City. We also noticed all three trucks were trading places with each other, like a giant shell game. They were constantly passing each other and being passed. We could also see the manager following at a distance in the unmarked car. In addition, the helicopter was always above us. Whatever this was, it was big.

When we got near Kansas City Airport, the trucks left the main highway. We were met by an escort car with flashing lights. We were led through gates onto the tarmac itself. We drove out to a runway and sat there, with all three trucks running. We waited for a few minutes, and then a big airliner landed and came to a stop on the runway. All three trucks drove out on the runway and down to the parked airliner. When we came to a stop, we were all told to exit and stand guard. We all piled out, shotguns at the ready.

The people on board the airliner, crowded around the windows watching us, just as curious as we were. What we would learn later, was that two of our team, were on board the plane as well. They had flown out the day before and escorted this load from its inception to K.C.

The back of the plane lowered and exposed a cargo compartment. Chuck and I were ordered to hand over our shotguns, and a number of men were ordered to unload the contents of the plane into the back of our truck. I was taken aside by the manager, and he told me that from this time forward, I was the messenger. I was given the manifest and told I was responsible to make sure every item was loaded. When I looked at what I was responsible for, my jaw dropped. It was a cash shipment from the Department of the United States treasury, going to the Federal Reserve bank of Kansas City. There are only twelve Federal Reserve banks in the United States. They supply all the money to every bank in the surrounding states. The amount was staggering.

They loaded the truck from floor to ceiling, wall to wall. I was responsible to confirm every serial number of every bag. My truck was the only truck that was loaded. The other two trucks were decoys. When the truck was filled, I signed my name on the paperwork. Chuck joined me in the back. He and I were the only two in the back, we had to stand by the door, because the space was limited. When I closed the door, we both burst into uncontrolled laughter. Here we were two boys from seminary, standing in a truck with more money than we knew existed. This was utterly ridiculous.

Several months earlier, when a company bought a skyscraper from Prudential, I had previously signed a certificate for 160 million. I remember thinking to myself at that time, this would be the most I would ever sign for. Not even close!

Don't Poke the Bear

One of the men who worked at the Armored company, I will call Earl. Earl was somewhat of a bully. One morning while we were gathered waiting for checkout, Earl started mocking Charles Keeley. Charles was somewhat small, In his fifties and overweight. Earl was probably twenty years younger. Charles is white and Earl, is black. Earl started calling Charles a Honky.

Then he got in Charles's face and started mocking him, shoving him and asking him what he was going to do about it. Charles gave him a gentle warning to back off. This just spurred Earl all the more. Charles tried to walk away and Earl jumped in his path. Without warning, and seemingly out of nowhere, Charles hit Earl in the face. He laid him out on the floor. The punch was so fast that Earl didn't even see it.

Earl was still on the floor but moving, when the manager came walking through to his office. He glanced down at Earl and up at the rest of us. None of us were moving to help him, so in that instant, the manager must have sensed that whatever happened, Earl deserved it. He knew Earl, we all knew Earl....so he kept walking, as if he hadn't seen a thing.

Charles, told us later, that he was sure he would be fired. His heart dropped when he saw the Manager. It turns out, Charles had been a golden glove boxer, in his younger days. He knew how to throw a punch with devastating force. I have heard it said so many times, you can't read a book by its cover. Earl learned this truth the hard way.

Vertical Lights

Michelle and I shared our only car. We were still too poor to afford a second vehicle.

I was working the late shift at the armored car company, and Michelle came to pick me up around midnight. As we were driving back home on I-435, I noticed far up ahead on the freeway some vertical red lights. They were out of place, and I told Michelle, "I think that's an accident." Yet the traffic was not stopping, so she discounted my theory. She said if it were an accident, people would be pulling over. I protested, and as we got closer, I was even more convinced. "Look," I said, "that looks like a semi-trailer, rolled over on its side."

She assumed it must have happened a while back, because there were no police, and all the traffic, kept passing the scene.

As I neared the scene, I slowed down and Michelle asked me what I was doing. I told her, "I'm going to check this out." She tried to talk me out of stopping and complained she was tired and wanted to get home. I pulled over anyway.

I was in the fast lane and pulled onto the left-hand shoulder. Michelle was getting frustrated and protested that it was extremely dangerous, to be on the Left side of the freeway.

The Semi was a flatbed, hauling giant coils of rolled steel. The trailer was on its side, but the cab was upside-down and positioned between two overpass bridges. The bridges were over another highway, that ran underneath. I hurried around to the driver's side. I walked down the concrete bank, to get a better look. I peered up into the windshield and could see into the cab. To my shock, there was blood dripping on the windshield. I ran back up and screamed for Michelle to find a phone and call for help.

I ran back to the driver's door, and tried to open it. Both the cab and the sleeper were crushed pretty badly. It was dark, but I could see the driver hanging by his seatbelt, and he was not moving.

Just then, two off duty police officers, on the road below, saw the cab hanging upside down and rushed up to help me. The three of us, tried to break the windshield. It was already cracked and eventually, we got in the cab. We crawled into the cab, and positioned ourselves to lift his body, and cut the belts off. We lowered his body onto the roof of the truck. He was still breathing and we could hear the firetrucks on their way. Our next concern was to see if anyone else was in the sleeper. We tried to use a flashlight to see, but the sleeper was almost completely crushed.

I left the scene after the firemen and paramedics took over. I never heard if the driver survived or if there was someone in the sleeper.

When I got back to the car, Michelle was so apologetic. "What if you hadn't stopped," she said, "He would still be hanging there. I feel so horrible. I'm sorry I was so angry with you. I'm glad you didn't listen."

I could tell she felt terrible.

I have always been confused as to why no one stopped? Someone must have seen the accident happen. Why wouldn't they pull over? How long had that truck been there before I arrived? How many people drove right by that guy? Did they all just assume it was an old accident scene? With his lights on, didn't common sense tell them, it was a fresh accident? Do people just not want to get involved? Would they rather see a man die? What if it were their child in the driver's seat? It boggled my mind!

There is a story Jesus tells that is so similar to this incident. There is this Jewish guy who is beaten by robbers, and left for dead. A Jewish priest walks by and does nothing. Several others, that you would expect would help, refuse to get involved. Along comes a Samaritan, who is despised by the Jews. They are enemies. But low and behold, the least likely person, stops and saves the victim. Jesus asks, which of these people had genuine love for others?

Our actions are the true barometer.

Ambush

I arrive at work early one morning. As soon as I entered the door, someone told me the manager wanted to see me. When I walked into the office, there were two men in suits, seated in the office. The manager introduced me, and I found out they were FBI agents.

They explained that they had received an anonymous call, about an ambush that was being planned, at the Hypermart.

The Hypermart was one of Sam Waltons ideas. It was a Walmart on steroids. It was a store so large, it had 150 check stands. It had 2,000 grocery carts. There were over 800 employees. Many of the workers wore roller-skates. The store was so big, it had many other stores inside. It had a shoe store, McDonalds, a bank, and many others. It was like an all-in-one mall. Every day I took their cash deposit, from the in-house bank, to the main branch. I could understand why they had targeted this stop.

The FBI agents believed the report to be credible, because they had details, including the make and model of the car, including the license plate number.

There would be four black males, all in their early twenties. The plan was to wait until I exited Hypermart with the deposit, shoot me, grab the money, and take off. They even had the type of guns they would be using. They would be armed with automatic AR-15s and AK-47s. They would be wearing ski masks, and they described all four masks.

The FBI agents surmised the anonymous caller, was a girlfriend of one of the shooters, and she wanted no part in a murder. Either that or an x-girlfriend. She told them that the gang had decided to simply, shoot and kill the guard, before he had a chance to draw his weapon.

My manager, and the two agents, encouraged me to run the route like normal. I was told that when I arrived at Hypermart, I was NOT to exit the vehicle. The FBI and other law enforcement would be there, to apprehend the suspects.

Chuck was my driver, and he was brought into the meeting, and given all the information. He was to keep an eye out for the car, and suspects. We had radios and would be in constant contact, with dispatch. If we saw the car, at any time, we were to call in immediately with our location. They, themselves, would stake out the Hypermart. We were warned, that even though it was supposed to be the Hypermart, we should expect them anywhere.

At first it really didn't sink in, in fact, as we loaded out that morning, Chuck and I kind of joked about it. But as we left the building, I felt

158

vulnerable. I had an eerie sense that someone was watching me. I was on high alert. Chuck became tense and on edge. As we continued that morning, I started feeling sick to my stomach. Suddenly it hit me, these punks didn't even know me. They were going to kill me, and leave Michelle a widow, and they didn't even know who they were killing. They didn't care! They were going to leave me dead, in a pool of my own blood, so they could buy things.

I was just an obstacle to be dispatched. I wasn't even human to them. I was a video game creature, to be blasted. If that caller hadn't called, I would not have lived long enough to have lunch with Chuck. I would never have seen Michelle again. It started to gall me.

Why had that girl called, and ratted them out? I believe God put it on her heart. He had plans for me, his son. What Satan planned for evil; God was turning into my good.

When we arrived at Hypermart, Chuck took the time to drive through the parking lot, looking for the car. Nothing. So, I stepped out and walked briskly to the door, looking behind me, to make sure, I was alone. It also kind of irked me that I hadn't been given an extra guard that day.

We finished the route and nothing happened. The manager told me not to worry, "He had my back!"

That night I shared my day with Michelle. She wanted me to quit immediately. Nothing was worth my life. She went through the same anger issues; I had been dealing with. The utter senselessness of it all. I decided to stick it out, and assured her that the manager told me, "They had my back!"

We never saw the car, or the suspects that week, or the next. But my nerves were frayed. Chuck and I were not sleeping well. I went into the office at the end of the second week and talked with the manager. I asked him how long were they going to stake out Hypermart? He assured me that if we saw the car, they would be there in a heartbeat.

That following Monday we entered the Hypermart parking lot, and Chuck start screaming "They're here, They're here!"

He called it in to dispatch, and they told me not to exit the truck, help was on the way. We waited, watching them. They were sitting in front of the entrances to Hypermart, just like we had been told. We could see them, and they were just as they had been described. The license plate matched. They had not put on their masks yet, and I was looking intently at their faces, so in court I could identify them. They kept looking out the rear window at us. Chuck had his gun out of the holster. He was ready.

After a few minutes Chuck called back in, "Where are you guys? They are going to get suspicious, because Perry hasn't exited the truck yet." Sure enough, they took off. They knew something wasn't right. We asked if we should follow them, and were told to stay put, help was on the way. 10

minutes goes by...no one shows up. 20 minutes, still no one. 30 minutes, nothing! 40 minutes not a single cop car, no one from Brinks, no FBI agents. Not even a mall cop. I am furious. "THIS IS HAVING MY BACK????"

If that anonymous tip had not come in, my funeral services would have been over before they arrived!

Finally, after over 45 minutes the first cop car, finally arrived. I was angry, they had lied to me. My life meant nothing to anyone at Brinks. They didn't have the place staked out. They didn't even have a game plan. Where was the FBI? They put a cop at every construction site, to just sit there watching traffic, and they couldn't put a cop at Hypermart?

The sad truth was that just weeks later, a Wells Fargo messenger was gunned down leaving the mall by the same guys, in the same car. They followed the same M.O., that we had been warned of. He lost his life, because they let them go that day at Hypermart. He didn't have to die. Even now as I write this, I am frustrated, his death was senseless. They dropped the ball.

Someone who didn't drop the ball was God. He saved my life again. He was watching out for me, when others were not.

Ride Along

One of the requirements, for graduation from Seminary, is to check off a list of things, they felt we needed to experience. For example, Funeral, Wedding, soup kitchen, preaching, Catholic mass, Jewish synagogue, etc. One of the things was a police ride along. I had some good friends in Kansas City that were policemen, and I got permission to ride along.

We were just getting started, and we got our first call, a woman in distress. We arrive at the home, and walk up to the door. We were greeted by the daughter, who was in her sixties. She ushered us into the living room and introduced us to her elderly mother.

As the daughter is explaining to the officer her concern, I naturally took the elderly woman's hand and ask her how she was feeling. My thought, in that moment, was to comfort her until the ambulance arrived. She smiled at me and she said, "Not so good."

She closed her eyes and died. Her hand went limp, her face relaxed, and she was gone. I found myself holding the hand of a corpse. Just minutes into my first police ride along, and I was faced with death. Life had slipped away, so quickly and quietly, that the policeman and daughter were totally unaware.

It wasn't morbid, or gross. It was natural and peaceful. This was the first in a long line of times, I would be there by someone's side, as they pass into eternity. The Doctor, is there to greet new life, and God had chosen me to be a minister, to be there when He calls their spirit home.

Jumper Cables

I was sitting in our apartment one evening and listening to the drone of the traffic on I-71 which was just over the edge of a bluff from us. Our apartment sat on top of the cliff overlooking the freeway. I wasn't really even cognizant of the traffic, until I could hear sirens coming, lots of sirens. After living in the city, you begin to recognize the differences, in an ambulance siren, a firetruck wailing, or police sirens. You can also recognize a high-speed chase. That perked my interest, then I heard, a horrific crash. I ran out of the apartment and out to the edge of the bluff, to look down on the accident scene.

The car had burst into flames and the black smoke came wafting out of the trees just below me. The car had left the freeway, and ended up in the overgrowth just below our apartment. I could hear the police screaming and yelling, so I decided to walk down to the scene, and watch the action. They were looking for the young man, that had stolen the vehicle. He had jumped out and ran, but the car was in flames. It took a while before the fire department arrived and doused the fire.

They never did find the suspect. He had escaped in the lush undergrowth.

We all watched, as the twilight of the evening faded into night. I guess I was there for the better part of an hour.

I had been chatting with another bystander, who had pulled off to the side of the freeway. He was a grandfatherly type, and a super nice guy. In fact, he and I had been leaning on the hood of his car, the whole time.

When they finally loaded the burnt remains of the stolen vehicle onto the flatbed truck, the police opened the freeway, and traffic was once again on the move. We walked over to the driver's door and he jumped in.

I decided to head back to the apartment, the excitement was over. The older gentleman, called out to me and asked if I had some jumper cables. He had left his headlights and flashers on, and it had run his battery down. I told him I had walked down from my apartment, and didn't have a car, or jumpers. We were standing in front of his car.

As he lifted the hood of his car, I turned and started to walk away. Suddenly there was an explosion behind me. I felt the concussion of sound and wind. It was deafening. I whipped my head around, but the gentleman and his car were gone. There was nothing there. The side of the freeway was empty. In that first second or two, I couldn't wrap my head around what was happening. I continued to turn my body around, to see where the car had disappeared to.

To my horror, the car was sliding down the freeway and came to a stop in the grass median. Another car was also tumbling down the freeway.

The whole area was lit up like a Christmas tree, with all the emergency vehicles, but a drunk had been racing down the freeway, and without even

161

hitting his breaks, had plowed into the back of this gentleman's car, killing him in an instant. They quickly lifted the car off of his body, but he had no chance. He died on impact.

I had missed death by less than two or three seconds. I had just stepped to the side of the car as he lifted the hood, when it was hit.

I was talking with a state highway patrolman a little later. It struck me that his last words on earth had been "jumper cables." What an odd word to utter as your last word in life.

Just then over his police radio, I heard the dispatcher requesting an officer to an address. He was to notify Mrs. "Smith", to meet the coroner at city general for positive ID.

I realized, that in a few moments, a woman was going to walk to her front door, utterly unaware, that when she opens that door, her life will change forever. She has no idea what is about to happen. She will receive the worst news of her life. She will experience her worst nightmare. When she opens that door, nothing will ever be the same again.

I thought about the officer, who was tasked with the unbelievable duty, of informing an elderly wife, that her husband will not be coming home. My heart was overwhelmed with sorrow. I was grieving for a wonderful old guy; I had just met. And a woman I would never know. My heart went out to them. Yet again a selfish drunk, had killed innocent people, spreading devastating heartache in his wake.

As I walked back home, I acknowledged to My Heavenly Father that He once again had spared my life. I should have been killed once again.

Explosion

I have always been the curious type. Whenever there was an accident, I went to investigate. Whenever there is a siren nearby, I go look. Many times, I had given a helping hand.

Early one morning, while it was still pitch dark, I was awakened by sirens. Several minutes later we were jolted by a horrific explosion. It was so loud and violent it actually shook our bed. The brilliant white light that accompanied it, was so intense, that it seemed as if we had been hit by lightning.

But that explosion was not like anything I had ever heard in my life. It actually shook our building. No lightening had ever done that.

The freeway was under construction, and had been for several months. They had been blasting solid rock, to make way for the new lanes. I had already surmised, that it was some sort of accident with the explosives. Within a few minutes, we could hear more sirens down on the freeway, coming closer. I instinctively jumped out of bed, to put on my clothes and investigate. Michelle, was absolutely resolute that I not go. She had never been like this. "What is your problem?" I asked somewhat frustrated.

162

She looked right at me, and said, "I'm frightened. That wasn't normal. Whatever that was, I don't feel good about it. I'm serious Perry, for once, just let it be!"

I had never seen her like this before. Oh, yea she had occasionally encouraged me to ignore other incidents, but this time she was very serious and angry. You could hear the demanding in her voice. "NOT THIS TIME!" "STAY HERE!"

As much as I wanted to go down, and see what in the world was going on, I had learned to trust Michelle's intuition. I relented and gave her my word I would not leave. I then walked out to the kitchen, to watch the emergency vehicles, and see what else I could see. Unfortunately, it was still night, and I really couldn't see anything. Then came the second explosion. So loud our ears were ringing.

The flash was pure white. Blinding white. Again, this explosion shook the ground, and the concussion in the atmosphere was intense. Whatever this was, it was catastrophic.

Michelle ran to the kitchen, and almost screamed at me, "If you had gone down there, that blast would have killed you!" She was right. I knew it. God had saved my life again.

We turned on the radio, but no one knew what was going on. All the stations were talking about it, but no one at that time, knew anything. By the time the sun rose, the street in front of our apartment was lined with satellite trucks. Every major network was present. The trucks were parked directly in front of our building.

Law enforcement had closed freeways, and were evacuating the area. The second explosion, and shock wave, had been so powerful, that the police helicopter flying towards the area had nearly been blown out of the sky, so they had closed down all air traffic. No one was allowed into the blast area.

Just after sunup, I had to go to work. I knew they had closed all the major freeways, so I took an extra hour, to drive through the city. When I arrived, I was in for a huge surprise!

Law enforcement had contacted the Armored car company, and asked if we would be willing to use one of the armored vehicles, to venture into the blast area, and evaluate the situation. It just so happened, the entire no-fly zone area in Kansas City, was a part of my route. They asked me, If I would be willing to carry a radio, and drive into the blast zone, and give a report of what I was seeing. They needed eyes on the ground.

What I learned, at that moment was that even first responders, had been evacuated from the blast area. The second explosion had made it, potentially, too dangerous for emergency personnel, to safely enter the area. No one was allowed in, until they knew what they were dealing with.

163

Everyone had been evacuated. They felt that an armored vehicle, was the safest way to evaluate the situation.

Chuck and I agreed to go in, and assess the situation. We were allowed beyond the barricades, and this is what we saw. Buildings were hit so hard by the blast concussion, that they were leaning. The Sears warehouse building, had all their giant, dock, doors blown in. The ceiling tiles in buildings were collapsed onto the floors.

We drove slowly through the streets; it was like Armageddon. Eerily lifeless. We were the only humans in the area. We were telling authorities everything we were seeing. The streets and freeway were utterly empty.

We were giving a first-hand account of what we saw. As we neared the construction zone even the trees were shredded.

Although no one knew it at the time, this is what happened:

The first call came into the fire department, that a pickup and semi-trailer were on fire. That's all the fire department was told. No one, not even the fireman racing to the scene, knew what was in those trailers. When they arrived, they reported that perhaps someone had set the rear trailer tires on fire. It looked like arson.

The firemen quickly unfurled the hose and began to douse the trailer with water. Here is what those unfortunate firemen didn't know. The trailer was filled with ammonium nitrate, fuel oil, and aluminum pellets. There were actually two trailers filled with more than 50,500 pounds of explosives. To put that into perspective, Timothy McVeigh bombed the Murrah building in Oklahoma City, with only 4,800 pounds of the same stuff. This was ten times that amount.

The fire department sent two pumper trucks to the scene. Each truck had a three-man crew. All six were instantly killed in the first blast. The blast was so powerful, that the battalion chief, who was on the way to the scene, had the windshield of his car blown in. He was a quarter of a mile away. Another car, crossing a bridge almost a mile away was blown into the side of the bridge by the shockwave. Windows were shattered miles away.

Michelle and I lived in the closest building to the blast, less than 1000 yards from ground zero. The authorities surmised that the reason our building wasn't more seriously damaged was because of the cliff wall, that took the brunt of the shockwave. Then it curled up and over our building. There were actually buildings further away, that sustained greater damage, because they were not protected by the cliff wall.

They never definitively knew who set the fires. This incident was highlighted on the T.V. show, Unsolved Mysteries.

Chuck and I had no idea at the time, because nothing was known when we drove in. The explosion was so massive, it left two craters in solid rock.

Once again, our lives were spared.

No Brainer

One day, Michelle and I were driving on a divided highway, that was separated by a solid concrete median. When out of nowhere this car passes us on the median. She is actually driving up on the concrete divider. I realized, she had to be drunk out of her mind. I had seen the aftermath of such drivers. So, I knew she may kill someone, if I didn't do something.

I raced ahead of her, and started wildly waving my arms, to get her to pull over. I pulled in front of her and slowed down. I was watching her like a hawk, to make sure she didn't rear-end me. She tried to weave around me, but I kept cutting her off, and continued to slow down. The other traffic could see what I'm trying to do, and gave me lots of room.

When I got her stopped, I ran back to her car, and before she could back up, or race off, I reached into the car and grabbed her keys out of the ignition. The car reeked of alcohol. She started cussing me out in slurred speech, and she tried to exit the car. I told her to stay put, I was placing her under citizen's arrest.

Someone else drove up, and told me, that they would call the police, and to keep her there. A few minutes later, a state trooper pulled up, and I explained what happened. I told him I had put her under citizen's arrest. He warned me, that if I did that, and she wasn't drunk, she could come back on me and sue me for false arrest. I laughed and told him, I'm willing to take that chance. He again implored me "Are you sure you know what you're doing?"

He told me to wait there, then he walked up to her car and had her step out. She is cursing and arguing and being belligerent. He gets her to try a few sobriety tests, but she can barely stand. He puts the cuffs on her and puts her in his car. He walked up to me with this big grin, and said "I guess that was a no brainer!" and we both burst out laughing.

Tackled

On a summer afternoon, I heard this odd sound and glanced toward the freeway. There was a vehicle that had flipped over and was skidding on its roof. He must have slid several hundred yards. I ran down to see if I could help, as I often did.

I got down to the scene, just as this mountain of a man, was crawling out of the broken side window. He was obviously drunk and smelled of booze. He was a husky dude.

He sat on the guard rail, sulking, while we waited for a policeman. When the policeman arrived, I took him aside and gave him my suspicion, that this guy was inebriated.

The policeman walked up to the guy, but the guy instantly became agitated. The officer tried to have him stand and the big dude rushed him, and just started beating on the officer. I could tell the big guy was getting the better of the officer. I could also see that the big guy, was trying to wrestle the gun out of the officer's holster. The officer kept hitting his hand away, but the big guy was landing staggering blows to this policeman's head. I asked the officer if I could help, and he yelled, "HELP ME!"

The drunk had his back to me and I ran at him with everything I had. I hit him so hard, he went flying in the air, and sprawling onto the pavement. My adrenaline must have been off the charts. I jumped on him and grabbed one arm, as the officer jumped on the other. While the fight had been going on, the ambulance had arrived, and the two of them joined the fray. It took all four of us, to subdue the guy. When it was over the officer thanked me profusely. He said he didn't know what he would have done, if I hadn't been there.

He laughed and said "You must have played football the way you tackled him, that was textbook. We need you playing for the Kansas City Chiefs!" I knew he was kidding, but it felt amazing all the same. Michelle had to put up with my swollen head for a few days.

God seemed to put me in situations where someone needed help. God knew he could count on me to get involved. I have been privileged to save a number of lives.

Life-Saving

I walked out of the main office of Brinks and was standing at the intersection by myself. A car on my left was creeping along at a little less than walking speed. I looked but there was no driver at the wheel. I keep watching for a few seconds, as the car was getting even nearer the intersection. It was barely creeping along, but I could tell it's about to enter the intersection and I needed to do something.

I ran out to the vehicle and I saw that a woman was lying unconscious across the front seat. I did a couple of things simultaneously. I start waving my arms at the traffic, and ran behind the car and raced up towards the driver's door. But it had already entered the intersection. The traffic could see me running and slowed down as I chased the car. The cross traffic thankfully stopped as the car neared the crest.

Downtown Kansas City is located on a high hill. All streets go downhill from the city center. This car had made its way to the top of the hill but was about to crest the hill and coast down the other side.

I reached the door handle and instinctively pulled with all my might to stop the slow roll, but the car kept moving. I could see that it was picking up speed as it started over the center of the intersection and back down the other side. I then tried to open the door and thankfully it opened. I quickly pushed her body over and out of the way, then jumped into the driver's seat and put on the breaks. I then pulled her car over to the curb and put it in park.

166

She started moaning that she needed sugar. I ran into the breakroom, picked up a soft drink and candy bar. Then returned to the car. She recovered rather quickly.

She told us she was staying at a hotel in the downtown area. She went out to grab something to eat, and began feeling faint, because of her diabetic condition. She had left her insulin at the hotel, but couldn't make it back in time.

We gave her a candy bar and she seemed to be back to normal. We gave her directions to her hotel and she left. I thanked God, he put me in the right place at exactly the right time. Nothing happens by accident. The scripture is true; Man, may think he is making all the plans, but it is the Lord that directs his footsteps. Five times in Proverbs alone God reminds us that He is directing everything in our lives.

Going for a Spin

The winters in Kansas City can be brutal. Especially when there is freezing rain. Chuck and I started out that morning and the Roads were icy. Like I've said before, Kansas City is on a hill and all roads lead down from city center. We were headed downhill on Truman Avenue, down to the viaduct, that crossed the railroad tracks.

As we were nearing Winchester Avenue the light turned red. When Chuck tapped the breaks, the truck started into a spin. I was sitting in the back, utterly helpless to do anything. Oddly enough, the ice was so smooth that when we were sideways, it became almost silent, with no road noise. I braced myself for the crash, which I was certain, we were about to have. We entered the intersection almost completely backwards. The truck continued in a slow-motion spin. The truck was sliding downhill, so we weren't slowing down at all. The truck had very little suspension. It was solid and heavy.

We were completely backwards, as we slid through the intersection. The truck continued to spin as we glided out onto the viaduct. As we were almost pointed forward again Chuck was frantically trying to find some steering. The truck straightened out and we were driving forward, as if nothing had happened.

We had just done a complete 360-degree spin, through a major intersection, on a red light, in an Armored truck, and hit absolutely nothing. Chuck turned to me and casually says, "You like that?" We both burst out laughing. Chuck looked at me again and said, in a nonchalant tone, "I see no need to mention this to anyone." I couldn't stop laughing.

Yet again God had saved my life.

167

The Honda

Michelle and I bought a little blue Honda, one of the early models that looked like a Volkswagen. Whenever seminarians left for vacations, we would volunteer to take them to the airport, in exchange for the use of their car, while they were gone. For that week, it was wonderful to have two cars, and not have to work around schedules.

The reciprocal was also the norm. As a number of students would volunteer to take us to the airport, in exchange for our car, for the week. Chuck and Kim were also poor, and could only afford one vehicle.

On this particular trip, Chuck drove us out to KCI in our car, and we flew out to the west, for a much-needed break.

When we flew back the next week, I actually told Michelle: Knowing Chuck, I'll bet he can't resist a practical joke, and he will tell us he wrecked our car. Sure enough, as if on cue, as soon as we got to baggage claim, Chuck couldn't resist. He told us that he had to drive his own car, because he had totaled ours. We laughed and I told Chuck, "I knew you were going to say that. I even told Michelle not 20 minutes ago, you would try and pull this."

All the way from baggage claim, out to the car, he was telling this ridiculous story of how he had totaled our car. In fact, he said it happened, on the drive home from the airport, the week before. He had totaled it before we had even flown out of Kansas City. But Michelle and I were not buying it. I told him, you can say whatever you want Chuck, I know you. I'm not biting.

When we drove into the parking lot of our apartment complex, we saw our car for the first time. The Honda was parked in one of the spaces, and the engine was clear up in the windshield. Michelle and I were stunned! He wasn't kidding! The car was so badly damaged, the first thing I said was "Chuck are you OK?"

I asked him to tell me again, what happened, because the truth is, I was only half listening. I didn't believe a word he was saying. He told me again, that as he was driving back home from the airport, he decided to stop by the armored car company. He then proceeded to drive downtown. He was traveling through an intersection, when a van ran a red light. The van hit him broadside, and sent him head-on into a light pole. The impact was so powerful it snapped the pole in half.

He said he had to be helped out of the car. When the police came, they talked to the other driver first. The policeman came to him and charged him with running a red light. He protested and the cop said that he had two witnesses, that verified the driver's story.

Then some other people came up to the cop, and told him that the two witnesses were both in the van. After the accident they left and came back as if they had seen everything. The true witnesses said, that the van ran the redlight, and plowed into Chuck. Eventually the police got to the truth.

A month later, Michelle and I received a bill, from the city, for the light poll which was destroyed in the accident. We had to fight the city and the insurance company, but eventually got it cleared up.

While we were on vacation, Chuck and his parents, had decided to bring an extra car they owned, up to Kansas City, from Mississippi. When we returned, they had already brought us a mode of transportation. They let us drive that car until the insurance paid off. They were incredibly gracious and thoughtful.

Money Bags

Michelle and I had learned that wise men live debt free. We began our marriage with the express goal of paying off all our debt. I had school loans from my college days, and other debt that I had taken on. We were living debt free and paying down every debt. We started with the little ones, to free up some cash. We then paid off the ones that charged interest.

The day came when we were down to our last one, my grandmother! She had loaned me $2,500, nearly eight years earlier. She never mentioned it, but I had given my word, I would pay her back. I wanted to surprise her, and give the entire $2,500 all at once. I'm pretty sure she thought I had forgotten. I had not!

One day Chuck and I were delivering to the Federal Reserve Bank, and I asked them to sell me brand new bills. The ones still in the plastic. We call them bricks, because they are compressed and sealed with a plastic wrap. Bricks come straight from the mint in Washington DC. I ordered 25 bricks of one-dollar bills. Each brick is 100 dollars. I wanted it in a canvas bag, to make it look official, with the lead seal and tag, I wanted the works.

I took the bag home and Michelle and I put it into a box and wrapped the box as a gift. We took it to the post office, and insured it, so grandma would have to sign for it.

A few days later, I got a call from grandma and she playfully chewed me out. "I should whip your behind!" She playfully says, and then proceeds to tell me this story.

She had been getting ready to leave, when the postman, Lenard, knocked on her door. She and Lenard, have been friends for years. "Got a package for you Nettie, and it must be important" he said, "because they require your signature."

"Who would send me a package?" She asked him, and he tells her, "It's from Kansas City."

Since it was wrapped as a gift, the two of them walk into the kitchen, and she opens it in front of him. She told me, "When we first saw the Brinks bag, I was fearful that you might have done something nefarious. Of course,

I dismissed that thought, the moment it flashed through my mind. But now I was really curious! Lenard, cut the seal with his pocket knife, and we pour out the contents onto the kitchen table.

(Now at this point, I must stop the story and share something you may not know. With freshly minted money, one side is brilliant green, and the other is a striking yellow. It has not been subject to oxygen, or sunlight, or wear and tear. The colors are quite vivid. They seal it with the clear plastic and preserve the colors. If you doubt this, look at the back side of a one-dollar bill.)

Grandma told me when she saw the money, she just assumed it was Monopoly money or funny money, you buy at a curio shop. she told Lenard, it's just Perry's comical way, of letting me know, he has not forgotten some money he owes me.

At this point she scoots the trash can over to the table and dumps the "play" money into the garbage. She is running late for her meeting and they leave.

She tells me that when she comes back home, she had a friend with her. The two of them are going out to lunch. While my grandmother stepped into the restroom, the friend caught sight of the BRINKS bag, still setting on the kitchen table. She calls out "Nettie, what's the BRINKS bag all about?"

By this time, her friend, has walked into the kitchen and glances into the garbage can, that's still sitting by the table. My grandmother yells back, "It was filled with monopoly money!"

But her friend has now reached in and grabbed a brick and is examining it. She yells back to my grandmother. "No Nettie! This is real money!"

Grandma told me she almost fell running out to the kitchen. She scolded me on the phone.

They retrieved the money out of the trash, and decided to take it to the bank before lunch. Pendleton is a smallish town, and when you have lived there as long as my grandma, people know each other. So, she is telling her friends at the bank, the whole story.

Meanwhile, the employees are taking her deposit, but they have to count it, even though it's wrapped.

Now at this point in the phone conversation, my grandmother says to me "I should wring your neck!"

"Why?" I ask.

"Because those poor people down at the bank had to count all that new money by hand, because their machine was down! Do you know how hard it is to get those bills apart? They stick to each other. To make matters worse, those poor people, would be counting and start laughing and loose count. It took them a month of Sundays to count two thousand four hundred dollars by hand!"

Then she playfully says, "I kept one packet, so I can beat you over the head with it!"

The real reason she kept it, was to show it to all her friends, as she tells them the story. For a while, my grandmother was quite the celebrity around town. In a small community, a story like that spreads quickly.

Seriously Injured

One of the downsides of riding in the back of an Armored truck, was the toll it took on the body. Riding in the back of a truck, where you are tossed and bounced all day, eventually wears on the back. Add to that, lifting thousands of boxes of coin had seriously damaged my back.

I was in excruciating back pain. I had gone to the doctor, and the x-rays showed that I had damaged disks. All those years of basketball, Tennis, lifting, and bouncing around in the back of a solid truck, had done the damage, and the doctor told me that I should consider a new line of work.

I had just had my yearly evaluation at work, and the assistant manager, had written on the official paperwork, "They wished they had a hundred more just like me." I was humbled and flattered. I had worked very hard in those three years, but I wanted to finish school and get back into ministry.

We decided to go on vacation and evaluate what to do next. Before we left, I felt obligated to be honest with the manager. I went in with the doctor's paperwork and talked to the manager about the diagnosis. I felt that he needed to know that I might have to go out on disability. In retrospect, that turned out to be a mistake.

When I arrived to work the first day back from vacation, I was called into the manager's office. He informed me that I was being fired. I was dumbfounded.

He told me the reason was because I had failed to pick up a stop several weeks earlier. That wasn't true, and he and I, both knew it. Secondly, that's not a condition of termination. Thirdly, he mentioned that working for an armored car company wasn't going to be my vocation anyway. Which is irrelevant.

What I found out from Chuck, and several others later, was this: Part of the bonus the manager received each quarter, is predicated on having no workman's comp claims. I had sealed my fate the moment I walked into his office, and told him the doctor signed the paperwork, for a workman's comp claim. The irony was, on vacation I had decided not to file a claim.

Driving School Bus

Perhaps the worst job I ever had, was driving a school bus. There are several reasons. The first was, as the last person to be hired, I got the worst route on the board. Routes are taken by seniority. The only route left on the board was the projects and the inner-city schools.

Secondly, I was a young, white male. We were perhaps the most despised genre of human beings in the inner city. Thirdly, a school bus driver is even lower on the food chain, than a substitute teacher. Rodney Dangerfield made a living complaining he got no respect; he was royalty compared to a bus driver, in the projects.

On the very first day on the job, I pulled up to an all-black high school. A carload of gang members came racing up in their vehicle, jumped out, and beat up a camera-wielding teacher. When the police boarded my bus to ask what I saw, one of the kids yelled out, "You open your mouth and you're a dead man." Right in front of the officer. They didn't care.

They would snap pennies, into the back of my head and laugh. So, after several days of this I went to my boss and said if it happens again, I will stop the bus and not move until they calm down.

The next day, they were cursing me and snapping the pennies, so I just pulled the bus over and parked. I said, "The bus won't move until everyone is seated and quiet." This only served to fuel the fire. We sat there for nearly an hour, while they acted out. Some of the kids begged the others to calm down, so they could get home. But the majority of the bus was acting like out-of-control savages. As a rule, a bus driver couldn't touch them or leave the driver's seat, and they knew it.

Eventually some parents started to call the office, and my boss told them, that the bus was out of control, and it wasn't safe to move.

Eventually they got tired of just sitting on the bus, and realized I was serious. They could see that I was not moving, and I didn't care if I sat there till the next day. When they finally sat down, I began driving again.

The next day, they started in again and I pulled the bus over. This time my boss had another plan, if I was still sitting there after 10 minutes, I was to call him on the radio and he would send the police. Which is exactly what he did.

I don't think the kids had seen a guy like me before. I wasn't intimidated. I never raised my voice; I didn't make idle threats; I just kept my word. The bus wasn't moving until they settled down and were respectful. After the police exited the bus, the jeering started up again, and I pulled the bus over without a word, but this time some of the other kids started to become angry, with the punks, and not me. Peer pressure started to have impact. But it did not change the behavior of some of the kids. They fed off the attention they were getting. In fact, it got so bad, and the kids were getting home so late, that the parents called for a school board meeting, to get me fired.

I asked my boss for a tape player. I put it under my seat, and I secretly taped the cursing and their threats, towards me. My plan was to play the tape, at the PTA board meeting. I was delighted to see my boss came through. After a couple days, we had some amazing audio, showing just how out of control these kids were.

At the meeting the parents just railed at the board, to have me fired. I was white, they were all black, reverse racism it just as real. These black women accused me of everything under the sun. Some of the woman, tried to say, I was coming onto their daughters, and their daughters were afraid to board the bus! REALLY? YOU GOT TO BE KIDDING ME! It was sad, how low they stooped.

When it was our turn to be heard at the meeting, my boss, simply pushed play on the recorder and let the tape play. Everyone could hear the kids cursing, calling me every name in the book, yelling profanities, threatening my life, and dropping the "F" bomb, you could hear the sheer pandemonium.

As soon as the tape stopped, one of the vocal mothers, started yelling: "You see why he needs to be fired? He has no control of that bus!" She had missed the point completely.

The school board met privately, after the meeting, and decided to do something that had never been done in the state of Missouri. They decided that my life was in danger, and they could see that the parents were of no help. So, they decided to prosecute the parents, of the kids that were the troublemakers. They also put a video camera on my bus. The first of its kind in the state. It had been done in other states, but never in Missouri.

The camera was put in a large black box, with a dark-tinted window hiding the camera. There was a blinking red light on the front. As soon as the kids got on the bus, they were all curious as to what it was. I told them, it was a camera and everything would now be on video. It was absolutely amazing, how different they acted. Now they knew their parents would see them. We got home in record time.

Because they were so well-behaved, I was extremely complimentary. I told them how proud I was of them. Their attitude changed towards me. Prior to this, they hadn't even seen me as human. They wouldn't even acknowledge me or greet me. But now, every morning, I was my cheerful self and they grew to genuinely like me. I had gained their respect because they realized, I wouldn't be intimidated. In fact, when they learned I was a youth pastor, and actually a pretty cool guy, some of the kids would sit behind me, and share their stories and ask for advice. At the end of that first year, the seniors asked the principal, if I could be their driver for the senior skip. God was using me in ways, I never dreamed possible.

The camera idea worked so well, that they put the same box in all the buses. What the kids didn't know, was we only had one camera. They began to circulate the camera from bus to bus. You couldn't see inside the box, so the driver never knew, if the camera was actually on their bus, or not. This had an added benefit, because the drivers were always on their best behavior as well.

Cameras are standard on buses now, but back then, it was the first.

No Camera

The following year, I took a bus driving job in Grandview, a suburb of Kansas City. It was still the worst route in the bus company, but it wasn't as dangerous as the inner city. Unfortunately, they didn't have cameras yet in their district.

One afternoon, I had just finished my last grade school run, when I received a radio call from Larry, my boss. I was told to return to the elementary school. When I drove up to the front of the school, there were several police cars. When I exited the bus, I was met by a couple of officers and put in handcuffs. They told me I was not under arrest, but being detained. I was confused, and a bit defensive. What now?..was my thought.

I was taken into the school and escorted into the office. As we entered the room, this black guy, jumps out of his chair, and charges toward me screaming he'll, "kill me for what I've done!" The other officers intercept him and restrain him. He sat back down, glaring at me.

I looked around the room, The superintendent of schools is there, a number of officers, my boss Larry, the principle, and the father who attacked me, and two third grade girls. All black, except Larry and I.

Let me stop here and explain something. I grew up in Burns Oregon. We didn't have anyone of color in our town. I didn't have a racist bone in my body. When I went to college, my closest buddies and roommates were black. We were all athletes and delighted in the brotherhood of competition. One of my roommates was Robert Donaldson, the brother of James Donaldson the NBA player for the Supersonics at the time. I loved these guys. I didn't grow up in segregation, so I was naive and oblivious to prejudiced thoughts.

The Christian college I attended, Northwest Nazarene, only deepened my appreciation and love of all people. People from all over the world were on campus, and they became dear friends. Some of my closest friends in life, are black.

My first introduction to hatred was in L.A.! I was hated for being white. When I moved to Kansas City, my closest friend was Neal Napoleon, an amazing black guy. The only prejudice I ever encountered was reverse prejudice. Some people hated me because I was white. I love people, and the love, that God put in my heart, only deepened the delightful acceptance of all humanity.

I only mention the fact that I was the only white guy, because of what happens next, and the level of hatred and racism leveled against me, simply because I was white.

174

The principal looks at me with utter hatred and disgust and says "I hope you rot in hell honky!"

Whoa! Where did that come from? I am asking myself. He is the principal? A professional? Yet here he is, fanning the flame of hatred! He doesn't even know me, but he is projecting onto me, everything he hates. I am stunned!

One of the officers asks the young girl, to repeat what she had told them before. The young girl is bleeding and has a road rash on her hands, face, and knees. Her dress is torn, and you can see pieces of gravel in the wounds. She is softly crying and with sobs, she tells them this:

"I came out to the bus, but I was late. The busses were about to pull out. I ran up to the front door of the bus, and when I tried to step up, the bus driver shut the door on my foot, and drove off, dragging me." The whole story came out between sobs of tears, and was very dramatic.

The father screamed "Look at what you did to my little girl, you piece of white trash?" (Not the exact expletives he used) He jumped at me a second time, swinging at my face, and if they had not restrained him, he was angry enough to have killed me. I was in cuffs. I was vulnerable.

The principle again yells at me, "You white punks are all the same. I think before they haul your @#$ to jail, you owe her an apology." This principle is out of control. He can't restrain his loathing.

Then the officer asks the other girl to tell her side. The young girl says, "She and her friend, ran to the bus and the driver saw them coming. He looked straight at her, and closed the door on her foot."

I sat there wondering if I had inadvertently, or unknowingly, closed the door on this girl's foot. But several things didn't add up.

First of all, the front door on that particular bus, was extremely hard to close. I had struggled with it all year; the tolerances were so tight, that you really had to throw your weight behind it to get it to close. If there had been a foot in it, it would have been impossible, utterly impossible to close.

Secondly, she said, "I looked at her," before I closed the door. I knew that wasn't true!

Thirdly, the protocol at all grade schools is the first bus in line, is not allowed to pull out, until there are no children present on the sidewalk. There is a teacher who checks the entire sidewalk, confirms that no child is outside the building, and then walks to the first bus and waves them on.

All This was running through my mind. I am in a state of panic! I can't think straight. What had happened that day? Did the first bus leave early? Was there no teacher on duty that day? My mind was racing.

In my heart, I knew I was innocent, but I was having a hard time thinking. I was panicking. My heart was racing, my chest felt like it was going to explode. I was terrified of going to jail. My life was collapsing and there was nothing I could do. I couldn't even speak; I was so confused. In my mind, I called out to God, "Please help me."

Instantly a calmness came over me and I relaxed. The officer put his hand under my arm to help lift me to my feet, when suddenly everything flashed in my mind in an instant. I actually shouted, "She's lying!"

Probably not the best choice of words, but I had just remembered everything that had happened. The father was beside himself, and went into a rage, because I had called his daughter a liar.

The principal was now yelling at me, "Take a good look at this girl. Look at what you did to her....and you dare to call 'her' the liar."

I look straight at the principle, and asked him, "You had an Assembly at the end of school today, correct?"

He nodded, "Yea so?"

I continued, "The speaker was a D.A.R.E. policewoman, right? (Drug Abuse Resistance Education)

The principal sarcastically sneers, "So? What's your point?"

"Call her, she will prove I'm innocent." I pleaded. Everyone was naturally skeptical, but they listened as I told them what happened:

"When busses arrived at the school, the first bus drove clear to the end of the sidewalk and parked. The second bus pulled in behind the first and actually bumped the first bus with the rubber stops, so that there is no gap, for a child to get in between. Then the third bus, bumps the second and so forth.

Today, I was the second bus in line! I just happened to be blocking the only exit, out of the teacher's parking area. You had the D.A.R.E. policewoman, park in that lot, with her patrol car. She couldn't get out, because I was in her way, and she asked me to move my bus. I explained that we were not able to move, until all the busses were loaded, and no more children were present. In fact, I went the extra mile for her, and told her I would ask the bus behind me, to let her out, when I pulled away. She was sitting in her car, looking straight out her windshield at my door, not four feet away, when I left today. If I had been dragging a girl, she would have seen it."

We all waited for the policewoman to arrive, and the tension was thick. But I was relaxed. When she came into the office, she cheerfully greeted me with a smile and a quizzical look, because I was in cuffs.

The other officer explains the situation and she simply said, "That's impossible! I was sitting facing his door and I watched him pull away." "There wasn't a child in sight. In fact, this gentleman actually apologized to me, for blocking the exit. He was kind enough to ask the bus behind him, to wait, so I could pull out."

At this, the father looks at his little actress and says, "All right, I want the truth!"

She starts crying again, and spills that she and her friend, had skipped out of the assembly. They were on the playground playing tetherball. They lost track of time, and when they heard the busses leaving, they ran and she fell on the asphalt. She didn't want to get into trouble for missing the bus, so they came up with this story.

As the officer is taking the cuffs off my wrists, I turned to the principal and stated, "I think she owes **me** an apology."

His prejudice was so engrained, he snaps back, "She owes no whitey, nothing!" This principle, was stuck in the 60s, and his racism was so deeply ingrained, he felt justified.

As I am writing this, I still marvel, at what God did for me that day. God saw what Satan had planned for me, and before I was even aware I would need an advocate, He provided one. Not just any advocate, but the best witness I could have dreamed up. A black woman! A policewoman! A respected D.A.R.E. officer! Sitting facing my door! Just 4 feet away! I had talked with her! She had seen my face! She knew it was me! She knew it was my door!

When God is for us, who can stand against us? This is what God promises us.

The IRS

In 1985, I filed a form with the IRS. It was accepted and I saved the paperwork in a file. The following year, the IRS froze my bank account and fined me. I took a day off of work and fought with an IRS agent. It took the entire day to get it resolved. I received a letter from the agent, that the problem had been solved. I saved that letter and put it with the other.

The following year the nightmare happened again. This time the fines were doubled and added to the first fines. Instead of hundreds, the fine, was now growing into thousands. I waited sometimes, three hours to actually get an IRS agent on the phone. I eventually had to meet personally with an IRS agent. I was required to bring all the substantiating paperwork. It took several weeks, but it was resolved, yet again. I received documentation of the resolution. And I filed it away, with all the others.

The following year it happened again. I had to miss days of work, hours of arguing with paper pushers, but eventually got it resolved. They apologized and sent more documentation confirming, I was correct, and they were wrong. Every year, I was assured by the IRS agent on the case, you will never hear from us again, it has been resolved.

Yet every year the nightmare would begin anew. By the seventh year, the fines were astronomical. The threats from the IRS were more intense, and my blood pressure over the top. I realized this was never going to end. So, I came up with an innovative plan.

I had worked with the IRS agents, and learned that they hated it when they knew, it was going to be a hassle for them. So, I decided to use that to my advantage.

When I finally got an agent on the line, I told them I needed to talk with their supervisor. They of course, would say, "Before we do that, why don't you tell me how I might help."

I was ready for them…I replied, "I hope you have your coffee because this is so complex, it's going to take about eight hours for me to explain, and several weeks to resolve! We have been dealing with this since 1985." When they heard that, you could feel the wheels turning in their heads, and they would say, "let me contact my supervisor."

As soon as the supervisor would answer the phone, I would say, "I need to speak to **your** supervisor." They would reply, "Before we do that, why don't you tell me how I might help."

Just as before, I would launch into "This is so complicated, it takes over eight hours to explain……and they would say, "Let me see if my supervisor is available?" Then I would be put on hold. Eventually I would get someone higher up the food chain, and I would go into my routine…" I need to talk to your supervisor; this is so complex it normally takes at least eight hours to explain and weeks to resolve!" Cha-Ching, I would be passed up to the next level.

Eventually, I reached the level where a secretary answered! I told them I needed to speak to her boss.

I think because I had gotten to that high a level, she assumed it must be serious. So, she patched me through to her boss. I went into my routine, "I need to speak to your supervisor…., this time, however, he told me, he was the regional supervisor for the western United States.

I explained that this situation is so complex, that they had passed me up to him. I apologized, and reiterated, that it was now going to take over eight hours to explain it. It would be better to talk to his supervisor, rather than taking up that much of his time. He agreed, and he passed me up the chain of command. As the day went on, the higher I climbed.

I had been on the phone for hours by this time, but it felt wonderful. I was getting really good and sounded more professional, as I made my way through the calls. Finally, I was patched through to a gentleman and I could tell immediately, he was different. He asked how I had gotten through to him

I didn't know who I had been passed up to, so I went into my spiel, I need to speak to your supervisor… yada yada. There was this long pause…then he said in a slow questioning voice, my supervisor is the President.

"Just the man I need to talk to!" I said confidently.

He graciously listened as I told him, I had tried to resolve this issue for seven years. I told him, I was in my Master of theology program, and that this had taken a toll on my life. He not only listened, he asked questions, and marveled, that I hadn't sued the government, or gone to the press. I was honest with him, and told him how I had played the game, to get up to his level. He actually laughed, and told me he admired my ingenuity.

He agreed that I had done the right thing. He actually apologized to me, that the government had harassed its own citizen, so badly. He told me, that it had been one of the president's priorities, to eliminate red tape and needless harassment.

I told him, that the file I had been keeping, was now over two inches thick. I shared with him that I had all the originals. He believed me and told me; he didn't need any documentation. He would get to the bottom of this, once and for all. He told me, "No citizen should have to go through, what you have gone through!"

True to his word, weeks later I received a personal letter from him. It was written on presidential stationary. He explained that the original forms, were archived in an underground facility, in Fresno, California. But to retrieve them, takes effort, and has to be manually found. Whoever was tasked with that job, simply blew it off and dropped the ball!

He said, what they discovered in their investigation was unconscionable. He promised me that I would never hear from the IRS again.

I don't know for sure, but I believe he somehow flagged my name, because too this day, I have never been audited. I have never heard about this again.

I learned some valuable lessons over those many years fighting the IRS. Always save the original paperwork! Never send the original. Even if they demand the original, never, ever send the original. Only send copies. When it is lost, (and it will get lost) You lose! There is nothing you can do to prove you sent it. They WANT to lose the original! Then they don't have to deal with the problem anymore.

You have to realize, that when they lose your original, they rule! They are now in control. They can make any demand they want because you don't have the original paperwork. You have nothing to stand on. You are at their mercy. And the government has no mercy.

Save ALL the paperwork, even if it seems trivial. Have a filing system, so you can find the documentation quickly. That paid dividends over and over again.

Be gracious with the people on the other end of the phone. I was always kind, even though I was angry over the harassment. I tried to be Christlike. If you yell or get snippy with them, the phone will simply go dead. They will simply hang up on you and claim you got disconnected. You will have to start all over again, and you can never get the same person again. You will have to explain the entire story to someone new.

When you are nice and you honor them, they will want to help you. If you make them mad, they will leave you on hold for hours. They will drag their feet and leave you hanging.

Get the name and badge number of the person you are talking with. If possible, get their phone number at work, so you don't have to work with someone new. Keep a journal by the phone, put the time of the call, write down the date you called. Notate when they answered, and how long you were on hold.

Remember, they are recording the conversation. Make your words sweet, because you may have to eat them. Threats are useless. Do you know how many times a day they hear empty threats about how they are going to lose their job? It's laughable. Government employees are almost impossible to fire. So don't rattle off useless threats.

Use their first name, it shows that you acknowledge they are important. Whenever I had someone on the line, I would say, "Good morning, Susan," or, "Hi Sam, I hope you're having a good day." By using their first name, it brings in an air of freshness and friendliness. It becomes personal, rather than a nameless voice on the other end of the line. It shows them, that you care about them, as well as your problem.

Kindness goes a long way, with people who may hate their job. They deal with angry people all day long, and it gets old. When you are kind and cheerful, it is like fresh water in a desert. Remember they are God's children as well. God sees how you are treating His child! If you want God to work on your behalf, treat his kids with honor and respect.

Armor Limousines

As I have stated before, I detested driving a school bus. I hated getting up at five in the morning! It was a hassle to come back later that afternoon, and do it again. So, I decided to quit and get a better job.

I love to drive. It was easy, and I enjoy windshield time. I was sitting at the kitchen table, asking myself, what were the best driving jobs I could think of? It occurred to me, that driving limousines would be perfect. I could drive the nicest cars. I already had a suit. I could study while I waited.

I opened the yellow pages and the first name listed, was Armor Limousines. When the owner answered, I told him about my driving experience with the armored car company, school bus driving, and that I had a chauffeur's license. He asked me to come down for a driving test.

When I arrived, he told me to jump into the limousine, and he would be right back. I sat in the driver's seat and marveled at how elegant it was. I had never been in a limo before.

Mac Armor came walking out, with a fish bowl in his hands. He jumped in the passenger's seat and set the fish bowl, full of water, in his lap. He grinned and said, "Drive on, and if we get back and I'm still dry, your hired!" That was it, I drove around a while, we chatted and laughed, and when we got back, he asked me, when I could start. I didn't even fill out an application, I don't think Mac even had one.

I told him I would only be available Fridays and Saturdays. He said, "That's great, most all our runs are on those two days anyway."

That Friday, I was getting ready for my first run, and Mac was filling me in on little details of what the customer was expecting. Then suddenly the back door of the Garage opened and in marches Sandy, Mac's wife.

She was an angry person, growling and snarling. The other drivers are obviously avoiding her and they scatter in all directions. She came across as bitter and cantankerous. Sandy was obese, unkept, and loud. Everyone seemed afraid of her, even Mac. She came across as a bully and somewhat intimidating.

Mac had a deformed arm. I learned that Sandy's son had shot him. Later, I was told that the marriage was one of convenience, not love. The two of them were always at each other.

Several months later, I was alone in the garage, prepping the car. Sandy came stomping in, "Where's that good for nothing," she snarled, referring to Mac. But I detected a glint in her eye, and I said with a grin, "Sandy, I just want you to know, you don't scare me. I know you put on this big act, but you're really a teddy bear." A wry smile came across her face, and she put her finger up to her mouth, in a shushing manner. She warned me not to tell anyone. That was the beginning of one of the most endearing friendships in my life.

Sandy and I, would talk for hours. Somehow, she felt safe confiding in me. She didn't have another friend in the world. Her angry persona was just her way of protecting herself. I think she felt, that if she could keep people at arm's length, they couldn't hurt her. For some reason, she let me into her world. It was a sad and tragic world.

Her son, from a previous marriage, was in prison for the attempted murder of Mac. Mac blamed her for being crippled for life.

Throughout life, she had always been rejected by the world; a world that rewarded good looks and a thin body.

Sandy had so much love to give. Sometimes, she would make cookies or brownies and give them to Michelle and I, as a gift. Sandy and I kept in contact, long after I left Kansas City. She was a delightful woman, with a great sense of humor. Once you got past the protective barrier, she was an amazing person indeed.

All Night Long

I had many memorable trips, driving limousines, but here are some of my favorites.

On one particular Friday night, the customers were actually at the garage, waiting for me when I arrived. The couple spent nearly an hour, explaining all that they were hiring me for.

I was to wait until nine O'clock. They told me their mom had a routine. At exactly nine O'clock, she would be in curlers and bathrobe, getting ready for bed. I was to knock on her door and when she answered the door, I was to tell her, that she had a surprise gift in the car.

I was warned, whatever you do, don't let her go back in the house. I was to take her, just as she looked, curlers and all.

I was to act like I had no idea who hired me, or what was going on. Just tell her; "I was simply told to come to this address, ma'am. I was kind of hoping you knew what was going on."

The couple, had a VCR tape, wrapped as a gift, that they handed me. I was instructed to give it to their mother, and have her play it in the car. The tape would have a riddle and she was to figure out the riddle, and I was to drive to that location, and find the next hidden VCR tape. Each tape would have another mystery riddle. She had to figure out, where to find the next tape. This scavenger hunt was to last all night long.

I was given all the answers and locations, but I was not to let on, that I had any clue what was going on. I was to play dumb. If she couldn't figure one of them out, just play along until she figured it out. If she got completely stumped, I was to make "guesses" and try to help her, guide her to the right answer, but she was never to know, that I knew. I was to act just as surprised as she was.

If she got way ahead of schedule, I was to stall, get lost, lead her in another direction. I was to take her all around Kansas City, and the hunt was to last all night long. My final instruction was, to make sure I arrived at the Lake, at Nine AM the next morning. That was where all her family, friends, and classmates, were having a surprise "This is your life" party for her.

They warned me over and over, don't let her go back home and change clothes. They wanted her to arrive in her curlers and a bathrobe.

When I arrived at the house, this delightful old lady, came to the door in fuzzy, pink, bunny slippers, bathrobe, and a big towering head of hair, in curlers. My clients were going to be delighted.

I talked her into coming out to the car, where her children had gift wrapped a present for her. It was sitting on the seat, in the back of the Limo. She crawled into the car and opened the present. When she found it to be a VCR tape, she showed it to me and I turned on the VCR.

She was all giggly, like a little girl. She played the tape and the riddle was clearly leading us to the Country Club Plaza. She was a gamer, and put up no fuss at all. We jumped into the front of the car and off we went. She was truly a free spirit; these kids knew their mom!

We traveled all over Kansas City, from KCI airport (a 45-minute drive north) to Olathe Kansas. At one point she got hungry and we went through the drive-through at Mcdonald's. She had the place laughing up a storm. Rather than being embarrassed about her attire, she embraced her appearance. She was having a blast. What a lady!

I made up my mind, that when I grow old, that's how I wanted to be. Cheerful, playful and laugh at whatever comes. I didn't want to become a grouchy, crotchety old man. I wanted my grandchildren wondering, are we going bungy jumping or sky diving grampa? I wanted my kids terrified to leave the grandkids with me.

Finally, we arrived at the last stop, out at the lake the next morning, and what a surprise. There must have been two hundred people there. This lady was loved, and she was obviously the life of the party.

Ultra-Rich

During the summer my schedule was a bit more open, and when Mac asked me to run an all-day special, I jumped at chance to bring in some extra cash. Mac told me that the tip was already included in the price of the car. That never happened, and the tip was generous. I was thrilled.

Mac told me, to report to the headquarters of a large nationally known Insurance agency. The president of the company, wanted to see me in his office, as soon as I arrived.

The Insurance company had a very beautiful building. Very elegant, very stately. I was impressed. When I pulled into the circular entrance, they were already waiting for me. I was ushered to the elevator, and escorted to the office of the president. The room was everything you imagine in a president's office.

Two walls were pure glass, and you could see a panoramic view clear to the far horizon. The door was over ten feet high, and solid dark hardwood. It matched the desk and bookshelves. It looked like something straight out of a James bond movie. It was the quintessential penthouse scene. The only thing that was off-kilter, was the president himself.

He was a nervous wreck. He kept fidgeting with his hands, he couldn't sit still. He was up and down constantly. He was jumping up and walking around the office as he explained what my assignment was that day.

He told me that; "In a few minutes were going out to the Johnson County airport, to meet a private jet." He explained that the insurance company, he was the president of, was just a small part of a larger conglomerate. The insurance company was just one spoke of a bigger wheel. The plane we were meeting, was the owner and CEO of the conglomerate. He owns corporations all over the world. He was actually from Great Britain, but he was visiting the United States. He was a multi-billionaire. One of the richest men in the world.

"OK," I thought, "That somewhat explained why this guy was anxious and fidgety."

He went on to explain, that this billionaire was bringing his wife with him. I was told that while all the executives were in meetings that day, I was to take her, wherever she wanted to go. He told me, that the billionaire, had called him personally, and tasked him with the responsibility of keeping his wife entertained.

So, he put his hand on my shoulder and looked me straight in the eye. With a very serious look he said; "This is your job today, please make me look good. I'm counting on you. Your boss recommended you, and told me your perfect for this assignment, please don't let me down."

He kept looking at himself in the mirror, straightening his tie, primping his hair, he was a nervous wreck. So, I became a gentle cheerleader. "You look great, I love that suit, it looks great on you." I put my hands on his shoulder and assured him he was going to make a great impression on the guy. He thanked me and told me he appreciated my encouragement.

I learned that day, that no matter what strata of life, men need encouragement. We're all little boys inside. We may put on the mask of pretense, but we all need to be assured, and encouraged from time to time.

He rode up front with me, on the way out to the airport. The plane hadn't arrived yet when we reached the Airport. Johnson County Airport is laid back, and they allowed us to drive the limo out on the tarmac. I was expecting to see a beautiful Lear jet, or a Cessna Citation. I was shocked when this guy, flew in on a private Boeing 737.

After the plane taxied up to the car, the airport personnel, rolled out an elaborate staircase. They positioned it at the front door of the Jet. A small entourage exited first. Just behind them, an unassuming, average looking elderly couple, made their way down the steps. She was somewhat diminutive and plump. He was easily in his late 70s. What struck me, was she was carrying her own bags. One of the richest women in the world and she was humbly carrying her own bags down the steps. She looked like any grandmotherly type.

She walked straight up to me, and asked if it would be all right, if she rode up front. She had a big smile and complained that the conversation, in the back was boring. She didn't want to listen to all business talk.

I placed their luggage into the trunk, and the men all load in the back. She was already sitting up front.

These are not the normal type of people who hire a super stretch limo. They are unassuming, and have nothing to prove. Normally I worked with the uppity people, who are somewhat arrogant and want to flaunt.

The ultra-rich are so wealthy, they don't give a whit, whether you know their rich or not. They don't have to prove anything to anybody. They truly don't care what others think. They are just normal people.

We in the industry, had a pet name for those who demanded the "Works". Hat, white gloves, kiss their feet. These are the insecure ones, that need everyone to know they have money. They are demanding, arrogant, shallow people. They are new money. We call them "Beamers!" They think their halos shine and they normally brag that they drive a BMW.

Old money on the other hand, have gotten past all that ridiculous nonsense. They frankly don't feel they have to prove anything. They act like they've been there before.

This elderly lady was no different. She and I chatted and carried on like we had known each other all our lives. I asked her what she would like to do? She said she loved to quilt. She wondered if there were quilt shops in the Kansas City area?

We arrived back at the Insurance complex. When all the men exited, she and I went to her hotel, so she could check-in. While she was checking in, and the porters were taking her bags up to their room, I flushed out a number of quilt shops in the area. She finished at the front desk, and I walked her out to the car, and off we went.

She was delighted. When we arrived at the first shop, I ran around to catch the door, but she was already out of the car. I put out my arm, and cheerfully said: "Grab my arm young lady, and let's go see if they can impress us!"

We had a wonderful time, going from shop to shop. Sometimes she would find a beautiful quilt, and call me over, "Hey Perry, what do you think about this one?" (I just loved her English accent.)

I would give her my honest opinion, and she appreciated that. She could see right away; I wasn't just a "yes man!" I gave her my serious critique of a quilt, the workmanship, the stitching, the pattern, the harmony of colors, and originality. She could see that I wasn't intimidated by her what-so-ever, and she truly appreciated that.

I think they get tired of being fawned over. They grow suspicious of the truthfulness of someone's opinion. I utterly disagreed with her sometimes and she delighted in my genuine candidness. I was just being me, and because I was authentic, she grew to trust me.

As the day went on, she found out, I was a Seminary student, studying for the ministry. Some of our conversations turned more serious. And since she now trusted my opinion, she opened up, and we spoke on a deeper level. I found myself genuinely caring for this wonderful woman. She

185

could sense it also, and for the rest of the day, we had some amazingly candid conversation.

At around dinner time, we picked up the executives, and I took them all down to the plaza. I studied my schoolwork, while they ate. When they came out of the restaurant, the president came out first and took me aside. "I don't know how you did it, but you went beyond my wildest expectations. She couldn't stop talking about the day you two had." Then he slipped a hundred-dollar bill into my hand. I protested and told him the gratuity was already included in the service. He just patted my shoulder, and said "I know" and walked away.

When the elderly husband came out, he walked up to me and said, "Young man, you made a huge impression on my wife today. At dinner she couldn't stop talking about you. She told me privately, that she had one of the most blessed days in years. You were a breath of fresh air to her. I just wanted to say thank you." He handed me another hundred-dollar bill. I was so humbled, I told him, "I wasn't doing it for a tip." Then the biggest grin came across his face and he said "Exactly what she said!"

When she came out, she walked up to me and took my hand and pulled me down, and I thought she was going to whisper something to me, but she kissed my cheek and said "Thank you hon, we had a day didn't we!" It had only been hours, but we had made a connection. And it would remain with us for the rest of our lives. I'm sure she never forgot that day, I know I never will.

World War II

One of the most beautiful and iconic areas in Kansas City, is called "The Country Club Plaza," or as the locals called it "The Plaza!" It has been featured in every mainstream magazine for years. Especially during the Christmas season, the lights are jaw-dropping. They actually have entire calendars made from the beauty of the plaza lights. If you live in America, you have probably seen pictures of this special place, and didn't realize it was, "The Plaza!"

One of the questions a limo driver is often asked is, "Where is a good place to eat? Are there any really special restaurants, you would recommend?" I had an amazing place, I liked to take all my clients. It was a German restaurant down on "The Plaza." I knew the owners personally. Two wonderful ladies that had immigrated to the U.S. after World War 2.

Many times, while the clients were eating, I would spend several hours visiting with the elderly sisters. I got to know them, and they appreciated that I was bringing them customers.

One day I received a call from Mac Armor. He had just received a phone call, requesting me as a driver. It was the younger sister, from the German restaurant. She had asked Mac to have me drop by the Plaza, and visit with her, and she would explain what was going down.

When I arrived, we sat down at a table and this is what she told me; (I will tell the story from her perspective as she told it to me)

"My sister and I grew up in a small German village. My sister was 16 years old and madly in love. She was engaged to be married, and we were making wedding plans when World War 2 came to our village. Late one night the German military trucks, came rumbling into our village. They searched every home and loaded any able-bodied man or boy. They rousted the men from their beds and loaded them onto trucks. It happened so fast, that we didn't even have time to say goodbye. The military was conscripting all men into the army, they needed bodies at the Russian front.

My father, and brothers were basically kidnapped by our own German army, in the middle of the night. Unfortunately, so was my sister's fiancé. We didn't know it at the time, but we would never see any of them again. They were either killed or captured and taken to a Russian prison camp.

Shortly thereafter our village was bombed by the allies and completely decimated. Most everyone in the village was killed. My sister and I ran, during the raid and watched in horror as the village was leveled. Only a handful of us survived. My mother was killed and my sister and I were orphaned and alone. We scavenged like animals for anything to eat.

Just after the bombing, the allies came through and we were taken to a refugee camp. We were eventually shipped to a processing camp. Right after that came the end of the war, and they moved us around to a few places until we were put on a ship to America. Eventually, we ended up in Kansas City. We have lived here ever since.

Last year, my older sister, received a phone call that turned her world upside down. It turned out that her fiancé, had been captured and taken to a prison camp in Russia. When the war was over, the Russians simply opened the gates of the prison camp. They knew that the Russian people would kill them on sight, for the atrocities the Germans had done to Russian prisoners of war. So, he hid during the day, and at night he walked across the country. He would hide under haystacks to keep warm.

He snuck his way across borders, and after nearly six months managed to make it back across the German line. When he finally made it back to our village, he was devastated to see it in total ruin. His family as well were all killed.

For several years, he did everything he could to stay alive, and finally found a steady job. He saved everything he could, and bought some property. He began to buy and sell properties, and found he had an amazing knack for making profit. He eventually became wealthy and bought bigger and bigger properties. He formed a company, and began renovating damaged Castles. In later years he began to rent them out, and made millions from oil companies. The Castles were modernized, and turned into elegant palaces. OPEC would pay millions of dollars to rent out an entire castle for meetings. The privacy these castles provided was unequaled, anywhere in the world.

He never married, and his heart always yearned for my sister. He never lost hope that perhaps she was still alive. He hired investigators to find out what had happened to her. He had been told, we all had been killed. Yet he could not find her burial place. For years he tracked down every lead, and eventually found that perhaps she was in the United States. He hired a team of investigators in New York to scour the archives and see if they could find any trace of her.

Last year he discovered, that not only had she survived the war, but that she was still alive, and living in Kansas City.

He called her, and when she heard his voice, after all those years, she recognized him. They talked for hours.

He was shocked to find out she had not married either. He now calls her every morning. He does not speak English, but he learned to say "Good morning my darling!"

About four weeks ago, he called her with a stunning proposition. He told her he still loved her, and he had always loved her. He asked her, if she would be willing to take a giant step of faith, and leave her life in America, and give him a chance to win her heart again.

He told her; he would understand if she was hesitant to leave the life, she had made for herself. He also had put half a million dollars, in her account, so that he could be sure the decision was not based on financial fears. Even if she decided not to come back to Germany and renew the relationship, he told her, the money was hers.

He asked her, if she would be willing to come live in one of his castles, with him. She would live in one half and have complete privacy, and he would live in the other half. For one year they would date. He promised that if she was willing to take the risk, he gave his word, and assured her, there would be no "Hanky Panky!" These were the exact two words he used.

That was four weeks ago. My sister has decided to take the chance. He is flying over here to pick her up. That's where you come in Perry. She is waiting at the house and you are taking her out to the airport. It will be the first time they will have seen each other since she was 16."

I drove over to the address the sister had given me, and as I drove up, she was already standing at the door. She came out and it was obvious she had been crying. I naturally put my arms out to give her a hug. I asked her if she was, OK? She just fell into my arms and started sobbing. She was literally shaking in fear.

"I'm so scared." She said in between sobs. "What am I doing? I feel like a teenage girl going on her first blind date. What if he finds me unattractive? What if he sees me and has regrets? I've dreamt of this day for a year, and now that it's here, I can hardly stand up, my legs are shaking so badly."

I assured her, she was still, a stunningly beautiful woman, and she truly was.

She asked if she could ride up front with me, and I took her hand, and we walked to the car.

We talked all the way out to KCI airport. She turned to me at one point, and jokingly said in a stern tone, "He better not be a fat, balding guy, or I'll send that boy packing!" We both started laughing, and couldn't stop. Every time we would stop laughing, we would get this picture in our mind, and break out laughing again.

When we arrived, I drove to the front doors. (Back then, you could park right in front of where they exit the ramp.) The walls were solid glass, and I could see her standing at the gate. She turned to me and showed me her crossed fingers. She was smiling now. The laughter had done her good.

I was watching as the passengers were walking up the ramp. I spotted a very sharp looking guy, in a suit, that looked like he had just walked off the pages of GQ magazine. I thought to myself, it would be cool if that were him….and it was.

When he saw her, his eyes lit up, and the broadest smile swept across his face. He dropped his bag and she ran into his arms. He was a lot taller than I had expected. She looked so tiny and frail in his arms. When he turned to pick up his bags and wasn't looking, she glanced out at me and gave me a big thumbs up.

I had the door open and as they exited the airport, I took his bags and put them in the trunk. They climbed in the back and I closed the privacy window and we drove back to the restaurant.

They had closed the restaurant that night, for a private party in his honor. The place was packed with other German people who had immigrated to the U.S.

After the party, I drove the two of them, to his hotel. He kissed her goodnight and she hopped in the front of the car with me. On the way back to her house, she shared with me, all that had happened.

She was absolutely beside herself with joy. She told me he was even dreamier than she had imagined. He was such a gentleman. He was so refined. She bragged that "He couldn't keep his eyes off of me." She told me she could, "See the delight in his eyes. He still finds me attractive."

Several days later, I had the privilege of driving them back out to the airport, for the return to Germany.

After that, whenever I would visit the restaurant, her sister would fill me in on the latest developments. She told me that her sister, found that it was exactly as he had said. She had one side of a castle, and he had the other. She had a large staff, that did everything for her.

In the evenings, he would call on her, and they would go out on dates. He courted her and won her heart.

A year later they did marry, and when I left Kansas City, they were happily making a new life for themselves in Germany.

I have often wished they could make a movie of these two, and their story. I was privileged to be a small part of a true fairy tale.

I have one more memorable story, from my days as a limo driver.

Field of Dreams

The premier of the movie Field of Dreams was accompanied by a tour of many of the cities of the mid-west. When the cast came to Kansas City, I picked up the ball players and we made the rounds. Radio shows in the morning, luncheons, press conferences, interviews at the Kansas City Star, and Dinner with dignitaries.

Throughout the day, I became more and more a part of the group, they included me in a lot of the activities. They were a great bunch of down to earth guys. At the end of the day, they all signed a baseball and presented it to me wrapped in a hundred-dollar bill. I still have that baseball on display at the house.

These are just a few of the memories of those years driving limousines. I made double or triple the money that I was making driving school bus. Just another example of how God took a bad situation, and turned it into an amazing blessing. I was wrongfully let go at the armored car company, but made far better money, for half the work, driving limo.

Bully Judge

I drove all over Kansas City for six years. Working for the armored car company, I learned all the shortcuts and back-alley ways. Driving school bus, for the school district, I had traveled and memorized all the different ways to get from school to school. Driving the limo, took me into some of the nicest areas the city had to offer. I knew the streets, freeways, alleyways, and backroads. I knew the city like the back of my hand.

One Monday morning, I drove down to the Seminary, like I had hundreds of times before. In six years, perhaps even a thousand times. This particular Monday morning, was as routine as any other. I could drive it in my sleep.

I was on Paseo Avenue, and I pulled into one of the two, left turn lanes. I was waiting for the green arrows and made my left turn. I glanced into the rearview mirror, and a policeman turned on his emergency lights and pulled me over.

I hadn't been speeding, so I was really at a loss as to why he would light me up. He came to the window, and asked for my Driver's License, registration, and proof of Insurance.

"Sir," he said, "I'm writing you a ticket for making an illegal left turn."

"Excuse me" I protested. "I was in the left turn lanes. I've been turning left there for six years."

He condescendingly said. "So, you admit you ignored the no left turn sign."

"What sign?" "There has never been a 'no left turn' sign at that intersection!" I state emphatically!

"There is one now…," he said with a grin, "…. we put it up this weekend."

I pointed out a few things to him, "What about the arrows, in the left turn lanes, that's entrapment, you can't give me a ticket for that." I was incredulous.

"You need to pay more attention, when you're driving." He states, with an air of superiority. Then he went back to his car, and returned with a ticket. "Sign the ticket," he demanded.

"This is not fair, and you know it," I tell him. "I will fight this."

"Tell it to the judge," he said, in the most condescending tone.

I was so angry, at the injustice of the situation, that I drove down to the police station and asked to see the officer in charge. I explain that they have a patrolman, giving tickets for left turns, on Paseo. He just brushes me off, and says you will have your day in court, tell it to a judge.

I had to wait several weeks, for my day in court, but I was ready when the day came. It was scheduled for the first court session of the morning. I was hoping to be the first one called. The courtroom was packed. People were standing. The patrolman was sitting with a lawyer, at a table upfront.

When the judge walked in, he was visibly upset. He was obviously in a foul mood. He was shouting at one of his own court clerks. He was given a hand full of paperwork. It looked to be six to eight inches thick. He started yelling at the room, but not to anyone in particular, "Don't you people know the rules of the road, Look at all these tickets!

He then called the first name, it was a young woman and she walked up front, through the small swinging gate, and stood at a podium.

He shouts at her, "IT SAYS HERE YOU FAILED TO USE YOUR BLINKER! WHY ARE YOUR TAKING UP MY TIME, PAY THE FINE, AND GET OUT OF MY COURT!

She started to say something, but he cut her off and he screams "I SAID PAY THE FINE!"

He was being a bully! He was being a complete jerk. He was totally unprofessional. He was also out of control. People in the courtroom were looking at each other with a "Can you believe this guy?" look.

I was getting angry. He hadn't even given that poor lady a chance to speak. He railroaded her. I have always detested bullies. I grew up with a bully.

Then, he yelled my name. I walked through the gate and up to the podium. I could feel that my face was flushing, I'm was so angry at the injustice of this courtroom.

He screamed at me the same way he did to the poor lady before me. "IT SAYS YOU MADE AN ILLEGAL LEFT TURN, PAY THE FINE!

I start to say something, but he cut me off, and shouted at the top of his lungs, "PAY THE FINE, AND GET OUT OF MY COURTROOM!"

"Let me explain!" I plead.

He rose out of his chair, livid that I dared to speak. "WHAT'S TO EXPLAIN, YOU MADE A LEFT TURN, PAY THE FINE!" He shouts.

Something in me just snapped, I was not going to let this Judge use his position to bully me. I yelled back at him, "I THOUGHT THIS WAS SUPPOSED TO BE A COURT OF JUSTICE!" You could hear the audible gasps from the other people in the courtroom.

His face turned bright red, and he rose back out of his chair, he was screaming so loud, he was spitting. "YOU WANT TO SPEND THREE DAYS IN JAIL!"

I yelled back at him, "GIVE ME 60 SECONDS."

He was still standing, and he glared at me and started yelling a countdown, trying to intimidate me.

"59! 58! 57!" He yells out.

I yell even louder, I MADE A LEFT TURN OUT OF A LEFT TURN LANE, HOW IS THAT ILLEGAL?

He stopped counting down and looked down at the ticket, which gave me the opportunity to say, "AND BOTH TURN LANES HAVE ARROWS POINTING LEFT!"

He turned to the cop, and through clenched teeth, he angrily demanded "IS THIS TRUE? The cop stood and started to say, "Yes, but...." Yet, before he could say anything else, the judge cut him off. "WHAT IN THE @#$% DID YOU GIVE HIM A TICKET FOR?"

The judge was now bullying the cop. Now it was the cops turn to squirm. He asked the judge for a moment to explain. He told the judge that there was a no-left turn sign, at the intersection.

The judge asked him how that was possible? How could there be two left turn lanes, with arrows in the lanes, and make it illegal? The cop then told the judge that the sign had gone up over the weekend, and they hadn't had time to remove the arrows, or the turn lanes. As soon as the cop said that, the judge just threw up his hands.

I took that moment, to point out that I had a class-A driver's license, and was a professional driver. I had been making that turn for six years. I added, that I had been given the ticket, the first thing Monday morning, after the change. I pointed out, that I wasn't even afforded a warning.

The judge looked over at the cop and reminded him, that the law read, after a change in traffic patterns, a ticket may not be issued for a minimum of 30 days. He then turned to the entire courtroom, and asked how many others were there, for the same ticket. The whole room raised their hands.

The judge screamed some obscenities and took the whole stack of tickets and threw them up in the air, as high as he could. The tickets flew all over the front of the courtroom. He told the courtroom; they were all excused. He then turned to the cop and started scolding him, like he was a child.

When the judge finally finished chewing him out, he told the cop, "You disgust me, now get out of my court, and take your counsel with you!" The cop was furious, and when he stomped out, he slammed the swinging gate, in anger.

The judge jumped to his feet and screamed for the policeman to come back. "How dare you disrespect me like that!" He yelled!

"I want you to walk through that gate 10 more times." The judge demanded, "…and if I so much as see it swing, I will hold you in contempt of court, and you will spend three days in jail." He warned the cop.

The cop walked through the gate and carefully held the gate, so it wouldn't swing.

Like a Sargent in boot camp, the Judge demanded that the cop count out loud. So, the cop started counting. But the judge was trying to humiliate him, so when the cop didn't say it loud enough, the judge made him start over. He demanded that the cop yell out the numbers.

I was still at the podium and the courtroom had emptied. The courtroom bailiff and secretaries were picking up all the tickets, the judge had tossed across the floor. I asked the judge if I was free to go. Without a word he waved his arm, gesturing me to leave.

The cop was still counting when I exited the back of the courtroom.

To my astonishment, the crowd was still waiting for me, outside the courtroom. When I entered the hallway, they start cheering and patting me on the back. People were genuinely appreciative, that I had stood up to the Judge. They were making comments like, "We couldn't believe you yelled at him like that, we thought for sure, you were going to jail." "That was awesome, thank you!" "Thank you for standing up to him, you were amazing!"

The Cop had been a bully! He had bullied everyone he had given that ticket to. As a person in authority, he had misused that office to bully the public. He had been condescending and arrogant. God gave him a piece of his own medicine, by putting someone who was in authority, above him. He received what he had been giving out. God, is a God of Justice.

I took that lesson with me into my marriage, parenting, and ministry. I never used my position as a husband, to bully or ride over Michelle. I never used the pulpit, to bully people. I knew that whatever measure I delt out, would come back on me. It's not karma, it's a Just God, who sees everything.

Let's hope that officer learned his lesson. If not, God will bring others into his life, until he does learn. God is constantly, re-parenting His children.

Mazda 323

When we were in the last year of my master's program, we had not only paid off our last debt, but we had been able to save $4,000. We had been married for seven years, and that whole time, we only had one car. What a hassle.

At the end of the month, we went to look for a used car. We had always heard that at the end of the month, the salesmen were eager to make a deal. They needed to make their quotas.

We were walking the lot when we came across a funny sight. Someone had completely trashed a new car with fresh paint. They had been painting the building and inadvertently covered the entire car with overspray.

The car was a new Mazda 323. It looked ugly, but I thought to myself, at least it's new. The car sold new, for around $12,000 at the time. The dealership was asking $8,000, because of the paint.

I surmised, that the dealership, had turned it into their insurance company, as a total loss. I only had $4,000 and I told the salesman that. They countered with $7,500. I told them $4,000. They came down to $7,000. I asked them how long it had been on the lot? I asked the salesman to be honest. Had anyone, even one person, ever even looked at this car? I answered my own question. "NO!" I said, "they hadn't."

He knew it and I knew it. No person, in their right mind, would come to a lot, looking for a new car, and even glance at such a hideous sight. At one point, we actually walked off the lot, when they came running after us.

I told them, I was offering $4,000 and that was all I could do. I told them that I didn't want to waste any more of their time. It was futile to dicker any longer. I wasn't going to compromise my convictions about debt, and they weren't serious about getting rid of the car. I told them, that they could call me, in a few months, when the car still hadn't sold. And then I added: "That is of course, assuming I haven't purchased another car by then."

They finally relented and sold us the car. We still had to figure out how we could drive it home. It was covered in paint, and you couldn't see through the windshield.

We took a razor blade and cleared off a patch on the windshield. We needed to be able to see enough, to drive it home. When we arrived, I went down to the apartment. Michelle stayed up with the car, to clean more of the windows off. A couple of hours later, she came prancing into the apartment and asked me to come up to the parking lot.

At first, I didn't even recognize the car as ours. It was showroom shiny. Not a hint of paint on the whole car. Even the tires and rubber trim were perfectly clean. I looked over at Michelle and she was gleaming ear to ear. She said, "I got some WD-40 and was wiping down the windshield wipers when I discovered the paint just wiped away. The overspray was dry enough when it hit the car, that it didn't stick. It just wiped off. No residue, no streaks, no scrubbing, it simply wiped off"

Sitting in front of us was a perfectly new car, with a showroom shine, and we only paid one third of what it cost new. God gave us that gift. Some of you are skeptical, I understand that. If it had happened only once, maybe it could be considered coincidental. But this will happen over and over and over, until its almost laughable.

The mathematical odds become so astronomical, you simply have to concede, it had to be God! Later in my life, we would experience even greater miracles than this.

Waving Goodbye

Being raised in the great basin of Oregon, I was used to dry heat. The high desert air has no moisture. Moving to Missouri was a shock. The humidity was oppressive. During the dog days of summer, it was like walking into a sauna. Instead of Missouri, we called it Misery.

After finishing my last class in seminary, we were packed up and headed to Carmichael, California.

As we were driving, we came upon the "Leaving Missouri" sign. I pulled over and asked Michelle to take my picture, while I was making a "waving goodbye" motion to the sign. Michelle snapped my picture. A highway patrolman, just happened to be driving by, and thought I was waving him down.

He pulled up, and asked us if everything was, ok? We laughed and shared with him that we were leaving Misery, and moving back to the west coast. We had just pulled over to wave goodbye, one last time, to the oppressive humidity. We joked with him, that it was our hope, that God would never call us to live in a humid state again. He laughed and wished us a safe trip.

Carmichael

During the previous Christmas break, I received a call from the Sacramento District superintendent, Walter Hubbard. Dr. Hubbard knew

195

me, from my time as a youth pastor in Yreka. He told me that he had been watching my progress. That surprised me, I had assumed I would find it hard to overcome the bad press, I had received in Bellflower. He evidently knew I had been cleared of those false accusations.

He asked us if we would like to interview at a church in Carmichael California. We accepted the interview, and they flew us out to meet with the church board. After the meeting, they extended an offer for us to become their new pastor.

I finished the last class of my master's program, during that winter interim. The timing was perfect. Within a week of my last class, we left Kansas City to start our new life in California.

Our first Sunday was February 14th, Valentine's Day. When we arrived that first Sunday morning, I walked into the back of the Sanctuary, and there was an old man sitting on the back pew. There was no one else at the church yet. He looked tired.

My first official day of senior pastoral ministry. The first opportunity to show encouragement! The very first family member, in our new church. In an effort to be cheerful and pastoral, I greeted him. "Good morning, you look as though you've lost your last friend?"

He looked at me, and with a totally straight face, he said, "Today is the one-year anniversary Blanch Maude was killed by that ambulance!"

I started laughing! What a sense of humor this guy possessed, and such quick wit. Blanch Maude, who comes up with a name like that, on the spur of the moment? I liked this guy. What a response, I could only dream of having such a quick and spontaneous retort.

"I don't see what's so funny, I miss her terribly." He says, keeping the humor rolling. Then this twinge of fear enters my heart, and I'm waiting for the "Gotcha!" "I had you going there for a moment, eh pastor?"

Now I am wondering, is this just more of his dry wit, or is this guy serious? I studied his face, to see if this guy was ribbing the new pastor, or could this actually be true?

To my horror, it turned out to be true!

The previous year, on Valentine's Day, Blanch had been walking in the fog, when she tried crossing the street, but she was struck and killed by an ambulance!

My first effort as a pastor was a complete disaster.

How do you recover from such an insensitive gaff? I tried to apologize to the old guy, but he never came back to church again.... I wonder why?

Going in the Wrong Direction

The church was in a devastating situation. The previous pastor had started a construction project without permits. He had taken the roof off the building. When the county building inspector found out, they red-flagged the building. (No Occupancy) The pastor bailed, and left the mess, with no monies left in the bank.

No heat, No electricity, No roof, No permit. No phone, No money, No Occupancy!

At the same time, the government was closing military bases across the country. McClellan Airforce base, with its 14,000 personnel was closing. Our church was located next to the base.

The congregation was decimated. To make matters worse, the largest church in the entire district, was 7 minutes away. That church offered all the bells and whistles of ministry. We had no youth pastor and zero teens. Our music consisted of three older women in their 80s.

When the remaining few members of the church, found out they were getting an inexperienced, new, straight-out-of-seminary, pastor…. that was the last nail in the coffin. They left the church.

Most of the leadership team had left before we arrived. Even those on the board, that had interviewed us, were gone before we arrived. Less than twenty-five people remained, and that included children and nursery. NOT what I had envisioned, as my first pastoral call.

Yet I was determined to take on the challenges of the senior pastorate.

Catch 22

We transferred all our banking to First Interstate, the bank the church used. Michelle and I went down to the DMV to get our new driver's licenses. We waited hours, but they closed before they could call our number. The next day we returned and waited several more hours before our number was finally called. When we arrived at the window, we let the woman at the counter know that we are there for new driver's licenses. She asked us for our old driver's licenses, we complied, and she promptly destroyed them.

We were expecting a bill of around forty dollars. When it came in at $1,400, we were shocked! It turned out, that the state of California, charged you sales tax on your car, even though you paid sales tax when you bought it. In addition, they were charging us three hundred dollars, (environmental impact fee), for each vehicle.

It was a bitter check to write out! When we presented the check, the cashier said that they didn't accept checks! They accept cash or credit cards only. Who carried that kind of cash? And because we lived debt free, we had no credit cards. We had to leave the DMV and go to the bank.

When we got to the bank, we were told that to withdraw money, we needed a current driver's license. We told them that our current driver's licenses had been destroyed. We of course let them know, that was why we needed the money. They turned us away.

We returned to the DMV and because we had left the building, we needed a new number. So, we waited again for several days.

When we finally made it back to the window, we told them of the catch-22 situation we were in. We told the lady at the DMV, that our bank wouldn't release our money, without a current driver's license. We were told, No cash, No Driver's License! They suggested we go to the manager of the bank, perhaps he would release our money?

We left the DMV again, exasperated. We returned to our bank and waited to see the manager of the branch. He came out to the lobby and told us that without a current California driver's license, there was nothing he could do. "It's my money" I reminded him. He was not amused. Once again, we left.

We didn't know what to do. We had to get a driver's license. We returned for a third time to the DMV and took a number. The next day when we finally made it to the counter, we asked to speak to her manager, because our bank was refusing to work with us.

May I just say right here, that when it comes to government agencies, like the DMV, they cannot think outside the box! They are on a script, and they become stone cold! You are a nuisance to be swatted away. "NEXT!"

We had mistakenly hoped we would find a human. One, that could see the impossible situation, the catch 22, the roadblock we were in. We thought there might be one compassionate and understanding person at the DMV. We thought to ourselves, surely someone will have common sense. Someone will help us work this out. How naïve we were back then!!!

After being laughed out of the DMV for the third time, I had the distinct notion that perhaps this is what Hell is like. Unyielding demons, that fully understand the situation, but somehow get a gleeful delight out of it. They condescendingly pat you on the head, and tell you to go away!

Several weeks passed by, and we were driving with no driver's license. I had always been a law-abiding citizen, but the system created a lawbreaker.

I asked our church treasurer for an advance, but the church was out of funds. Coincidently Joyce also worked at my bank, so I asked her to talk to her manager, and see if there was anything she could do. She told me, "I have already told him you're my pastor, He knows full well, you are who you say you are, but he is unbending."

I asked her, "Why is he being like this?"

"Because he can!" That was all she could say.

I reasoned with her, "Surely there are people who bank there, without a driver's license. How do they get their money out?" She came back and told me that if I could get an ID card, with my picture, then the bank would accept that.

Where do you go to get a picture ID? I asked. "Are they not also, going to need proof of identity? How do I pay for a picture ID, without money?

We found out, that the only agency that will give you a picture ID, is the social security department. Oh yippee, another government agency…. this ought to be fun!

It took us days, to find "Original" birth certificates, and our marriage license. We had jumped through a number of hoops, and filled out all kinds of paperwork. What a nightmare! It was one of the most exasperating experiences of my life…. Oh wait, I had dealt with the IRS for years!!!!

We finally got our ducks in a row, and within a couple of days, we finally had our new California Drivers License's. Thankfully we were not stopped by the police during our unlawful lives on the lamb!

I truly do not understand people like this. They all knew who we were. What do they get out of this, but the perverted pleasure of seeing others squirm? I learned that, "Letter of the law people are cruel! They are bullies!"

I learned that there is spirit of the law, and letter of the law. I understand trying to thwart lawbreakers, but when they know full well, you are just an average citizen, trying to do the right thing, why not use common sense? Jesus dealt with these type of people in His day, and He called them "A brood of vipers."

God knows how bitter it can be to live on earth, with these types of people. So, throughout the New Testament, Jesus begs us to be compassionate, show mercy, avoid being unyielding. Don't be rigid. Be flexible.

If you show compassion, is there a chance that someone might slip through? Of course, but the damage done to the other 99%, in the meantime, is immeasurably greater. Think outside the box people. Use wisdom and discernment, but please, please I beg you…. let common sense rule the day. Don't be a "letter of the law" individual, just because you can! Life is unbearably harsh, but "Letter of the law" people make it so much worse.

From Bad to Worse

When Michelle and I went to the first Wednesday night service, we were the only two that came. None of the six board members, none of the teens, none of the music team, No one!

The following Sunday morning, one of the men on the church leadership team approached me and told me of a dream he had. He said, "I was driving into the church parking lot and there was a tombstone in the front of the church, and it read:

This is the house of God
or so they said
But they would not obey
So now it's dead

199

Then he left the church for good. "Wow" I thought to myself, "I guess we can scratch off 'Encourager' as **his** spiritual gift!"

The church had been without a roof, or a pastor, for nearly a year. The people that were still attending, were tired and exhausted. Without any money, the church faced a grim prospect. In those first few weeks, I had discovered that the costs, to get the permits, fix the roof, and occupy the building, was going to be approximately $36,000 dollars. The church had no money.

At the first board meeting, the truth of what was really going on, came out. They had no money to pay us. At the meeting, two of the five board members informed everyone, that they were moving out of state. They were part of the financial backbone of the church.

Within months, two other board members left, for a larger church. They told me, that the only reason they had stayed on, was because they were on the board, and were only waiting until the new pastor came. Now that I had come, they were leaving.

At the same time, one of the last two remaining board members died. She had been one of our biggest cheerleaders.

The church tithe had dropped to around $200 a week. We needed at least $1,000 a month for basic operational costs. It looked obvious that the church would have to close. Michelle and I went on half salary to keep the doors open.

"Stand Back and Watch What I Will Do"

I was praying one morning, and God spoke to my heart, not in an audible voice of course, but in a thought. "I must weed the garden for it to grow, remain faithful and pray, then stand back and watch what I will do!" These were some of the things God told Moses, in his day as well.

We began to emphasize prayer in our services. Some people became angry with me, and left the church, complaining that prayer was boring! We were down to less than 15 people. But I believed my wonderful Heavenly Father. He had told me to remain faithful, and I trusted Him.

A general contractor, Howard Patterson knocked on the door. He was a Christian, and he had heard we were in deep trouble. He volunteered to help us for free. He went down to the county and got the permits.

We had no men left to be laborers, so we prayed to God for help, and He sent us two volunteers to work with Howard.

We needed new gas lines to be installed. New gas lines require a certified plumber! We began to pray, and God sent Ron Hopping a licensed plumber. Ron not only donated his time, but the materials as well.

When the roof was ready to be put back on, we prayed for a roofer, and God sent a roofing contractor, Galen. He volunteered to give his time, if we would pay for the materials and labor. He measured the roof and determined that it would be thousands of dollars we didn't have. We began to pray.

Then, God sent a manufacturing rep to Galen. Galen called and told me that a roofing manufacturer, was willing to donate the materials. All we needed was monies for labor. We began to specifically pray for this.

I was sitting at my desk, when I heard a car pull up in the parking lot. An old man got out, and I walked out to greet him. He was a gruff old guy. He looked up at the church roof, and then back at me. "Why haven't you people put a roof on this building yet? I've been driving past here for over a year, and it's an eye sore!"

I explained that we simply didn't have the money. He yells out "That's nonsense! You contact a legitimate roofing contractor; get a bid, and send me the bill. I don't want some cheap volunteers; I want a licensed contractor!"

I told him I already had the materials and contractor; we were just waiting for God to supply the monies. He grinned and his exact words were, "Well then let's get humming!"

The old man turned out to be Ernie New. He and his family became an integral part of the church in the years to come.

We were also in need of a licensed Electrician, to completely re-wire the church. The wiring was so badly damaged, and the water damage so extensive, we needed to start from scratch. Starting with a new panel, and totally rewiring the building. This was going to be tens of thousands of dollars. This was God's church; He could do miracles. So, we started praying for an Electrician.

God sent an electrical contractor, Donald Hodson. When Donald heard of our plight, he was so moved by God. Donald took a weeks' vacation, came down from his home in Redding California, and rewired the entire church.... For free!

The water damage was so extensive that the mold was in layers. All the drywall was taken out. This made it easier for Donald to put in the new wiring, light fixtures, outlets, and switches. Now though, we needed to re-sheetrock the building. We prayed and God sent us Rick List. He donated his time, and his boss donated all the materials. In the end, his boss even donated a texture machine, and came and helped Rick and I finish the job.

When I arrived at Carmichael, it was February. The rains destroyed the interior of the building. We actually had mushrooms growing out of the carpet. Howard and I tore out the old carpet, but we had no money to replace the flooring. So, we continued to pray.

God sent us Mary, who donated the carpeting for the Foyer.

God was touching the hearts of new families. They could see God's hand at work. These new families came forward, and not only recarpeted the rest of the church, they went far beyond that. One woman bought brand-new cribs for the nursery. She also purchased a changing table. Then she took the time to renovate and paint the restroom and nursery.

I am fully convinced that God was getting delight out of our awe, at what he was doing. He was bringing glory to his name.

We needed new hymnals and an organ. So, we prayed and God put it on Ernie's heart to purchase all new hymnals and a brand-new organ. I love gruff old men!

Far and away the biggest obstacle was the city's bureaucracy. The previous pastor had made them angry. He had gone behind their back, and started the project without permits or inspections. So, we had to tear out all the work that had already been done, and start from scratch.

We were forced to remove the new sheeting and were required to put in fire breaks. They fined the church over $7,000, for the previous work that had been done, without a license or permit. At every turn God provided.

Some bureaucrat decided to stick it to the Church. He made our occupancy conditional. He demanded that the church supply the neighborhood, with a new Transformer. In addition, he wanted it placed on a concrete slab. He also added a new power pole. This of course had nothing to do with our church per se. He simply saw an opportunity to take advantage of the church and blackmailed the church. He simply refused to sign off on our occupancy permit, unless we put in their transformer for them. So, we went to prayer about this, God saw what was going on!

I know by now that it gets redundant, but each miracle was astounding on its own merits. Once again, with the city, we were facing an impossible situation. It just seemed as if we had done all that work for nothing. The city was holding us hostage.

They say you can't fight city hall. They may be right, but God owns city hall and everyone in it. God touched someone's conscience, because we received a phone call, and were told that the entire project was scrapped, and our permit would be signed!

Perhaps the most emotional moment for me was yet to come.

As a pastor back then, the phone was far and away the most important tool in ministry. Imagine how difficult these projects were to accomplish without a phone. They couldn't get ahold of me, and I couldn't get ahold of them. Cell phones weren't around yet, only landlines. And the church didn't have landlines.

Remember that the church was only bringing in $200 a week. So, when the phone company told us that it would be a minimum $100 service call. It was out of the question. Yet God prompted Jim Holmes from AT&T to drop by one day. He had been seeing all the work being done, and felt that he should drop in.

We walked around and he gave me the bad news. The entire church would need new wiring. Most of the old wiring had been broken or torn out. I thanked him, and he left.

The next day, Jim Holmes called and asked if I could meet him at 5:15 that afternoon. I told him I would be there. I assumed that he wanted to look at something he had missed, or that he might have an alternate plan.

At 5:15 a caravan of large AT&T trucks and vans started pouring into the church parking lot. I stood there amazed as they just kept coming. I panicked, perhaps Jim hadn't understood, that I couldn't even pay for a service call.

God had spoken to Jim's heart. It turned out, Jim had posted a note on the bulletin board that morning, asking for volunteers to help a church out. They came as an army. Within hours they had completely wired the entire church and put in new phones. Jim came up to me at the end of that evening, and told me that he had inexplicably lost the invoices. After they left, I went into my office. I was so overwhelmed, I broke down in tears.

Logan, Paul, and Brad

Now that the building was completed, Howard was gone. The two volunteer laborers had found jobs. We needed some heating and air units. We prayed about it and God sent Logan Devasier. As Logan and I sat up on the roof, looking at options, I began to share the good news of Christ, and the miracles God had been performing. God had been speaking to Logan before he met me, and we both knew that this was a Devine appointment.

The next Sunday Logan brought his wife and several friends. Paul, Brad, and Larina, they had all grown up together and had been High School friends, in Roseburg Oregon. One evening a few weeks later, I was sitting with Brad Ellison, and God so moved in his heart, that right there, he gave his life to Christ. Logan and Paul soon became believers as well. God was not only building a building, but His family as well.

I Stand Humbled

Our property needed a lawn Tractor, and God gave us a brand-new one. It should have cost $2,600, but God got it for less than $200 dollars. Another new believer was so moved by the Lord, that she paid for the entire fellowship hall to be renovated. In all, there were 36 separate Miracles, and direct answers to prayer, in that first year of ministry.

We went from closing the doors to flourishing, in a matter of a year. No human could have pulled that off. Remember the two volunteers that came to help. One of the volunteers was my brother-in-law. He was also a pastor. But Steve and Barbra and their children were in between ministry assignments. They lived with us, that summer waiting for something to become available. While he waited, he volunteered his days, working with Howard. At the exact time when we needed help so badly.

On the last day of work, Howard's job was completed. The inspector came that afternoon and signed the permit for occupancy. We were putting away the tools for the last time. 30 minutes later, Steve received a call from a church. He had been waiting for months. Yet, God had that church call, half an hour after he was finished at our church.

God told me to watch what he would do, and I did. You may think I went out and drummed up all these people, but remember I knew no one. I was new to Carmichael. I had no phone! They all came to my door. Howard was just as amazed as I was. These people were not Howard's friends. None of this was Howards doing either. They were all sent, one by one, by the prompting of God.

You might convince yourselves, that it was a mere coincidence. I ask you to consider the mathematical odds of Thirty-Six coincidences in a row, at just the right time?!?

Sam Parsons

Back when I lived in L.A., an old gentleman, who didn't like to golf by himself, took me golfing. I liked it, so he gave me a set of golf clubs. He was a wealthy man and he paid the green fees every time. It was a win-win. I got to learn the game of golf, and he had a friend to accompany him. I became a decent golfer.

When we moved to Kansas City, Michelle bought me a yearly student pass. It cost less than a hundred dollars a year. The real beauty of this pass was I could golf as many rounds a day as I pleased. During the summer, I would often golf 36 holes.

In golf, you show up as a single player and the starter would put you with others, to make a foursome. This particular day, I had been paired up with three other men. We were out on the course and a thunderstorm hit with all its fury. The hail began pelting us and we took off running toward the parking lot. I yelled at one of the men to jump in my car. The rain and hail came in torrents, it was a good old fashion gully washer.

The roar of the storm was impressive. We were just excited to be out of the deluge. We were both soaked to the bone. I introduced myself and met Sam Parsons. Sam began telling me about himself. When he found out I was a pastor, his demeanor changed. He felt safe to take the mask of pretense off, and he shared with me, that his life was falling apart. His marriage was ending.

I knew almost immediately, that God had set up this Devine appointment. We talked for a long time, as the storm refused to let up. Something far more important was happening in that car. Sam committed his life to Jesus that day.

He began to attend services, and we found out he could sing. It turned out his whole family sang. His dad had sung with Jake Hess years before, and Sam's uncle was Squire Parsons.

Sam was blessed to meet Ron Guffnet, a gifted pianist, who also attended our church. It didn't take long before Sam and Ron, had assembled a southern gospel quartet, called the "Sons of light." They began to perform and eventually cut a CD. Sam loved to sing, and God opened that door for him.

Sam and I remain wonderful friends, to this day. We have often talked about that Devine appointment. We went out for a round of golf that day, but God had other plans. It changed Sam's life! It also saved his marriage. But most of all, it changed his eternity!

God was still saving my life as well.

Tracks

Michelle and I decided to join the Arbogast family for Christmas. It would be the first time in our married life, we would get to spend Christmas with my grandmother. Now that she was a Christian, Christmas would be even more special. We left Carmichael and headed to Pendleton Oregon.

It is a seven-hundred-mile trip. When we finally made it to the I-84 freeway, it had been snowing for hours. The lanes were mounded. There was a large hump in the middle of each lane of hard-packed snow. The snowplows hadn't been able to keep up. The big semi-trucks kept the tire tracks somewhat clear, but it created a tire rut. You could let go of the steering wheel and the car would stay in its own lane.... like driving by braille.

At around 2:00 am, somewhere near Boardman Oregon, I fell asleep at the wheel. When I woke up, I was laying over on Michelle and she was sound asleep as well. I sat bolt upright and realized that we had been traveling down the freeway for some time. The freeway is straight for nearly 28 miles. No turns, No deviations. Almost completely level ground. The last thing I remember was Boardman. I have no idea how many miles we traveled; all I do know is God woke me up, before I came to the corner. My foot had been laying over on the gas pedal and we were traveling at a fairly high rate of speed. In all those miles, we had not rear-ended anyone. The berms had kept the car in its lane.

God had saved both our lives. I felt as if my life was spared by God's hand. He could have allowed us to crash, but I felt that he was not finished with us yet. That realization followed me the rest of my ministry. Many times, I would remember that night, while we were sleeping, the car drove for miles by itself. God could have taken our lives that night, but he spared us. Every minute thereafter is a gift.

We made it to Pendleton and enjoyed a blessed Christmas. Since my grandmother had become a Christian, there were others in the family that had become Christians as well. More and more family members were coming to believe in God.

We returned to our ministry in Carmichael, rejuvenated.

Up in Smoke

I have performed countless weddings, but three stand out. My first wedding was a complete disaster. After the father of the bride handed his daughter off to the groom, I was supposed to have the congregation sit. I forgot, and the entire church remained standing, for the complete wedding. Then to make it even more of a disaster, the bride caught her veil on fire. She burned her eyebrows, singed her hair, and we were beating her head to get the flames out.

In my defense, I had told them, and even shown her how to take her candle, and tip it forward toward the groom, so the groom could blow it out. We had even practiced it at the rehearsal. Yet during the wedding, she brought it under her vail and whoosh, it vaporized in flame.

With this wedding, only the bride felt the heat, but there was one that everyone felt.

Fastest Wedding

The temperature was 108 degrees that day. It was made even hotter on the concrete. The bride had planned an outdoor wedding in the middle of the summer. The venue was a backyard patio. They had set up the seating with metal chairs. The sun made the chairs too hot to touch. But it got worse, the groom had come down with chicken pox. He was lying upstairs in bed, with a high temperature.

The older people couldn't venture out on the concrete. The radiated heat off the concrete, was truly dangerous.

When everyone had arrived, the bride's family decided to go through with the ceremony anyway. They asked the older ones to stand at the windows and they could watch from there.

Unfortunately, I was wearing my black suit, as was the custom. The bride's family came up to me, and asked if I could perform, only the vows and do it as fast as I could. We cut out everything, the music, the processional, and the unity candle. The only thing they asked me to do was the vows.

We gathered all the guests and told them our plan. We would all run out on the patio together, and do the ceremony under the arch and return immediately to the airconditioned house.

They dressed the groom in his black tux, and when he came downstairs, he was so weak that several groomsmen were holding him up. We all rushed out to the patio. In less than a minute I had them repeat the vows. The bride was holding the groom up on one side and the best man was holding him up on the other. They quickly exchanged rings and I pronounced them husband and wife. The heat was intense, and as they were taking him back into the house, the groom passed out.

They were putting cold water and ice on him to cool him down. I was miserable in my black suit; I couldn't imagine how horrible the groom must have felt. They carried him back up to his room, as I filled out the paperwork. The family was so apologetic, and thanked me profusely for being so quick. It was the fastest wedding I ever performed. No one had a stopwatch, but I believe it was less than two minutes.

Grandma Mary

One of the dearest woman I ever met in my life was Mary Fyffe. She had a servant's heart. She was so humble, and kind. I had often wished I could have had a mom like her. We at the church called her Grandma Mary. She loved Michelle and I.

Grandma Mary became part of our family. She was so genuine and authentic. She didn't have a mean bone in her body. When you meet people like her you marvel at their kindness. She was always kind, never cross! She was always cheerful, and when she was around the church you could hear her singing. She would stand at the door of the church on Sunday mornings and hug everyone. She was so full of Love, and she passed it out freely.

Among other things she did around the church, she was the custodian. I marveled at her spirit. She would be cleaning the restrooms and you could hear her singing. She told me one time, cleaning the church was a privilege, that it was like washing Jesus' feet. She loved cleaning the church. Who thinks like that?

Over the years, I got to know her family. Some of her children and their families began to attend. Mary would bring her grandchildren in from time to time, when she was cleaning. I got to know them. They loved being around Grandma Mary, they would even volunteer to help her clean. That's just how contagious her love was.

I have found over the years, that the kindest people have often experienced the harshest circumstances, life can dish out. Yet those trials, tend to prioritize the things that are truly important in life. These people don't tend to be shallow, vain, or trite. They tend to have depth. This was certainly the case for Grandma Mary.

She was raised in the mountains of West Virginia. He maiden name was Higginbotham. When she was 16, she got married. But the man she married was older, and brutal. He would get drunk, and beat her like a dog. One night he got drunk at the bar and was killed. Mary met and married another man, but just after they were married, he was drafted into the army. He was killed in action. Mary was not yet 18 years old and was twice widowed. She married a third time, but this man was even worse. He was a child molester.

Mary became a Christian, and her life changed for the better. When I met her, Grandma Mary had been a part of the Church for years. She had a tenderness and warmth, that can only come from God. She was deep and authentic. Everyone, and I mean EVERYONE, loved Mary.

I first met her granddaughter, when she was in grade school. I watched as she grew up and graduated from high school. She then entered the military. While she was in the service, she met and married a young man.

One day, Grandma Mary came into my office and asked me if I would be willing to perform a church wedding for her granddaughter? She would be coming home on leave, and Grandma Mary wanted them to have a proper church wedding. Of course, I was delighted to accommodate.

Grandma Mary and her daughter handled all the arrangements, and for months plans were made and carried out. They asked if I would do the customary marriage enrichment class with them, even though they were already married. I agreed.

When they arrived in town for the wedding, we spent an entire afternoon together, discussing all the premarital issues you find in marriage. I found out that as a honeymoon gift, her parents had promised the couple a paid trip to Hawaii. But only if they would agree to a church wedding. The plan was to marry them the next day, and they would be off to Hawaii later that same evening.

Their military leave, would be spent on their honeymoon, on a tropical island.

Mary and the family had gone out of their way to make the wedding special. They had spared no expense. It was an elaborate affair. The couple exchanged rings, and celebrated at the reception, then left for the airport.

The next day, I arrived at church to find Grandma Mary crying and almost inconsolable. In between sobs, she kept saying "My heart is broken." All I could do was hold her as she just wept.

After a long while she said; "I'm so embarrassed, I don't even know where to start. I don't want to have to tell you, pastor, but you need to know."

We have all been played for fools. My granddaughter and her former husband, had been divorced, before they arrived. The whole thing was a sham. That whole afternoon you were asking them questions? It was all an act! She just wanted the vacation, so she agreed to the church wedding, her mother and I wanted for her. It turned out, she had talked her X-husband into playing along. She got over to Hawaii and called to say, she is a lesbian. She and her girlfriend lover, exchanged one of the tickets and they flew over to Hawaii together.

The parents, (whose names have been purposely left out), never returned to the church. They were too embarrassed to come back. My heart broke for them and I tried many times, but they just wouldn't consider returning.

I loved Grandma Mary, and it broke my heart. It never ceases to amaze me, the level of hurt we humans inflict on one another.

Carylon Clark

In ministry, there are certain types of people, that are in every church. In fact, pastors have certain names that we use, and every pastor in the room instantly knows what we mean. Just like in life, when someone says they know a Benedict Arnold, that means a traitor. John Doe is an unknown person. Jezebel evokes the thought of a wicked woman.

In ministry, every church has a Mrs. McGillicuddy. This is the woman who makes life miserable for the pastor and his family. They are critical and make it their mission to complain about the pastor, his wife, their children, or the message. There is no pleasing a Mrs. McGillicuddy! It doesn't matter what you do, she will find fault. She is always angry about something the pastor has done wrong.

Her name at Carmichael, was Carolyn Clark. She loathed the sight of us, but Carmichael Valley Oaks was her church, and she wasn't about to leave. She especially took a dislike of Michelle. She would complain that Michelle should play the piano, "Every pastor's wife should learn to play the piano."

Carolyn was best friends with the previous pastor's wife. In fact, they were so close, that Carolyn vacationed with them every year. Whenever she would return from being with them, we knew in our hearts, that the attacks against Michelle would begin again in earnest. Carolyn would complain: "Why couldn't Michelle be more like -----!-----?" (Insert previous pastors wife's name here)

With that background, let me share what happened one morning at my office. My office was next to the parking lot. Right outside the window, facing the parking lot, are the steps leading into the building. Many times, someone would come up the steps, and if the double glass doors were locked, they would rap on my window, and I would exit my office to open the double doors.

We couldn't afford a church secretary, so the only two employees were Grandma Mary, our custodian, and myself. Most of the time, I was alone at the church. This particular morning was no exception, I was alone in my office studying. Suddenly I heard this woman screaming, "Help me, he's going to kill me."

She came running into the parking lot. Still screaming out to the neighborhood, "He has a gun, Help me!" My car was in the parking lot, so when she spotted it, she ran up on the steps and started pounding on the glass doors and screamed for someone to let her in.

I opened my window, and was stunned to find, that she was also almost completely naked. She was barefoot, all she had on, was a skimpy see-through negligee' It left nothing to the imagination, you could see everything. I could also see that she was dead serious. She was terrified! I didn't have time to think, so I ran to the double doors and opened them. I told her to use my office phone, and call the police! I realized in that same instant, that I should stay outside, so I let the doors close.

I could hear her talking to police dispatch. I sat down on the steps, outside in the parking lot, and waited for the police to show up. The window was still open so I was listening, as this hysterical woman tried to communicate with dispatch. They were trying to calm her down, so they could get a picture of the situation. But she was to rattled to make much sense.

As I sat out on the steps, I felt exposed, and was also concerned about this gun-toting maniac. What might he do when he discovered she was in the office, talking to the police. Would he come at me?

Just then, who should drive into the parking lot? My Mrs. McGillicuddy! Don't tell me God doesn't have a sense of humor! There I was, with a naked woman in MY office, and Carolyn, of all the people in the world, pulling into the church. I thank God that He gave me enough wisdom, to be outside on the steps.

When she drove in, I could see the curious look on her face. As she got out of her car, I told her I was glad to see her, and I needed her help. Partially true. I needed her to comfort that poor woman until the police arrived.

You could see the wheels turning in her head. She was trying to piece together the naked woman in my office, me sitting out on the steps, and she could hear the conversation with dispatch. So, even though she still gave me the stink eye, she unlocked the door and went in to sit with the woman until the police arrived.

The police came and took her to a safe house. Her boyfriend had gone into a rage, when he found out she had dented his vintage car. He had chased her with a gun, but when she ran into the church, he took off.

Carolyn eventually came to Michelle, years later, and apologized for how she had treated her. She asked Michelle to forgive her. Carolyn confessed that her heart had been broken, when the previous pastor had left. She deliberately didn't want to befriend Michelle, because she didn't want to be hurt again. Instead, she attacked Michelle. Her hurt and anger were actually towards -----!-----!

Just like my own mother, sometimes we are just the lighting rod, that attracts the anger. It's not us personally they may be mad at. We are just the recipients of their anger. Give grace, because you never know the whole story.

God wants to show the world, that he is real. How can he show a sceptic? He uses His servants, to prove that He is real.

Let me explain. If you want to know what's in a cup, bump it, and what is in the cup will spill out. God allows his servants to be bumped, to show the offender that **love** pours out. The offender realizes, that perhaps there is a God, because what pours out is **love,** not **hate**! **Kindness**, not **bitterness**! **Soft words**, not **cursing**!

Our response baffles a skeptic. When we show patience, or gentleness, or a soft word, perhaps compassion, or even an apology, the sceptic is not expecting this. They become puzzled. They begin to wonder if we could be telling the truth, when we say God has changed us.

Yet all too often we do irreparable harm, when we respond anger for anger, cursing for cursing, bitterness for bitterness. When we are bumped, what spills out?

Bank Robbery

Our Church treasurer, Joyce Trawick, worked at our bank. She was also my neighbor. Every Monday morning, I helped her out, by bringing the church deposit to the bank. The routine was always the same. I would drive to the church, retrieve the locked bag from the safe, and take it to the bank. Every Monday morning, Joyce would greet me with a hearty hello, and I would hand her the bag.

On this particular Monday morning, I had driven to the church and retrieved the bag.

When I entered the bank, my cheerful greeting to Joyce, was met with stoic silence. Immediately I knew something was different. I looked around and took note of everything. I still didn't realize anything was wrong, just different. My first thought was, she must be deep in thought or concentrating on something, or perhaps just haveing a bad day.

Two guys came up behind me and it gave me the creeps. They seemed to be standing too close. One guy was on my left and the other was on my right. I didn't recognize any of the four guys in the bank that morning.

Suddenly they all took off running out the door, and Joyce shouts, "We've been robbed." I had walked in on a bank robbery! I instinctively made a mental note of everything I could remember, because it might be important. I was the only customer in the bank, so I was trying to recall everything I saw, over the previous few seconds.

Without warning the police came bursting in the door, and for the third time in my life, I was thrown to the ground, and put in handcuffs. At least this time I was not behind the counter. Joyce had set off the silent alarm, even before I had walked into the bank. The police had arrived without sirens, in an effort to catch them in the act.

Joyce told them, that the four men had just run out the door. She told them that I was her pastor, and an innocent customer. At first, they left the handcuffs on, until they could sort out if Joyce was actually an employee.

The police began asking me questions. They wanted me to tell them everything I could remember, as they took off the cuffs. They patted me down and made sure I was not armed, but they were kind and professional. I pointed out a magazine, that one of the robbers had picked up, and told them, his fingerprints would be on it.

Joyce was shaken, but she and I told the same story. Our descriptions were perfectly in sync. One of the officers approached me, and asked if I would be willing to step outside and identify the suspects. The police believed they had the suspects surrounded at gunpoint, in the parking lot.

I agreed, and the police led me out of the building. I was surprised, there must have been 15 to 20 police cars. They were from every law enforcement agency in the area. Carmichael police, Sacramento PD., Sheriff's deputies, Highway Patrol, and State police. I was truly stunned at the response. I remember thinking to myself, "It's too bad these guys weren't in Kansas City when I needed them." "It could have saved that Wells Fargo messenger his life!"

I was directed around the building. The police had a car surrounded. There were four men inside, all with their hands up, touching the roof. The police had every gun drawn down on them.

I turned to the officer, who was escorting me and said, "That's not them!" He seemed disappointed, and asked me to take a good look at each individual, "You're sure none of them is someone you saw? He pleads.

"None!" I told him, with absolute certainty.

The four men in the car just happened to pull into the parking lot, ahead of the police. I felt for them. I've been there! It's scary having guns drawn on you. Those guns look huge when they are pointed at your head. You're just praying, that someone doesn't accidentally get startled. All it would take is a car to backfire and all those guns could start putting holes in you.

They took me back inside for more questioning. After just a few minutes, one of the officers approached me, and once again asked me, if I would be willing to take a ride? They believed they had the suspects. So, they loaded me in the front seat of a police car, and we drove down to the intersection of Madison and Auburn. It's a large intersection. Six lanes on Madison crossing with six lanes on Auburn.

As we drove up, we could see a large crowd has gathered. Everyone had come out of the nearby businesses, to see what was going on. The officer blipped his siren, to get people to separate and let us through. In the middle of the intersection was a vehicle, completely surrounded by police cars. The officer with me, was on the radio with the officers at the scene. I was scanning the crowd and spotted two of the suspects, standing in the crowd! I yelled at the officer in the car, "Hey, those two over there, were in on it."

"Are you certain?" he asked.

"Absolutely!" I responded.

He was on his radio, and directed officers to come up behind the suspects. He was telling them "No, more to your left, a little further, ok just in front of you, in the hat." Suddenly the suspects heads dropped out of sight, and just disappeared as the police tackled them.

People were standing in the road, and the officer had to keep hitting his siren to get through the crowd. When we finally got close enough to see the car, it was completely surrounded by police. I could see the remaining two suspects, hands raised, sitting perfectly still in their car. I recognized them immediately. Within twenty minutes, they had captured all four men.

The officer took me back to the bank, and they took my statement. They were extremely appreciative of my willingness to help, and I was caught off guard. They told me, that most people won't help the police. They refuse to get involved. I was disappointed to hear that, it saddened me deeply. I hoped that wasn't true.

Edmund Burke was right when he said; The only thing necessary for evil to triumph, is for good men to do nothing!

Later I learned, that all four men pled guilty, and there was no need for a trial.

Drex Archer

One of the difficult aspects of ministry, at least in America, is the skepticism aimed at the church. It is difficult to overcome the barriers, and defensive walls people build up against anything Christian. Pastors are always looking for creative ways to reach people, that won't be offensive. The average American hesitates visiting a church service. It's just to uncomfortable and intimidating. They are not against God necessarily, but they struggle with church.

To overcome these hurdles, we are always trying to find, none offensive ways, to reach out. People might not attend church, but they might try a Superbowl party. They may not come to a church building, but if it's on a beach, they might give it a try. They may not come to a structured service, but they might come to a concert. Members in our church may not feel comfortable inviting their family to a church service, but would have no problem inviting them to a cookout.

With this in mind, I came up with an idea to have a friend of mine, do a concert for our church. Every year, my friend Drex Archer, would come to our church for a concert. The problem was, no one from the community,

213

would come into the church for the concert. So, one year, in an effort to reach our community, I asked Drex if he would be interested in an outdoor concert.

Instead of a Sunday Service, we would have the concert outdoors, which was less intimidating. After the concert, we could serve Ice Cream. People love music and ice cream. Drex was all for the idea.

So, I approached our church leadership about the idea. I suggested to them that, "Your friends and neighbors may not attend church, but what about a concert and ice cream?" The leaders and members of the church seemed to embraced the idea as well.

We paid a company to make us a flyer, and we bought a package deal they offered, which would include the company sending the flyer to 5,000 addresses in our area.

We were doing really well at the church, and this could be a springboard to even greater ministry. I was genuinely excited. I expected about 300 to 500 people. So, we made provisions for a crowd that size. We borrowed chairs from surrounding churches. The flyers were sent out and we were set.

We planned the event for months. I encouraged everyone, to invite at least a couple friends or family members.

Drex, set up his sound system outside, in the open air.

I was excited and expectant. I was thrilled to see what months of work would accomplish. Michelle and I had put many hours of work into this event. In all our ministry, we had not invested as much time and energy, as we did for the Archer concert. I had personally invited a number of people, and they had all agreed to come.

As the time for concert approached, I kept looking at the parking lot for the crowd. When 10:00am service time came, there were zero visitors, none of those who agreed to be there. Even worse, our normal attendees were absent. Not even the ministry team showed up. Only a couple board members showed up, without any friends.

I was overcome with disappointment!

When Drex started to sing, the neighbor behind the fence turned on his table saw and started to take a 2 by 4 and cut it, making a loud racket. When Drex would end his song, the neighbor would stop cutting, but the saw stayed on. As soon as Drex started singing, he started cutting pieces of the 2x4. After the second song, it was obvious that the neighbor was doing it on purpose. Every time Drex started to sing, or say something, the neighbor would look over the fence and start running the end of the 2x4wood through the blade, drowning out Drex's voice. The neighbor would be looking straight at us the whole time.

Evidently, when we sent out the flyers, this neighbor decided that he would do everything in his power to destroy the concert. Sometimes when

Drex would try to say something, the neighbor would quickly slide a board through so we couldn't hear what Drex was saying.

As soon as Drex was finished with the concert, the neighbor wheeled his saw back into the garage and gave us all, a huge grin, as if to say, mission accomplished.

We had a freezer full of ice cream, and only 10 or 15 people. I didn't feel like Ice Cream. I just wanted the nightmare to end. I was embarrassed for Drex, and disappointed in the leadership of our church.

For nearly four months, I had been under the illusion, I was leading the church. I foolishly thought, they were on board with the idea of a concert. It turned out I was bobbing out in the ocean alone.

Testimonies

I realized after that bitter event that people, may say they want to see the church grow, but they have no intention of being a part of it.

"That's what we pay you for, pastor!" they say to themselves.

Scripture teaches us that "We are all the priesthood of believers."

I started an evening class, on how to share your story. Five sentences of what life was like before God, five sentences of how you accepted God into your life, and Five sentences describing how God had changed your life. We had almost 40 people attend that class for eight weeks. It was one of the most successful and well attended classes, I had ever done.

I wanted them to share their story with each other. I asked them to be prepared to share the following week. On the Sunday evening we were to begin, no one showed up! Zero! NaDa! Zip! (Insert the sound of crickets here)!!!!!

That was very insightful to me. If they won't even tell their story to one another, how was God going to encourage them to share with others? Is it any wonder why the church is dying in America?

Ministry in the United States has become very difficult. It is not for the faint of heart. Yet when God calls you, it is the greatest privilege He can bestow on you.

Canada

I had been trying for years to start a relationship with my dad. He was always aloof and rejected every effort I made. So, when he called me and told me he had a proposition for me, I was all ears.

He told me that he and I, hadn't gotten to know each other, and he wanted to do something together. He asked If I would like to join him, on a deep-sea fishing trip to British Colombia, Canada? "It will just be the two of us," he added. I have already purchased our tickets; would you like to join me? he asked.

He outlined his idea. We would take his pickup, and drive into Canada. We would then drive aboard a ferry, and make our way to the port on Victoria Island. From there, it was an eight-hour drive, up to the northern-most tip of the Island, where we would meet up with our guide. The guide would take us the rest of the way by boat.

They have all the equipment, cabins, bedding, food, everything. He assured me. He seemed genuinely excited. He was paying for the two of us to spend a week together, I was thrilled. I agreed and told him I was really looking forward to it.

He told me, all I needed for the trip was my own rain gear.

For several months I got prepared for the adventure. Making sure my passport was ready, getting my gear ready.

A few days before the trip, he called back and told me he hadn't gotten my check yet. "What check" I asked. "For your half of the trip of course," he said, with an incredulous air.

He had manipulated me. He purposely played on my desire to spend time with him, acting as if he desired the same thing. He deliberately waited several days before the trip, so that I had taken the time off, got pulpit supply, had my passport ready. Then when it was too late to back out, he called demanding that I pay half.

I couldn't believe my own father would pull such an underhanded scam. It turned out that he had bought the tickets months earlier, for he and Marie to go. But she didn't want to go. He didn't want to lose the money, so he asked my brother, uncle, some of my cousins, and anyone else he knew. When he couldn't find anyone else to buy the other half, he had called me as a last resort. All the while claiming that he had done all this, for the two of us. I was deeply hurt, but I decided that regardless of his motive, It would still give the two of us some alone time together.

When I arrived in Oregon, we packed the pickup. The next morning before sunrise, we said our goodbyes, and headed for the freeway. He turned towards me and informed me that we needed to fuel up. That's odd I thought, why hadn't he had the truck fully fueled up beforehand. Then came the second bombshell! When we arrived at the gas station, he informed me that it was my responsibility to buy all the fuel for the trip. "If we're going to use my truck, the least you can do is buy the gas!" he said, in an angry tone. I was speechless.

The third bombshell, came when we missed the turnoff for the freeway. When I mentioned to him, that we just missed the entrance. He turns to me, and with a wry smile said, "Oh, I thought I told you; we have to pick up Floyd, he is also going with us." It turned out that Floyd and Bud, had bought the trips at the same time, and he had lied to me, about it just being the two of us.

When we picked up Floyd, Dad told me to sit in the back. I am a big guy, and the truck only had half a seat in back. I had to sit utterly sideways on a hard bench seat. When Floyd climbed in, the conversation was just between the two of them.

The trip took all day. That evening we were taxied to the fishing camp by boat.

There were about fifty other clients at fishing camp. There were about twenty boats, each boat came with a two-man crew. I would guess about a hundred men at camp.

The next day, we went out on the ocean and I got seasick. Dad and Floyd had both been in the navy, so all day long they mocked me. I can take a ribbing, but after hours, it grew on my nerves.

The following morning, they all got up at 4am, and I was still pretty sick. I apologized and told them I would sit this one out. About mid-morning, I was finally feeling human again, and went into the cafeteria and visited with the owner of the entire operation.

He asked me if I would like to take his private boat and do some fishing on my own? I told him that I had gotten pretty sick the first day.

He told me, "Just take it out to the bay, don't venture out into the ocean and you'll be fine." He was being so kind that I took him up on it.

He was letting me use his private boat. Wow, what a boat. It had two, two hundred horsepower Evinrude outboards. He encouraged me to give it my all, because it was fast, and the wind in my hair would be just the ticket. He informed me that even if I gave it full throttle, I couldn't do it any harm. Just give it full power, and enjoy the ride.

He set me up with some poles, and I took it out on the river. The camp was located about five miles upriver from the ocean. The river was calm as ice. I had no problems with seasickness.

I made my way down the river, and to my astonishment, I saw black bears everywhere. I would pull up to them and they wouldn't even acknowledge my presence. They were so used to boats that they took no notice of me. I came right up to them and they just ignored me. I was having a blast. When I got near the ocean, the river was about half a mile wide. I stayed in the inlet and just puttered around.

Around noon, something extraordinary happened. I was parked, setting bait, when a whale came up and swam right next to the boat. I was amazed, it was an Orca whale. To my utter shock, other whales started to come alongside the boat. They were on all sides of me, and not just Orca, but Humpbacks, and gray whales. The bay was full of whales, and they were all around me.

I got out my video camera, and started filming the incredible spectacle. A part of me was fearful, these giants could easily knock my boat over. I felt insignificantly small. I was wrestling with the fight or flight instinct.

One flick of the tail and I would die. But I felt as if God were saying, "This is my gift to you, I did this just for you Perry." "Enjoy."

There were no other boats on the horizon. I was the only one who got to experience this amazing display. It was a deeply moving experience.

Eventually I returned to camp, and ran up to the cafeteria to tell the owner what I had experienced. I thanked him for encouraging me to venture out to the bay, because of what I saw. I told him about all the different types of whales I had seen in the bay.

Suddenly he stopped me and went into an angry rage. I don't remember all he said, but I remember distinctly what he accused me of. I will leave out all the expletives, but here is the gist of what he said;

"You young city punks, come up here to the wilderness, and think we must be idiots. How dare you come in here with such a ridiculous story. Listen I have been coming here my whole life. I live in this camp half the year. I've owned this place for over 30 years. First of all, this is not the migrating season for whales, that was two months ago, secondly Orcas don't run together with other types of whales. Thirdly you wouldn't know a gray whale from a humpback." He was genuinely angry.

I waited until he was finished with his tirade, and then said, "I guess you wouldn't be interested in seeing it on video then!"

"WHAT!" he jumped up. "LIKE {#%^&} YOU DO!

I whipped the camera out of the backpack and flipped open the screen and pushed play.

What happened next was poetic justice as he ate every single word. Let me share it with you, it went something like this:

"Well, I'll be {@#$%}, that is a Humpback. {$%#@#} what's a gray whale doing in these parts? Those {#$%$} Orca are everywhere! If I hadn't seen this with my own eyes, I would never have believed it. In all my years I have never seen anything even close to this. That IS right here in OUR bay!!! I recognize the shoreline. YEP, that's my boat. UNBELIEVABLE! Well, you know your whale's son, I owe you a huge apology. I'm seeing it, but I still can't believe it!!!"

That guy watched that tape all afternoon!

He and I talked the rest of the afternoon, as he watched the tape. I shared that I was up there that week, trying to connect with my dad. There was no one else around, just he and I.

Suddenly, he slapped me on the back and said, "No one but you and I know about this tape, right? Ok I have an idea. I want to set my guys up, the same way you set me up. Tonight, don't say a word to anyone. Not even your dad, no one! Don't even tell them you went out on my boat. I want to set them up at dinner. You sit there and no matter what I say you just follow my lead. When I'm done, I will show your video on the big screen up front."

Later that night all the men were seated in the cafeteria when the owner gets up and winks at me. He walks over and picks up the mike, and starts this tirade about how gullible some of the city slickers think they are, "I was in here this afternoon....," he says, "....and some city boy starts pulling my leg about all these whales he saw." The room erupts into laughter. "We all know the migration happened a couple of months ago, but this idiot thinks he is talking to a country bumpkin! Then this Einstein starts in on how there were Grays and Humpbacks, and Orcas..." The group is laughing and jeers are being directed my way. Everyone in the room knows exactly who he is talking about. So, they are all looking at me. The tirade continues, "He must think I was born yesterday..." The owner is milking this story, for all its worth.

Then my dad joined the jeers, "He's college-educated too, he's always been a liar, and what makes it even harder to stomach is, he is a religious nut!"

The room got deathly still.

The pain in my heart was so intense, I felt as if my chest walls were caving in. My eyes were burning, I got up and walked out.

I could hear the tape beginning to play as I walked back to the dormitory cabin, but the damage had been done.

Later that night, when the men came into the dormitory, many of them walked up to my bed, and one by one, let me know how extraordinary the video was. Many of them said, how sorry they felt about what my dad had said, and acknowledged that, it had to have been a kick in the teeth!

My dad hadn't come back yet, and wasn't in the room, but when he did show up, the owner was with him. I could tell by the look on the owner's face, that he felt bad, about how everything went down. So, in an effort to make things right he offered us his boat again. "Why don't the two of you take my boat out tomorrow," he pleaded, "Just the two of you." He was desperately trying to make amends. "The salmon are running, or the two of you could just explore up river, and make a day of it. No cost! It's on me!"

"Not interested!" My dad snapped back, "I didn't pay good money for a guide, to run around in a boat!" and walked out of the room.

The men in the room were silent, then one man speaks up, and quietly said.... "I would pay any amount of money in the world, if my boy was willing to spend time with me. He hasn't spoken to me in years. It's his loss son, your dad is a $%#$ Idiot."

That night as I lay awake, my Heavenly Father spoke to me in my thoughts. He said, "I have always been Your Father, I'm the one who created you in the womb, Bud was only a sperm donor, but he has never been a true father to you. I have always been there! I have always protected you! I will be there, walking beside you, for the rest of your life, and beyond." My mind drifted to the amazing hours with the whales, and remembered the gift it was to me.

Cliff Hanger

I loved riding dirt bikes. I rode in high school, and bought one in college at BMCC. When I was living in Carmichael, I decided to buy a big bike. A Honda 650 Enduro. It was what I had always wanted. Logan, Paul and I loved riding sand rails, four wheelers, and dirt bikes.

Up in Auburn California, in the Sierra Nevada mountains, they have trails that go for miles. In Forest Hill, they even marked the trails, for their level of difficulty. Just like in skiing runs. Double black diamond was for the expert riders.

One day I was riding with Paul, and as always, was wearing my gear. I had the full set, including my racing boots. I wasn't used to walking in boots and at one point in the day, I was on a bluff and lost my footing. I fell off the cliff. I remember flying through the air and thinking "Ok this is how I die!" I didn't have time to be especially scared, almost a resignation of "this is it." Then total blackness!

Paul watched in horror, and later described what he saw; "You were falling through the air and your body was tumbling. At the bottom were huge boulders and I watched as you landed. You hit one of the biggest boulders, square on your back. Your body bounced up like a ball, and you fell in between two boulders, your body kind of dangling."

When I was coming to, I could hear Paul's voice, but it seemed really distant. When I opened my eyes, I heard his voice as normal. I still had my helmet on and was trying to reach up and take it off. Then Paul's voice got distant again and almost a tinging sound, like a high-pitched sound. I was unconscious again.

When I regained consciousness the second time, I felt very relaxed with no pain. Paul's voice came back into focus, and he was asking me to drink some water. I could talk for a little bit, and then I remember telling him I was going out again, and I could actually hear my voice slur. Blackness again.

I could hear Paul yelling for me to open my eyes, and he was telling me I was going to be ok. It seemed comforting. But his voice was so far away. Then it came closer and closer and I came to again.

I began to drink the water he was offering me. I was beginning to feel a bit queasy, but other than that I felt fine. Paul helped pull me out, from between the boulders and sat me up. He helped me take off my gloves and helmet. The fresh air felt rejuvenating.

I sat there for about ten minutes and Paul was trying to assess if I had any broken bones. I told him outside of feeling a bit vomitous, I felt fine. He didn't know if he should leave me, and go get help, or stay with me. I stood up and still didn't feel any real pain, so we hiked back up to the top of the cliff.

I got back on the bike and asked him to follow me and we slowly rode back to the truck. By the time I got to the truck, my stomach felt better, and I continued to hydrate. I ate a few snacks as Paul loaded the bikes. He drove me back to Carmichael and dropped me off.

I told Michelle what had happened and she was none too happy. I told her we couldn't really afford an emergency room visit, and just to keep an eye on me the rest of the day. I promised her that if I began feeling weird, I would go immediately to the hospital, no argument.

My only guess is, I hit so perfectly flat on that rock, that my whole body spread the impact, and it was not concentrated on any one part. I was wearing my helmet and pads, so that took some of the hit, like pads in football.

God had saved my life, again, for the umpteenth time. Coincidence? Come on, after a while even a skeptic, has to scratch their head and admit that God must be watching out for you. If 100 people were tossed off that cliff, almost none would survive. The few that might have lived, would have been broken to pieces. To fall and walk away.... a pure miracle of God.

"Trip" of a lifetime

A wonderful friend of mine, Merlin Hunter, was building a parsonage in Lemon Valley, near Reno. It was nearing winter and He needed help. I was thrilled to be able to give him a hand. I had been doing so much construction around Carmichael, that I was used to pounding nails.

We were on the roof finishing for the day, and it was bitter cold. The temperature was near freezing. The ground was rock solid, and it was getting dusk. I came down the ladder and was jumping in the truck when I happened to glance up to see, that I had left my leather nail bag on the roof. I was in a hurry and scurried up the ladder. I grabbed my bag and when I turned around to put my foot on the ladder, the nails that were holding the ladder in place gave way.

My foot got caught in the top rung of the ladder and I fell backward off the roof, head first, like a dive. I couldn't see the ground and I thought, in that instant, if I hit head first, I will snap my neck. So, I extended my arms over my head and when I hit, it shattered the bones in my arm.

The entire tip of the humerus (elbow) bone snapped off. A spiral fracture from the elbow to the wrist. But I didn't hit head first, and that saved my life. I ended up in a cast and sling for months, but once again God saved my life.

Uncle Jack

I was asked to conduct a funeral service for an elderly gentleman. I noticed an old man there in denim coveralls, wearing a T-shirt. Not exactly appropriate attire, for a funeral.

I was told that his name was Jack, and he was the son of the man who had just died. So, I walked up to him and tried to engage him in conversation. He was shy and frightened, staring at the ground. It became immediately obvious; he was socially awkward. In the process of trying to draw him out, I invited him to come to our church.

Several weeks later, I was utterly surprised to see him sitting in the furthest back row of the sanctuary, near the door. He was again wearing a pair of coveralls and a white T-shirt. After the closing prayer, I looked up to find that he had disappeared. This went on for several weeks.

I was on to his game, so I deliberately walked to the back of the sanctuary before the ending prayer. I caught him off guard, but it was the only way I could see to catch him.

In a diminutive shy voice, his first words were, "Do you like NASCAR?"

What an odd question I thought. The Perry in me, almost blurted out something, but I felt the quiet voice of God say, "Don't say it!" Instead, I inquired; "Why do you ask?"

He looked up at me and our eyes met, "I like NASCAR," he replied. "I taped it on my VCR, and wondered if you would like to come over, and watch it with me?"

This shy little man was being vulnerable. He was inviting me into his world, so without hesitation, I accepted his invitation. I asked him to give me a couple hours, and I would be there. At lunch, I told Michelle, I had been invited to this gentleman's house, and would be gone a few hours.

When I arrived at the address, all the shades were pulled down. The house looked closed and locked up tight. There were signs on the front door that read; "Go Away!" "No Solicitors!" "House guarded by Smith and Wesson!" It was clear he felt that the world was dangerous, and he had isolated himself. He was an utter recluse.

I knocked on the door and heard a faint yell, "Come in." So, I tried the door and it was open. But the house was dark, no lights. It took my eyes a few seconds to adjust. When I closed the door behind me, it felt creepy and a little awkward, and eerily dark. I walked down a hallway and looked to the right, into a lightless room, and I could see him sitting there, rocking back and forth.

The moment I stepped into the room; he switched on the VCR. I saw that he had set up a chair near his, so I sat down. He hadn't said anything, He just stared straight ahead at the TV. I could see that he was very uncomfortable. He wasn't used to having someone in his house. He rocked back and forth utterly frightened.

For a few minutes, I sat there in the quietness, listening to the commentary on TV, and finally broke the awkward silence, by asked him, "Do you have a favorite driver?"

"Yes." Was his only response. So, I tried again, "Who is it?"

"Earnhardt!" he says. Silence. So, I try yet again, "What number does he drive?" I asked

"Three" he responds, then....... more silence.

There were a few more one-word answers and another round of silence. His fear is palpable.

Finally, he said in a quiet monotone voice, still staring straight ahead; "I heard you say in one of your sermons, you like ice cream. I'm a diabetic, but I got you some ice cream. You'll have to help yourself."

I found my way into the dark kitchen and opened the freezer compartment. In front of me, packed side to side, top to bottom, front to back, were pints of ice cream- vanilla, strawberry, coffee, mint chocolate chip, butter pecan, cookies and cream, rocky road, pistachio, and Neapolitan-every flavor you could find! Probably twenty-five containers! I could tell by the brands that he had gone to a number of stores Raley's, Albertsons, and Safeway.

He was so desperate for a friend; he had gone out of his way to make sure I would find something I liked. My heart was broken. After standing there shocked and stupefied a few moments, I chose Pralines and Cream, scooped it into a dish, and rejoined Jack in the TV room.

I thanked him profusely, and commented on how delicious the ice-cream was.

After I had finished the ice cream, Jack quietly said, "Thought you might want something to drink, so I got you a pop." Back to the fridge I went, and opened the door. Every shelf was packed with bottles of soda, orange, grape, Dr. Pepper, Seven-up, root beer, Shasta, diet Coke, Cherry Coke, Mountain Dew, Spite, Pepsi, you name it, it was there. I picked up a bottle of Pepsi, and went back to NASCAR.

My heart was overwhelmed. This man was so lonely, that he had gone the extra mile. No! He had gone a hundred extra miles to ensure I would like him. "You are an amazing host Jack, thank you!" I said, and I could see a glimmer of a smile on his face.

As I got up to leave, I commented that "I would have to come back for next week's race, If I had any chance to polish off all that ice cream." His face lit up, and he said, "I'll tape it for us!"

I continued coming over every Sunday afternoon from that time on. It became my Sunday ritual. Uncle Jack, as I began calling him, became more at ease with each successive visit. The rocking was not as pronounced. He began to use more than one-word answers.

About six months later, we were watching the race when out of the blue, he turned to me and asked, "Could I be a greeter?"

I was blown away. Of all the people I knew, this was the last person in the world, I would have suspected, wanted to be church greeter. This quiet unassuming recluse, wasn't even on my radar. I couldn't imagine what had prompted him, to make such an amazing request. What he told me, would change my life, and my ministry profoundly.

He looked over at me and said, "When I came to the church for the first time, Grandma Mary was greeting at the door, and she gave me a hug. That was the first time anyone had touched me in years. I have no wife, no children, no brothers or sisters, I have no-one. That hug was the first human touch I could remember, and it meant the world to me."

What I learned is people need touch. A handshake, a fist pump, a hug, something. I had never been one to hug or touch, but after that, I made a conscious effort to hug people.

It changed our ministry, instead of coming across as hard and plastic, people told me, I seemed warm and loving. The children began to wait in line to get their hugs. In the mornings, when families arrived, the children would race across the parking lot, to get their hugs from pastor. It had never occurred to me, that I had come across as starchy or rigid. That all changed, when God showed me through Uncle Jack, that touch is not only needed, its essential.

From that time on, Grandma Mary and Uncle Jack greeted everyone who came to church. Every person, regardless of age or social standing, got a loving hug from those two. Jack needed it as much as they did. They turned out to be phenomenal greeters.

Everyone fell in love, with one of the most gentle men I have ever known. We all loved him. As time went on, and he came out of his shell, we found out he was extremely intelligent. He became a board member and taught a class on Revelations. When I would walk by his class, and see him up front speaking, I would marvel. God changes lives!

Michelle and I adopted Uncle jack into our family. From that time on, he was at all the holidays. He just became a part of our lives. He was no longer an orphan, he had us.

Schwan's

One summer, while on vacation in Oregon with my brother, I joined him on a service call. Carl owns a cabinet shop, and he was out to do a measure-up. As we were traveling along a remote highway, I noticed a Schwan's ice cream truck, setting on the side of the road.

As we passed by, I didn't see a driver. I told Carl, "That doesn't seem right! What would a freezer truck, be doing in the middle of the summer, sitting on the side of the road?"

We went back and pulled up alongside the truck. I hopped out to see if I could find the driver. I climbed up, to look in the cab, and it was empty. I walked around the truck and found the driver laying on the ground semi-conscious. He had vomited on himself.

We didn't have cell phones back then, so we picked him up and loaded him into the passenger's side of his Schwan's truck. I ran around and jumped in and took off toward Walla Walla. Luckily the truck had a two-way radio, so I grabbed the mic and told them to, "Have an ambulance meet me on the highway, I was headed into town, and their driver was in serious shape."

When I saw the flashing lights, I pulled over and they took him to the hospital from there. I jumped back in the truck and got directions to their terminal and returned the truck. They took my name and number.

On the way back home, Carl and I were lamenting that "The least they could have done, was give us a quart of ice cream," and we laughed.

About six months later, back in Carmichael, I received a phone call from the driver's wife. She thanked me over and over for saving her husband's life. Evidently while he was out of the truck, he suffered a heart attack. She told me, it was only a part-time job to help pay the bills. I asked her "What does your husband do for a living?" She responded, "He is a pastor!"

I thought to myself, "Yet another Divine appointment you sent me on, Lord!"

The Healing

I was up in Bend Oregon, at a golf tournament for my alma mater. After the tournament, I was by myself, and decided to travel up to Hermiston to see my parents. I had not seen them in several years. When I arrived, it was in the late evening and it was just starting to get dark. I knocked on the door, and Marie answered the door. I had not let them know I was coming, because to be honest, I hadn't even considered it myself, until I was leaving the Golf course.

Marie's first words were, "Oh, you just missed Bud, he took Grandma back to Pendleton. Come in." The first twinge that came into my heart, was fear. I had not been alone with my mother since I was running for my life back in High School. I thought to myself how ridiculous to be afraid; after all, your six foot two, and she is a frail old woman now. But the thought of being alone with her, was still daunting, rational or not.

She offered me a chair, and she sat on the couch, on the other side of the room. It was fairly dark in the room, and I found it odd that she had not turned on the lights.

She and I talked for a while, and then she mentioned something about her traumatic incident and being raped.

225

I found myself in a counseling role, and I felt compelled to ask her "How do you think that incident shaped your life?" My heart was filled with compassion for this damaged woman. After she shared some pretty insightful observations, I asked her to join me for a mental journey back in time. "I want you to walk into that room again, but this time as a mature adult, I will be standing right beside you, as the two of us confront the rapist. What would you say to him?

I was not prepared for the level of intensity that she lashed out at him. She was cursing and screaming at him, telling him to get his filthy hands off that girl. It was as if I weren't even in the room. She raged on and on, and I began to realize why the lights needed to be down. God had set it up, to help heal a long-standing wound.

Because the room was dark, she didn't feel self-conscious. she was completely in the moment. She was in full emersion; she was in that room, with that pervert and she was venting years of vengeful anger.

When she finished, I asked her to join me again and we were going back into that room one more time as full-grown adults, and I asked her to "Tell me what you would say to that little girl?" Her voice became soft, and gentle, as she tenderly comforted the little girl, she began to sob, as she communicated to that little girl "It's not your fault, It's not your fault." She was so intently in the moment; she was unaware she was talking to herself! On her own, she moved forward and told the girl, "I believe you." "They should have believed you!"

What happened over the next few minutes, was life-changing for her. I listened, as she, for the first time in her life, brought justice, to a long-standing wound in her life. She wept, and because we were alone, and it was dark, she felt safe. I was thankful that Bud wasn't there. God knew the exact hour for my arrival. His timing was perfect.

Because the two of us had shared something so traumatic that night, she began to see me in a completely different light. I became her pastor. I was no longer her detestable little boy, but a gentle Shepard. She gained a deep level of trust in whom I had become. After that night, she felt safe in calling and seeking my advice.

Mother's Day

The following Mother's Day, I called, and she cheerfully answered the phone. I was still trying to wrap my mind around this new relationship. She was asking me questions about "What did I believe about this? Or what does the bible say about that?" We were about to hang up and I said "love ya mom." There was a pause, and then she quietly asked. "Do you really?" Without hesitation I said "I love you deeply" and it was true. God had so changed my heart that I had a deep and genuine compassion for her. I had been praying for her for years and grew to love her.

Then she said, "I can tell you do, but how can you, after all I've done to you?" Perhaps because of the conversation we had been having, I sensed in her question, something much deeper. She was asking me "How can God love me when I don't deserve it?

I told her, Mom it's the difference between a reward and a gift. A reward has to be earned, to receive a reward the onus or responsibility is on us. We have to perform something or do something extraordinary. A paycheck is a reward for hard work. A trophy is a reward for outperforming everyone else. A gift is completely different. It has nothing to do with the recipient. The decision is solely in the giver's heart. The recipient may not even know it's coming.

Then I blew her mind! Did you know that not one time in scripture is Heaven ever called a reward!? Every time it's mentioned, it's called a gift. I quoted my favorite scripture:

> *For it is by grace you have been saved,*
> *through faith, and this not from yourselves,*
> *it is the gift of God—not by works,*
> *so that no one can boast. Ephesians 2:8,9*

God loves you unconditionally mom!

She started to cry, and said to me, "If anyone but you had told me that, I would have scoffed. But if you can love me, after all I did to you, then it's within the realm of possibility that God could love me."

She called me on the phone later and shared with me what had happened to her in the night.

The Dream

I was walking up a valley. I heard the most beautiful music I have ever heard. It was coming from a giant tree, the only tree on top of the hill. I walked up the hill. The music became even more beautiful. The harmonies were perfect. The sound was crystal clear. I looked and I could see that each branch was an instrument and each leaf, a voice. I wanted to be a part of the tree so bad, that I was overcome with grief.

Please I asked, let me be a part of something so beautiful. The tree invited me to simply jump up and grab a branch. But as I looked, all the branches were far too high. I can't reach it on my own I complained. The tree said why don't you roll that wooden barrel over and stand on it. I rolled the barrel over to the tree and it had blood on it. It had nails in it. When I tipped it up, I saw the name, Jesus. I stood on the barrel but it was very wobbly on the ground. I reached up to grab a limb, but it was still just out of reach. I started to cry and the tree said Jump!

I looked down in the valley and dad was walking up the hill. I told the tree that if I jump, the barrel will roll down the hill, and break into pieces. Then my husband will not be able to reach a branch. The tree said that I had to make a decision for myself. The tree had been calling all my life, and if I wanted to be a part of the beautiful music, I had to jump. I wanted to, but I didn't want to leave my husband, I wrestled with the decision, and yet the desire to sing and be part of such perfection was stronger, and I jumped with all my might. As I touched the branch, I was so filled with joy that I sang out, and it was a perfect voice.

I had never been so full of all that is Holy, and pure. I looked and the barrel went tumbling down into the valley and was broken into pieces. I cried for my husband, but the tree asked why I wept? I have broken the barrel, I replied. But the tree said take a look, and as I looked my weight on the branch had brought the tip low enough for my husband to take hold, and he too began to sing.

She told me that she had accepted Jesus as her savior. That she was now a Christian. She was convinced that before dad died, he too would become a believer.

Dad
Dad called one day and told me that he and mom had been reading and studying the bible. He began to see that God loved him. He was letting me know that he had asked God to forgive him, and he was trusting Jesus for salvation.

God had mercy on a simple-minded man, who didn't have a clue how to be a father but was humble enough to realize he needed Jesus. God had answered my mother's prayers and fulfilled her dream, and the two of them will spend eternity together. I couldn't have been, more thrilled.

Mom's Call
After Dad passed away, I received a call from mom. I instinctively put the cell phone on speaker, so I could hear her better. Michelle was in the room and was listening.

Mom began the conversation. "I am calling you before I die, to tell you why I did the things I did to you." She said, "I have taken the time to write down every incident I could remember." "Every time I tried to kill you." "Every time I beat you. "Every time I was being cruel"

She went on to explain, "I was going to take your life because then you wouldn't have to experience the pain of life. It was because I loved you that I decided to put you to death." She continued; "I beat you that day because I was struggling with manic depression." "I decided to stab you to death on that day, because ...."

She started at the top of her list, and one by one she named every single incident, and it was an extensive list. She went into great detail and explained all the backstories of each incident. She put every incident in context so that I would better understand.

She was asking me to forgive her, but at the same time, she was trying to justify her actions. She told me the reason for the call, was to bring healing to me. That I needed to know that her motive, for all the abuse, was because she loved me. It was both heartwarming and tragic, innocent and delusional.

Michelle sat on the couch listening to the whole, odd, conversation.

Wisdom was telling me that Mom was justifying the call in her own mind, by telling herself that she was doing it for me, but it was blatantly obvious, she needed the soothing healing of being forgiven. I have learned that sometimes, you have to read between the lines.

She was trying to make amends in her own stumbling, childlike, backhanded way. I assured her that I had completely forgiven her and that I loved her dearly. She needed to hear that. We all need to hear that.

She couldn't go back in time and make it right, but she would acknowledge it, and deal with every situation, so she could put it behind her once and for all.

As I continued to assure her that I loved her, and forgave her for what she had done, you could hear the joy return in her voice. This had obviously been weighing on her mind. I had forgiven her years before, in college, when I released her out of the dungeon of my heart. Yet, she was still haunted by her memories.

She didn't realize it, but she was carrying out, several of the 12 steps in recovery. One of the steps in recovery is owning something you have done. Admitting and taking responsibility for your part. Then if it is possible, make amends to someone you have hurt. God was leading my mom in the healing process.

We spoke for a long time. When she had finished the long list of offenses, she asked if there were any that I could think of. She was desperate to cover every possible infraction. I assured her that all was made right, and I encouraged her to drive the rest of her life, looking through the windshield of her life. I had learned I couldn't move forward, driving through the rearview mirror!

After the phone call, Michelle was just looking at me. "I want you to know" she said, "I always believed you when you told me all those outlandish stories, of abuse, but it was amazing to hear your mom, recount each and every story you have ever told me."

I had always had this tiny fear in the back of my mind, that perhaps Michelle thought I had exaggerated, or embellished a story. Or perhaps didn't truly believe, a mother could do that to her boy. Michelle's comment washed over me like a cleansing. I had needed to hear those words; it was so validating! In God's amazing way, he had brought healing to me as well

Homeless

One afternoon, I happened to be walking through the church, when my eye caught movement in the field, out back of the church. I went out to explore and came across a homeless young man. He was emaciated and dirty. His face was gaunt and his clothes were well worn. He was making a camp for himself in the high weeds.

I invited him to our house for lunch, and found out that he struggled with a drug addiction. His wife had left him, and taken his little girls with her. He had lost his job, and apartment. He had been living on the streets, but they were dangerous, so when he found the back field, he felt he could be safe there. Michelle and I spent the afternoon sharing with him, how amazing God had been to us. That He truly did exist, and that God could work a miracle in his life as well, if he would simply allow God to take over. He humbly asked God to take over his life.

He felt the weight of the world lift from his shoulders. I told him he needed to find his wife, and heal the hurt that he had inflicted on her. He needed to be the father those little girls deserved. He told me that his wife would never trust him again, and I told him "You let God take care of all the impossible things you face." You just humbly do the right things, and let God handle the rest." He told me that his wife lived in the L.A. area and he could not afford a bus ticket. So, I bought him a ticket to L.A. and watched him leave on the bus.

Six years later, Michelle drove into our driveway, and was spooked by a van in front of our house. She was getting the groceries out of the car, when a big, good-looking man, came walking up. With a big grin he asked if could help her with the bags. She looked at him warily and said, "No thanks."

He said, "You don't recognize me, do you?" She looked more closely and apologized, but she couldn't place him. "I'm the young man that was in the back field, and you two brought me to your house for lunch, and bought me a bus ticket to L.A."

Michelle gasped and said, "You have put on so much weight, I didn't recognize you."

Just then I drove up, and he introduced himself to me. I was stunned. He didn't look like the man I remembered. He told us that after he arrived in L.A. he found his wife, and God worked a number of miracles, and they got back together. She had accepted God as her savior, and they attended church together. He had gone to college, graduated and was now a full-time pastor. God had so completely reparented him, that now he was helping others, as I had helped him.

He said that he was praying in his office that morning, and felt that God told him, "To drive up to Carmichael and share your story with the two of them."

He said, "I didn't even know your names, and I wasn't sure that you two would still be living here. I couldn't remember where you lived, but I have found that if I just trust God, he takes care of the rest." He broke out in a big grin. We both knew, those were the very words I had encouraged him with, all those years before.

Ordination

In the Church of the Nazarene, getting Ordained as an elder is a lengthy process. It takes years. To protect the sanctity of the pastoral role, the church has taken extraordinary steps to ensure that, anyone getting Elders orders, is truly qualified! For me, I had to complete my Bachelor's degree, then qualify for a district License. Every pastor must serve consecutive years as senior pastor at the same church, and a number of other qualifications.

The last big hurdle, was passing the interview and qualifications, of the Ministerial Credentials Board. You must demonstrate a high degree of competency in Theology, Scripture, Education, Polity, and the Nazarene manual.

After years of faithfully fulfilling all the requirements, I finally was recommended for Elders Orders. One of the last questions that they always ask is, "As a Nazarene minister, are you in complete agreement with everything in Nazarene Manuel?"

When I was asked that question, I answered "NO!" The District Superintendent was incredulous. "What do you disagree with?" He demanded!

I calmly explain my issue. "In the Manuel it states that when a person is sanctified, the sin nature within a man is eradicated! That is a poor choice of words. Eradicated means that it is gone. Dead! Doesn't exist! It can't raise its ugly head, ever again. I find that utterly ridiculous. That is tantamount to saying that once you are sanctified, you can never sin again. Everyone in this room knows full well, that the sin nature within a man, is always present until we die. Common sense and pastoral experience, prove this to be true every day. I cannot agree with the word, "Eradicated!"

That was the death nail to Ordination, and I knew it. But I couldn't lie and agree with something that I felt was utterly ridiculous. I was reprimanded by the board, and required to read a number of books. In addition, I was required to meet, once a month, and be tutored by one of the pastors on the board. So, for the next year I endured the gauntlet.

The following year I met with the board, and they fully expected me to agree. When I told them that I could not, in good conscience, agree with the use of the word eradicated, I was shot down yet again.

The following year, before the interview, one of the pastors who was on the board and a wonderful friend, took me aside and gave me this advice.

"Perry, we know you are called of God, that is quite obvious. Everyone in that room wants to ordain you. We are begging you to simply tell the superintendent what he wants to hear, and be done with it. You don't have to preach it; the truth is, most of us agree with you. Just tell him, "Yes" and let's get this over with!"

When I walked in and sat down, the superintendent spoke first. "All we want to know is Yes, or No? Do you believe everything in the Manuel?" I looked at them and said, "I love you guys, and I know your just doing your job, but I truly don't care if I ever get ordained! I will never agree to something so blatantly false!"

They excused me from the room. I knew I may have sealed my fate. The thought ran through my mind, that I would possibly be removed from ministry. They could strip my District License in the Church of the Nazarene, and remove me from the church.

A while later, I was summoned to return. The Superintendent spoke; "Perry, it is obvious you will never change your mind, and that you are a man of convictions. It is also obvious that God called you and that you possess the gifts and graces of a pastor. We therefore are in unanimous agreement, that you be ordained. Congratulations."

That year at district assembly, I was ordained an Elder in the Church.

There are many times in life when we may be asked to compromise on our convictions. Peer pressure is real. The temptation to relent is powerful. Especially in ministry, the pressure to cave to the latest social trend is powerful. The politically correct crowd mocks Gods values. They are on the march, and have put pressure on pastors to compromise Gods standards. Unfortunately, many pastors and church leaders have capitulated and caved in to peer pressure, or the latest socially accepted trends. Those pastors are committing ministerial malpractice.

God called me to be an ambassador. An ambassador is not afforded an opinion. A faithful ambassador, is only allowed to relay the opinion of their King. Anything less, is to abdicate the role of ambassador. My stance or opinion is irrelevant, the question is; What is my Kings stance?!

In an ironic twist, the next quadrennial General assembly, the Nazarene Church removed the word "eradicate" from the Manual.

Fraud

Michelle was stricken with severe endometriosis. It was so invasive, that it began to work into the other organs of her body, and began to tear and rip her insides. The only answer to stave off the advance was a complete hysterectomy.

She was also diagnosed with Lupus. An autoimmune condition, where your own body attacks itself. So early on, we knew that having children was out of the question. Instead, we explored Adoption.

We filled out our Adoption Resumé and waited. Our adoption attorney put our resume in the back of the file. As those in front are chosen or drop out, your file moves forward. When an expectant mother comes in, the first three resumes are examined. If she doesn't like any of the first three, then the next three resumes in the file are given to her, until she comes across one she chooses. It took nearly two years before we were chosen. We were brought in for the interview, and she questioned us thoroughly.

As the months clicked down the excitement increased. Michelle's arms ached to hold a baby. Finally came the due date, and Michelle was pacing the floor all day. She couldn't sit still, but the days came and went. Her anxiety increased. We of course were aware that the first baby, for many women, may come late. So, we weren't concerned. But after two weeks we called the attorney. He assured us everything was on schedule. He sent us pictures of the ultrasound to ease our anxiety.

Our expectant mother was living in a home for unwed mothers, in the San Jose area. Our attorney lived and worked in Santa Cruz, about a three-to-four-hour drive for us, depending on traffic. After the third full week, we suspected something may be seriously wrong. Even the Attorney was concerned. By the fourth week, and still no baby, the attorney contacted authorities of a potential fraud.

The investigators discovered the woman was never pregnant. The police had been looking for this con woman for a while. She had embezzled several hundred thousand dollars from one of her victims, and was hiding in the home for unwed mothers. Her level of cruelty was astounding. She had copied the ultrasound images and passed them off as hers.

Our Oregon Girl

My brother and his wife became aware of a woman, who wanted to adopt out her young girl. They wanted to know if we were interested in a two-year-old. We came to Oregon and met with the young mother and the precious little girl. The single mother was financially unable to care for the child and she had decided it would be better to adopt her out, rather than have the state take her away.

We made preparations to take the little girl home with us. We had to work through all the proper legal channels. This took some time, but by Friday, everything was in order. Saturday we were prepared to take full custody and return home. We had fallen for this adorable little girl.

On Saturday morning, we received a phone call from the State. That Friday night, they had arrested the woman and her boyfriend for selling the little girl for a porn video. The state's Child protective service had stepped in, and because of the circumstances, the adoption proceedings would be terminated. We were crushed

233

Money, Money, Money

Our adoption attorney called and told us that we were chosen by another couple. The mother and birth father wanted to interview us. We drove the four hours to meet up with the couple, and Attorney. The interview went well. We learned that the baby was due in less than a month. The next day they called us, excited to have their child in such good hands.

In the state of California, it is illegal to "auction" a child. There are laws in place to keep the mother from offering her baby to the highest bidder. That being said, it's within the woman's right to ask for "reasonable" compensation and costs. Our attorney assured us, at the beginning of the process, several years earlier, that he never allows any money to change hands, until the adoption is over. The State of California also has a provision, that allows the mother to change her mind up to a year after birth.

The couple asked us if we were able to provide $6,000, as her compensation? This is what we agreed upon at the interview. It was simply the amount that we agreed was fair compensation. Once that amount is agreed upon, it legally cannot be changed. The catch is this. Until the attorney types up the contract and it's on paper and signed, it's only a verbal agreement, and utterly inconsequential. Depending on the attorney, that can take days or weeks, to get it typed up and signed.

We had the amount set aside, but we only had enough money left over, to pay the attorney. Later we received a call from the attorney, that the couple were having second thoughts. They had found a couple willing to pay $12,000. Could we match that? Because we had not signed the letter of intent, the price was still on table. Michelle was beside herself in grief. She became very depressed and quiet. An extra $6,000 was out of the question. She cried all weekend. I was powerless to comfort her.

On Monday morning she was getting ready for work, and began crying, her heart had been broken for the third time. On her way to work, she cried out to God, "You own the cattle on a thousand hills, so what's one baby to you. You have the resources to pay for this baby."

When she arrived to work, she was preparing for her first patient. When Michelle was seating her, the woman looked up and gently said, "Are you ok? I can see you have been crying."

At first Michelle didn't want to talk about it, because she was afraid, she would break down in tears again. But the woman was persistent, and took hold of her hand. Michelle relented and quickly shared that the adoption would fall through if she didn't come up with the extra $6,000 dollars.

Michelle, then left the room and returned a few minutes later. When she walked into the room the woman said, "Here, this is for you," and handed her a card, and inside the card was a check for $6.000 dollars. Michelle started to object, but the woman stopped her. "Let me explain" she said, "I am a Christian, and this morning during prayer, God spoke very clearly to me about this $6,000. I have had it for years. It was just sitting in an account and I had wanted to bless someone with it. This morning while I was praying God brought it to my mind, and told me to use it today. I even put a card in my purse. When you told me the amount, I about fell out of the chair. $6,000 was the exact amount I had in the account."

God set up a Divine appointment that morning. He spoke to one of His children to bless another of his children. What are the mathematical odds, that on that particular morning, Michelle's first patient, or any patient would hand her $6,000 dollars? Michelle worked for twenty years as a dental assistant, and not one other time, in those thousands of days, and tens of thousands of patients, ever handed her a card. Much less with a check in it for thousands of dollars.

We contacted the attorney, but in the end, the couple had gone back to the other couple and got them to agree to $14,000!

We returned the check. And took the time to explain to this dear woman, what that check really represented. It was God's way of encouraging his wounded daughter. God had used her check that morning, to show Michelle, He had heard her prayer. He did care. He had seen the injustice, and that nothing was impossible for Him.

Mindy

We received another call from our attorney. When we arrived at the interview, the birth mother was accompanied by her mother's best friend. Kelly's mother had just died, and Kelly had no way of caring for her unborn baby girl, by herself. Kelly was quiet for most of the interview, her mom's friend dominated the conversation. We were told we were chosen, because of our education, and most importantly, that we were Christian.

On October 2nd, 1996 we had just arrived in the hallway of the hospital when I saw a nurse, come running out of a room holding a tiny newborn baby. I asked if that was our little girl? And she said, "follow me." We watched spellbound, through a glass window, as our daughter Mindy Lee Arbogast was washed off, weighed, and wrapped in a swaddling blanket. I bonded the instant I saw her. We were not allowed to touch her, or even enter the nursery until the social worker completed all the paperwork.

Hours later we were finally allowed to hold our daughter. We didn't know it at the time, but Mindy had several life-threatening issues with her heart. Many newborns have small holes in their heart that eventually close, but Mindy had holes that were life-threatening. Mindy also had pulmonary stenosis. One of her tricuspid valves was nearly 50% closed.

When it was discovered that she needed open heart surgery, we, of course went to God and asked Him to help. There were two teams of heart doctors assembled to do different facets of surgery. We were facing a quarter of a million dollars in costs.

In the hours leading up to the surgery, the last tests were run, and something extraordinary occurred. Mindy's Tricuspid valve tore open, allowing the blood to flow. Instead of 50% blockage, it was so perfect, that she has better flow than a normal heart. The flaps alone, for a normal heart, restrict around 11%. She only has 8%! To the doctor's astonishment, the holes that were to be surgically repaired, were simply gone! They couldn't explain it. The doctors themselves called it a Miracle.

Michelle

When we adopted Mindy, I had to deal with an odd consequence, that I had not considered. My wife Michelle had wanted children since she was in Jr. High. She always assumed she would have a large family. When we were dating, she told me she was eager to have at least four, perhaps five children. After we were married, and she found that she needed a hysterectomy, she went into a dark depression. For several years, I would find her softly crying. She was devastated. She could not come to grips with the fact, she would never bear children. She struggled with feelings of inadequacy. She felt she was only half a woman.

I, on the other hand, really didn't care. I wasn't particularly excited to carry the responsibility of a child anyway. It didn't bother me, and I tried many ways to convey it to Michelle. I don't know why, but I honestly didn't want children. "What a hassle," was my thought.

But I loved Michelle so deeply, that if she wanted children, I was all in. She was excited over the prospect of adoption. To say that Michelle was obsessed with having a baby, would be an understatement. She lived, breathed, walked and talked about having a baby. Her entire world centered around getting a baby. We looked into foster care, but that didn't work out. We were not comfortable with surrogate mothers, but we examined all possible avenues. I went along because I could see how passionate Michelle was.

When we looked into adoption, we found everything seemed to line up. Eventually the day came and we were called to the hospital, and our daughter Mindy was born. As I said before, when I first saw that little baby girl, I bonded instantaneously. I even changed her first diaper! We had gone through many heartaches on the path to having Mindy as our daughter. So, when she finally came, I was all in.

But something unprecedented happened with Michelle. I was not prepared to handle what happened next. Michelle, struggled. She became distant from Mindy. She would not bond. She was fighting emotions of anger. She had no idea what was happening to her either. We talked about it for hours, and she confided in me that seeing Mindy, only reinforced the fact that she could not bear children. It was bitter for Michelle, to have to concede to caring for another woman's baby. She told me she didn't want to be a glorified babysitter.

I was in a state of shock. Who was this woman, and what had she done with my wife? For years she had been a woman, whose every thought was consumed with having a baby! Yet now that we had a baby, she was struggling to bond?

One night she was quietly crying and I asked her to tell me what she was is thinking. She said, "For several years after we were married, I would lay awake at night trying to imagine what our baby would look like. I would picture my button nose and your beautiful blue eyes. I would picture her face with my eyebrows and those cute dimples you have in your cheeks. My baby is dead, and I am grieving."

This was way above my pay grade. I hadn't even considered this level of hurt. Words are completely ineffectual in times like these. All I could do is hold her and let her grieve.

Another contributing factor was, that a part of Michelle was afraid to bond. That one-year date was ever-present. Kelly could change her mind, at any time in that year, and simply take Mindy back, and Michelle couldn't allow herself to bond, and then have the baby taken.

Michelle had been unyielding in her staunch demand for a closed adoption. The welfare people were constantly pushing the liberal, open adoption, concept on us. But we were resolute!

One evening, Mindy was cheerfully cooing and giggling on the baby blanket and I turned to Michelle and quietly said, "It's not Mindy's fault, but you're making that precious baby pay the price for this injustice. Mindy needs a mother, and you're the only mom she gets. If you withhold your love, she will be the only casualty. You will hold her responsible to carry the "punishment" of your perceived injustice."

From that moment on, Michelle bonded. She loved that little girl, and cared for Mindy, with all the passion she had always carried. She released the floodgates of love, on that Gift from God.

Mindy's New Daddy

I was 36 years old when Mindy was born. I had grown up a lot since becoming a Christian. God had been reparenting me for many years by this time. I had determined not to pass on any of the dysfunctions to my children. The generational abuse would stop with me! I was passionate to begin a new family paradigm.

I read many books on child rearing. I had studied the entire bible over and over. I watched video series on parenting. I read a number of books by Dr. James Dobson. Some of the best material I found was from Dr. Ezzo and his wife. Their series on "Growing Kids Gods way", was invaluable.

Mindy was shown healthy love throughout her life. We disciplined her, but in a controlled and mature way, never in a fit of anger. She was a fairly compliant child. So, raising her was a delight. We had the typical conflicts through teen years, but we will always be close. I call her my precious jewel, and she calls me daddy.

Sometimes life has blind corners, you don't see coming. I had no idea, how deeply I could love a child. I wasn't prepared for Michelle's struggle to bond. Sometimes people you least expect, accept Christ. I never imagined when I was a little boy, that God would use me to lead my parents to salvation. I never knew from day to day, what surprises God had in store for me.

Last Call

Mike had invited an old man to church, and told the old guy that he would pick him up at the house. The old guy was rough around the edges. He had lived his life in the bars, but he agreed to go. That Sunday morning, was the first time the old guy had ever been in a church. But God spoke so powerfully to his heart that he accepted God into his life.

The following Sunday morning, Mike, went to pick him up and found him lying on the floor, fully dressed, ready for church.

At his funeral, we opened the mike and allowed people to share. His daughter walked up to the open mike and shared this story; *"I didn't like my father. When we were kids, he made us spend the day at the dump, collecting aluminum cans, and tearing out copper from appliances, just so he could spend the week at the bar. He was a drunk, every day of his life. I decided years ago I didn't want anything to do with him. We hadn't spoken in many years."*

"Then last week he called me. He apologized for all the cruel things he had done. He told me that God had filled his heart with love. I could hear in his voice a happiness and joy that I had never heard before. My dad broke down and cried as he asked me to forgive him. I never heard that man cry ever."

"He called me almost every day last week, just to tell me how much he loved me. He told me he had gone to a church, which seemed impossible to me. I just couldn't picture him sitting in a church. He told me that God was so real, that he had become a Christian. My dad, a Christian! That defies any logic I have ever known. Yet every day he called me, and I could tell he had changed."

Another daughter came forward to the mike. *"I also got a call from dad last week. He was so gentle and kind, and spoke so seriously, I didn't know how to process it. That man had always been hard as a rock. But on the phone, he was sincerely asking for forgiveness, for the father he had been. I thought, maybe he was going to hit me up for money, but every day last week, he just called to visit. I can't explain it, but something remarkable had changed that man's heart."*

One of his former drinking buddies came forward. *"I have known that man for forever, but something must have happened to him. Because Monday, he came into the bar and he was cheerful and happy. At first, I thought he was drunk, but he has always been a mean drunk. He told us all, at the Bar, that God was real. He told us, God had change him. He even brought in a new golf bag, and told us all, that he was raffling it off, so he could take the money and help his church. We thought he was kidding, but he was dead serious. I don't know what happened when he went to church, but it made a new man out of him. We offered him a drink and he said he didn't need it. He didn't take a drink all week!"*

There is a story Jesus tells of workers that are hired at different times of the day. One of the workers is hired at the end of the day just before quitting time. The boss pays him first and gives him a full day's pay. The other workers get frustrated when they also get a day's wages because it didn't seem fair. And the boss asks them, didn't you agree to work for a day's wages? Why would you be angry because of my generosity, to guys that came later in the day?

The point of the story, was that God, offers the gift of Eternal life, to anyone, even on the last day of their lives. That old man didn't realize it at the time, but he would never be in church again. God's mercy was so amazing, that He saved his soul, in the last hours of his life. Eternal life is a gift, and God doesn't give the gift because it is deserved, heaven knows that guy didn't deserve it, but God gives the gift, because He genuinely loves the little humans, He created.

When you open a parachute to save your life, it doesn't matter if you open it when you first jump out of the plane, or just before you hit the ground. Just as long as you open it before it's too late. Life is foggy, the danger in waiting is, we don't know how close we are to the ground!

Solo Flight

I love to fly, all my life whenever I got a chance to fly, I took it. When I got the chance to take ground school in high school, I jumped on it. Then later in life I went to Cessna flight school, and learned to fly, but couldn't afford to finish. It always bugged me that I didn't get a pilot's license. When I was finally able to afford flying lessons again, it was in Carmichael. But there was a new license that was available, called a sport license. It was far cheaper and allowed me to fly Ultra Lights.

I took flying lessons and finally qualified to take my first solo flight. The morning of my flight, it was foggy. My instructor wanted me to come out to the airport anyway, and take the written exam. He explained that by the time I had finished the test, the marine layer would lift, and burn off.

After I passed the test, the clouds had lifted some and I began the preflight of the aircraft. When that was finished, I looked up at the clouds, but they were still far too low. The instructor came walking out the hanger, and told me to jump in and get buckled up.

I told him that the clouds were much too low to attempt my first solo flight. He ignored my concern, and looked up and told me the clouds were at least four thousand feet, just stay below them. It didn't seem like it to me, but he was the expert instructor, and I was the student.

He had another surprise for me. He informed me, the radio in the aircraft was broken, and that we were going to rely on, two-way, handheld, radios. I was already anxious, so I didn't need any surprises. My stomach was churning.

I had always pictured my solo flight on a bright sunny day, on a weekend, with a large crowd of friends around, with a celebratory atmosphere. But it was a weekday. No one there but the instructor. The skies were gray and cloudy. The atmosphere was gloomy. Now the radios didn't work, and things weren't perfect. I was intimidated.

I knew that in a few minutes, I would lift off the ground, and my life would be in my hands. If I were to survive, I would have to do everything myself. My instructor had always said; Takeoffs are optional, landings are mandatory.

The Airport had two runways in the shape of a giant X. I was to take off and land on the same runway. The instructor told me that he wanted me to take off, fly around the entire airport, then land on the same runway I took off on. He was very forceful, "Just listen to my instructions," he told me, "And do everything I tell you to do!"

I had butterflies in my stomach. I was about to accomplish something I had always wanted to do.

Finally, he closed the door. He spoke into the handheld radio, and asked me if I could hear him? I gave him the thumbs up. He saluted, and I powered up the engine and let off on the breaks. The plane began to roll down the runway.

My mind was racing, I didn't want to forget anything, or it could cost me my life. I gently pulled back on the stick and waited until the plane lifted off the ground. I was flying by myself for the first time in my life. The right seat was empty.

The most important factor in takeoff deaths, is pulling up to quickly and stalling out the plane. So, it was imperative that I watched my airspeed, as I climbed in altitude, and keep it well above stall speed.

I was watching intently at my airspeed, altitude, and...... suddenly a complete white out. I was only four hundred feet off the ground, and I was already in the clouds. This is the most dangerous situation you can be in, because it causes complete disorientation. You have to trust your instruments, not your senses!

Several things went through my mind in that half second; First, I had been right, I knew the cloud level was no 4,000 feet! Secondly, GET BACK DOWN!!!! I pushed the stick forward gently until I could see that I was losing altitude. Thirdly, I watched my Horizontal situational indicator to make sure I was still in straight and level flight.

I couldn't see the ground; the fog was thick. I kept dropping and suddenly I was out of the clouds. I was a bit ticked off at the instructor. He had put my life at risk. I decided that I was going to turn and immediately land on the other runway before the clouds had a chance to drop any lower.

As I lined up on the runway, the instructor began screaming at me, "What are you doing? Not that runway" I told you to fly around! If you land that plane, ill flunk you! He was yelling, but I didn't care! It's my life, not his! All I could think about was getting the plane back down on the ground. He was yelling at me all the way to the ground.

When I taxied up to him, he had this grin as big as all outdoors. I was utterly confused. I shut down the plane, and he came running up to the door to congratulate me. "That was perfect, just what I hoped you would do." He said with an air of confidence. "I knew the clouds were around 500 feet and I knew you would simply bring it down and land! If you had listened to me and taken it around, I wouldn't have signed you off. I have always told you that you are the 'pilot in command' and it's your responsibility to make the right decisions. Air traffic control can't know all that you know. Why do you think I was so explicit about landing on the same runway?" "Oh, and by the way, he says, "The radio works fine in the aircraft, I did that on purpose, so you wouldn't talk to me. I wanted you, to do just what you did. Well done!"

I didn't know whether to accept his hug, or punch him?

Mud Boy

I had just purchased a plane and, I was out flying around the first afternoon with my new aircraft. Michelle was sitting in the hanger reading her book. I told her I was going to go up for one more flight. I had half a tank of fuel left, and I wanted to get some more practice with my take offs and landings. I took off, and was a couple miles away, when I started to turn back towards the airport, suddenly everything became deathly still. The motor didn't sputter to a stop; it was full power, then nothing!

My training kicked in, and I immediately did all the protocols, but the engine would not restart. I knew that the key to surviving, was to remain calm and keep the airspeed above stall. I had practiced this a hundred times on Microsoft flight simulator, but this was a real plane, and I had only one shot to get it right. There was no pushing the restart button.

I had lost power so I was a glider. I was too far from the airport, so I quickly scanned where I could safely put it down or crash. I saw a field and gauged my speed to keep it just above stall. I was gauging my glide ratio. I needed to clear the fence on the near side of the field, yet come to a complete stop before I crashed into the canal on the other side.

As I cleared the fence, I started to pull back, to get the plane as slow as possible before touching down. I kept pulling back until I was only a few inches off the ground. I kept it there until there was simply no more lift. The wheels gently set down, but unbeknownst to me, the ground in the field was muddy just under the surface. The landing was so soft I barely felt it, and then I simply slid quietly to a stop. It was the softest landing I had ever experienced.

I hadn't really been afraid, because you're thinking so rapidly, you don't have time to run all the possible bad outcomes through your head. Your concentration level becomes acute. You are simply doing all the things you have been trained to do.

I unstrapped and jumped out of the plane and stepped into the mud. It splattered up to my face. I walked through the muddy field, to the nearest road and back to the airport. Michelle was still reading when I walked up. I was covered from head to toe in mud. "What happened to you?" she asked, looking around for the plane.

"I lost power and had to crash land it in a field," I said, with an air of accomplishment.

I walked around the building enlisting a bunch of guys to help me. When I walked into the hanger one of the guys looked up and asked, "What happened to Mud Boy?" He had sealed my nickname. From that moment on, everyone called me Mud Boy.

We went back out and the crowd of us, walked the plane up to the road. The reason I didn't land on the road, was because I didn't have the airspeed to make it to the road. Gliders can't be choosers!

I was still curious as to why the engine had stopped. I explained to some of the more experienced pilots, that I had plenty of fuel. They asked me how I knew that? I showed them the clear panel where you can see the level in the tank. I showed them that it was a little less than half full. That is when I learned that on that particular aircraft, the tank is in a "V" shape. If you can see the fuel level, then that tells you you're nearly out of fuel. "Well, that would have been nice to know!" I said in an irritated voice. I was frustrated with the previous owner, for not pointing that out. That oversight could have cost me my life!

Once again God had helped me escape death. How many people in life, fall out of cars, fall off cliffs, fall off roofs, walk into bank robberies, have cars that drive miles on their own, or have an engine failure in their planes, and live to tell the story?

The House that Jack Built

Uncle Jack had become such a normal part of our family, that I saw him almost every day. He was always puttering around the church fixing something. For years he had been a fixture at holidays, and he had adopted Mindy as his granddaughter. Out of the blue one day, he asked us what we're going to do for a house in retirement. We told him that we hadn't seriously considered that yet. Then he said, "I want to get rid of dad's old house and wondered if you would like to buy it?"

"How much do you want for it," I asked.

"I want to give it to you for 60K!"

"Jack, you can't do that!" I protested. "You could easily get four times that."

"I know," he says. "But this way, I don't have to find a realtor, I don't have to deal with people. I don't have to clean it up. I don't have to worry about fixing it, you can have it just as it sits. The truth is I don't even need the money."

We took a couple of weeks to consider his offer and to be sure Jack knew what he was doing. Yet he remained insistent that we buy his house. We finally realized how much Jack wanted to do this, so we bought the house and completely gutted it.

We took it down to the studs and started by completely rewiring the house. We did all the work ourselves and spent 30K on the renovation. When we were finished, the house was stunning.

The Door

Just after we moved into our new house, Michelle came home with a door. She had bought it at a garage sale, for 1 dollar. At first glance, I thought she paid 99 cents too much. It was painted like the partridge family bus. It looked like it had come straight out of the 60s. Something you would see at a hippy commune! To call It ugly would have been kind. It was hideous!

As I helped her carry it into the garage, she could see the disgust on my face, she was smiling and assured me that she knew what she was doing. I remembered the Mazda 323, so I didn't say anything.

A few days later she came proudly bounding into the living room and told me she was ready for me to see the door. I walked out into the garage and my mouth dropped to the floor.

The window at the top of the door was ornate crystal inlay. The door was beautifully white. The handle turned out to be brass, and she had polished it to a brilliant shine.

When I had helped Michelle carry the door, I remembered it had been incredibly heavy. Now that we could see it, we realized it was a solid, metal, fire safety, door. When we discovered the make of the door, we found that the door alone sold new, for $1,800.

The handle was a Baldwin Manchester safety handle. From the inside, when you turned the handle, it not only opened the door but released the deadbolt mechanism, as well. It retailed for $360 dollars at the time. God had given us a $2,200 front door for 1 dollar.

The door was so beautiful, that when we put it on, neighbors stopped and asked us if they could take a picture of it. Several days later, someone stopped their car, backed up, and came across our lawn. He knocked on our door, and asked us, if he too, could take a picture of it.

Later when we sold the house, a relator actually mocked us for wasting our money on a door that was overbuilt for the neighborhood. His actual words were: "You spent too much money for a door like that in this neighborhood! Michelle gave me a wink and said "I doubt it!"

God delights in giving His children gifts

Caught in the Act

I had purchased a new pickup, from the police department. The chaplin of the police department, who happened to be a friend, sold it to me for a greatly reduced price. I needed a pickup for the renovation of our house.

All the emergency lights were still in working order. The police told me that I could take the truck, but not to use the flashing lights. The headlights flashed back and forth, and the taillights did the same thing. When it was all lit up, it was impressive. I took time to show Michelle where all the toggle switches were and warned her to be careful not to flip them on. Impersonating an officer is punishable by imprisonment and a hefty fine.

One day I was out in the yard, when she came driving up in my truck, with all the emergency lights flashing. When she opened the door, I asked her what in the world she was doing! You can't drive around with those flashing! She had no idea they were on, and she looked at me and remarked...." Now it all makes sense.... I drove all the way home and everyone was moving out of my way, I made record time!"

I was backing out of the new house with my new truck and I spotted four young black kids, dressed gang style. Hats on backwards, baggy pants. They were out of place in our neighborhood. I drove by them, and I knew they were up to something, just by the way they were carrying themselves. I quickly drove around the block and parked where I could see them, but I was out of sight. Sure enough, while one of them stood guard, the other three jumped the fence into Glen's backyard, and broke into the back door. I didn't own a cell phone at the time, so I had to wait till they came running out and around the corner. I ran into the house and called the police. Glen, himself, worked for the police department, and I knew he was at work.

When the officers arrived, they turned out to be a young female officer and an older guy. I described in detail all four individuals. The two officers went driving around, then came back complaining that they didn't see anything and left. I was frustrated, so I jumped back in my truck and drove around the corner and saw them coming out of another house. I backed up and into my driveway and ran into the house. I asked Michelle to call the police again and tell them to look for my police truck, I was going to follow the thieves.

I returned to my truck and drove slowly to where I could see them but they couldn't see me. While I waited for the officers to arrive, I witnessed them burglarize yet another house. I took the time to write down the address, so I could remember. It took a while but eventually the police car, with the same two officers, pulled up beside my truck. I pointed out the suspects and they told me to stay put, they would take it from there.

I saw the punks disappear over the hill and the police car as well. I couldn't see anything anymore, so I drove to the top of the hill, to see if I could see what was going on.

When I crested the hill, I could see that the four young men had decided to fight. The young female officer was on the ground fighting with one of the young men. Another suspect was sneaking around a hedge to come up and attack her from behind. I took off in the truck.

The gang member had his back to me and he was now running towards the female officer. I jumped the curb and hit him with the truck before he had a chance to attack her. I jumped out and got on top of him and she came over and cuffed him.

She started thanking me profusely. "I had no idea he was there. If you hadn't hit him, he could have grabbed my gun and shot the two of us." When the other officers arrived, the woman told the Sergeant that my fast thinking had probably saved their lives. She showed them how she had been facing, how the suspect had come up from behind, and that if I hadn't hit him with the truck when I did, things would have gone south in a hurry.

I hadn't hit him hard enough to kill him, but I did want to send him flying. When they were putting him in the car, he yelled out at me that I was a "dead man."

Later, when he was in court, that threat was brought up to the judge.

All three of the other defendants pleaded guilty, and truthfully, they couldn't fight it. The police had caught them, with all the stolen goods in their coats. But the guy I had hit with my truck, was facing twenty-five years to life, as a third time offender. He had nothing to lose fighting it in court.

I had been the only witness, and their only hope was to claim I was in my truck, and couldn't be sure of a positive identification. I told the court that I had driven by them several times because they hadn't realized I was watching them. I had been watching them for over an hour. I also reminded his attorneys, I had hit him with my pickup and got to see him up close and personal! I was absolutely positive It was him!

He was found guilty. I wasn't there when he was sentenced, but it was a minimum of twenty-five years.

Cabinets

When we gutted the house and renovated the inside, I called my brother. He owned a cabinet shop, and built some of the most beautiful cabinets I have ever seen. I asked him if he would be willing to give me a bid, to build cabinets for our new home. I told him to work up a fair bid and add the cost of delivery. (He lived in Oregon, and I lived in California.)

"That won't be necessary, we're brothers after all!" He responded. "Besides, I will take my vacation, and the two of us will spend the week at the beach and sightseeing. It will only take a few hours and if you help me, we can install them ourselves." Carl was adamant that the trip down was his "House Warming Gift" to Michelle and I.

I told him. "I understood that, but I wanted to make this a business transaction. I didn't want this to get awkward. I wanted him to make a bid, exactly as he would with any customer. I told him I had no problem paying him, market price."

Then I told him very clearly, my biggest frustration, with any contractor, was hidden "Dings!" I didn't want that. I told him several times, just give me the full bid, every cost, and I would pay it. No Dings, and no Extras at the end. I explained to him that if he would do that for me, I would do him a favor and pay for the whole project. That way, he didn't have to come up with the cost of materials upfront. I would pay him the Grand total before he even started the project. "Full price upfront and I would pay for everything in one check," I told him.

He agreed, but insisted that, "He would not include the labor cost to install, that was his gift to Michelle and I." He worked up the project on a computer and sent me the bid.

Carl had a truly amazing computer program. The software gives you the ability to show a 3-D image of the cabinets already installed. I simply gave him the dimensions of each room, and he sent me, 3-D images of exactly what the room would look like with the Oak we chose. The program also gives the price. It's actually quite remarkable.

The contract was quite extensive. Multiple pages, with every cabinet from several angles. The price was quite extensive as well. We could have saved thousands, but I wanted to have Carl do this. So, before we signed it, I called Carl and we went over it on the phone for nearly an hour. At the end I reiterated; "This is everything, no extras later?"

Carl insisted; "Pay this amount and you are 'Paid in full!" This covers Material, labor, travel, trims, and installation! You will owe me nothing else later." Carl was firm! So, Michelle and I signed the contract, and sent him a check for the full amount.

Carl picked the exact week that he would come down to install the cabinets and spend the week vacationing with me. He told me he chose that week because his wife would be in Portland, at a conference. So, for nearly four months we waited expectantly for our new cabinets and Carl's visit.

I wanted to bless Carl, so I had told him, when we first made the plans, that I would pay for his meals, fuel, and all incidental costs that week.

When Carl arrived, he had brought his truck and trailer. The trailer was not only for hauling, but he could work out of it. His table saw, drills, chop saw, the tools of the trade, were in the trailer.

To our surprise though, Karen, his wife, and three other adults had followed in Karen's car. Instead of one adult mouth to feed for a week, there were five adults. I felt he had taken advantage of me, and invited others on the trip.

We traveled to San Francisco, took in all the sights, and had dinner on the Warf. Because there were so many of us, we had to take two cars, which was a significant increase in costs. Plus, I had only budgeted for one meal, not five. Instead of twenty dollars, every meal was costing us one hundred. I decided not to say anything, but clearly, I felt they were taking advantage of my hospitality.

At the end of the week, we took a day and installed the cabinets. The cabinets were exquisite! Carl had made them perfectly. He then installed the trim throughout the house. He cut to fit, all the trim, and toe kicks.

I was in the kitchen and I noticed that something wasn't right. I went to the picture and noticed what the problem was.

I asked Carl, where the floor-to-ceiling cabinets, were?

"What cabinets?" Carl asked.

I grabbed the bid and showed him the cabinets that we had agreed upon. He had forgotten to build two entire pieces of the build. Several thousand dollars of Cabinets, I had already paid for, were missing. Karen walked out of the room and told Carl she needed to talk to him.

When Karen and Carl came back into the house, they confronted Michelle and I. Carl said that I owed him 50 dollars an hour, for the entire week he had been with me. Karen chimed in, "You didn't think he was going to miss a whole week of work, and not be paid. You owe him for the entire 40-hour work week, and that comes out to $2000 dollars."

I could tell that Carl was feeling pressured by Karen. I don't believe he would have done this on his own.

I reminded Carl that he himself had called it a vacation. He said I also owed him an additional $600 for fuel costs for the trip. I showed him on the contract, that the fuel costs were a line item, that I had already paid for.

Karen started becoming belligerent, and in addition to the 50 dollars an hour for the week she demanded to be compensated 50 dollars an hour for every hour it took to drive down and back from Oregon.

I went over to the church office to spend some quiet time, and seek Gods advice. This will probably not make any sense to you, if you do not have an intimate relationship with God, but those of us who seek the will of God, we pray. Prayer is simply chatting with our Father. It's not mystical or magical. It's not that God speaks in an audible voice. It's not like Christians hear voices.

What hearing from God is like, is akin to that sense you get, when you are leaving the house and you know you're forgetting something. It's a strong sense that you just "know" that you're forgetting something. It's like a mother that can't quite put her finger on it, but she just "knows" somethings wrong with her baby. It's like that feeling you get when someone creeps you out, you can't put your finger on it, but you just "know" that you "know", that guy is dangerous.

It is closely related to intuition. You just have this inner "knowing" that you can't legally prove, but you "know!" When someone is lying to you, you just have this solid sense, that they are not telling the truth, but you can't prove it.

I was seeking that "knowing!" After you've experienced it, a few times, you begin to recognize it more easily. Our heavenly Father just gives you this "knowing," of what you should do.

When you know what you should do, you have a choice. You can obey, or you can ignore it. When I was a young Christian, I would often argue with that inner "knowing" and blow it off! I knew full well what God was asking, but I would blow Him off. When you do that, things come crashing in on you. You learn fairly quickly, and the next time that you get that "knowing what He wants" you just do it! When you do, amazing things happen. With lots of practice, you finally learn to listen, to that inner voice, and obey.

Any married person knows what I'm talking about. When you are first married you don't know your spouse, but over time you "know" them well enough, that you don't even have to ask. You know full well, the things that will irritate them. So, when you're about to do something, there is this inner voice of caution. There is this moment of "knowing" and you have a choice. A fool will do it anyway and ignore that inner voice. A wise man heeds the inner "knowing" and changes course, so he doesn't make his wife angry.

Often times we know what to do, we know what God would do, and we know what we should do, but we ignore it. I got tired of consequences crashing in on me. So, I learned to listen to that inner voice, that intuition, that sixth sense, that "knowing." In fact, I found that when I did start obeying that "knowing voice" my life dramatically changed for the good. My life was constantly blessed. I heard the "knowing inner voice" and followed its advice.

It may sound odd to you now, but really, it is quite simple. You start asking God to lead you and guide you. You start seeking His will. You start asking His advice. You get used to wanting **His** will to be done, not your own. Whenever I chose my own, I always paid a heavy price and suffered consequences. But when I followed His will, He always worked it out.

In scripture, He tells us not to lean on our own limited understanding but to trust Him. The advice is, don't trust that you know better than God. Knowing God's will eventually becomes easier. Especially when you know scripture because He flat out tells you. You also learn what Jesus did, and simply do the same things. You also learn what not to do. What to avoid. In addition to all that, the bible shows us that, there are principles in life. You can take those principles into many different situations. These principles cover a whole gambit of life situations.

I went into my office to seek what God wanted me to do. Logic tells us, that I send Carl and all the others he brought with him packing, but I was sensing that God told me to pay him. Just give him the money. So, I obeyed and they left. I never mentioned it again.

For years after Carl and Karen avoided us. Not only had they taken the money, Carl never did make the two missing cabinets. In addition, I had sold them some furniture and a pool table that was never paid for.

Years later, I received a phone call from Carl. The first phone call in many years. Karen had been killed that afternoon in an automobile accident. Later that night, around two AM, Carl called again. He informed me that they had sent Karen's body to Seattle to harvest her organs. She was an organ donor. But when they went to prepare her, they found she had regained brain activity. She had been left on life support so that they could keep the organs alive, but her brain was swelling and since she had activity, they put everything on hold. Carl decided to travel up to Seattle, to be with Karen.

I jumped on my Goldwing, headed to Boise, and flew up to Seattle to be with him. Imagine his shock, when I walked into the hospital room, especially after so many years of estrangement. We spent the following week together, but I never mentioned anything about the incident. Michelle and I had written it off. It was behind us, and we had moved on, driving through life looking out the windshield, not the rearview mirror.

Karen was still in a deep coma that week. What the doctors thought had happened, was that the brain had sustained a blunt shock and stopped the brainwaves for nearly 10 hours. It was like the brain was stunned, then began again. Karen started breathing on her own but remained unconscious. The news outlets began to hear of Karen and came to the hospital to do a story. Carl asked me to do the interviews. KING news, the NBC affiliate aired the amazing story of the woman who came back to life.

After a week, the doctors came into the room and informed us that Karen's condition, although amazing, would not end well. They shared with us that Karen, if she would happen to live, would be a complete vegetable. The human brain cannot go without oxygen for 10 hours. Carl didn't know what to do, so I suggested that he wait one more week. If she improved then it would be self-evident. If she continued to deteriorate then the choice would be easier.

I left the next day to return home. The following day, I went to retrieve the mail, and found a letter from Carl. In it was a check, for the full amount of everything that he and Karen had owed Michelle and I. I had never mentioned it! Yet it had obviously been weighing on his heart, for the entire ten years. How sad!

Carl's decision to remove Karen from life support was made easy when Karen's condition worsened. She could no longer breathe on her own. She never regained consciousness; she was still in a deep coma. He signed the papers to disconnect life support but she was already dead. I love my brother Carl, and we have stayed close, ever since.

Sensing a Change

Michelle and I both felt that after eleven years at Carmichael, God was about to make a move. I loved the people there, especially Grandma Mary and Uncle Jack.

I prayed that God would let me know when it was time to move on. I was sitting in Uncle Jack's living room, watching NASCAR when out of the blue Jack turned to me and said; "If God ever calls you away, I want you to know I'm good with that!" I had never mentioned a single word to Jack.

Then came the worst news imaginable, Grandma Mary was diagnosed with inoperable cancer. When I went to see her, she took my hand and said: "I have been looking forward to Heaven so long, I'm actually excited. I want to see Jesus."

At her funeral the church was packed. I shared a story about an old cat I grew up with. We called that cat "old feller." Dad had it before we kids were born, and we grew up with that old cat. It was the fattest, laziest, slowest cat I had ever seen.

Now it just so happened that Grandad had purchased a bird dog. "Barney Google" spent most of the time cooped up in a dog run in

Pendleton. But Grandad had decided to bring it out to our property, and let it run free for a few days.

When he drove up Old Feller, came out to greet him. But as soon as the door opened Barney Google came bounding out, and took off running full speed. When Old Feller saw that dog, headed his way, that old cat took off across the yard and straight up a tree in a flash. We were shocked!

Barney Google continued to run full blast all over the area. He had no place to go, but he was making good time. Old Feller on the other hand, just sat up in that tree, giving that Dog a wide birth. That cats' eyes were wide as saucers, and you could tell he had no idea what just happened. We couldn't get that cat to come down for days.

I told the congregation; heaven is reeling the same way right now. When that glory train opened the door, and Grandma Mary was released into heaven, those poor angels had no idea what just happened! She probably has them treed and no tell'n when they may come down.

There was a roar of laughter, because we all knew, to some extent, it was true!

I don't have a death wish, but when my time comes, I am so looking forward to seeing Grandma Mary again.

With her passing, Michelle and I knew it was time to move on. That was confirmed just a short time later, when the District Superintendent and I agreed that the Church needed a new start.

Embezzlement

Satan can't resist getting his jabs in. We Christians may wear a cross, but to Satan its Crosshairs. We are a target, and he is relentlessly after us.

When we announced to the Church that we were leaving, one of the Church members, stood and demanded to know if Michelle and I were going to return the money we embezzled? Before we could respond, he continued; *"It's obvious that these two took money from the church, because they bought Jack's house, and paid for it with cash! There is no possible way they could afford that. I know how much we pay him, and it would be impossible, without stealing a large part from the tithe. I kept my mouth shut, because I thought they might pay it back. But now that I learn that they are leaving, it's obvious they took the money, bought the house, and are running away."*

I had to explain that even though we were only being paid a thousand dollars a month, we had lived debt free. We had been putting money aside, and it had grown over the eleven years. We also hadn't paid market price for the house. The member stood up and yelled; "I don't believe a word of it. They will say anything to hide the truth. Don't say I didn't warn you!" And he stomped out. That was a somewhat bitter morning, and those who knew the truth, went and explained it to that member.

251

The Newlywed Game

Most of the Church understood and accepted our leaving, as part of the dynamic and ever-changing life we live.

Michelle and I saw an odd advertisement, in the want ads. The want ad, was asking If someone was willing to take over payments for a new car. We went to find out the rest of the story, and discovered that a gentleman had purchased a car for his girlfriend, and then she dumped him. He was simply asking someone to take over payments. In addition, the apartment complex was taking the parking spot, and the car had to go.

The good news was the price. He only had a few thousand to go, but he told us, he just wanted it gone. It reminded him of her, and it was a bitter memory. So, we bought the car.

Just after we purchased that car, we found that we would be moving. We accepted a pastorate at a church in Elko Nevada. Elko is a mile high, and the winters are brutal. So, we needed a four-wheel drive vehicle. The car would not fill the bill.

Now it just so happened, that at the same time, two of our great friends, Sammy and Matt Dussel, were in a car bind. They could only afford one car. The problem was, they had three teenagers. Trying to juggle one car around five schedules, was a nightmare.

We saw the horrible situation the Dussel's were in, and came up with a really fun idea. Michelle and I wanted to bless this wonderful family. We wanted to simply surprise them and give them our new car.

This was our fun Idea. At our going away party, we would play the Newlywed game. At the end of the game, we would give out prizes. I had placed the keys, and the title, in a small box, and gift wrapped it. I contacted three other couples and outlined my devious little scheme. They would be given all the questions in advance, so they could get every question correct. The poor Dussells, would have no chance of winning and would be given a "booby prize," which was the tiny unimpressive box. But of course, inside would be the title and keys to their new car!

Sammy Dussel, was in charge of the party, and when I interrupted her plans, and suggested we play the newlywed game, she was put out. She went along with it, but you could tell she was miffed. Of course, losing every round of the game only made her "already sour mood" turn ugly. She couldn't understand, why the other couples knew each other so well. Of course, every time Matt got the wrong answer, she scolded him, and pointed out that the other husbands, knew their wives!

One of the questions was; "If your wife were a cartoon character, which one would she be?" All the other couples matched their answers and Sammy was beside herself. "How do you guys know each other that well." She complained.

So, when Matt was asked what cartoon character is your wife? His answered "Grumpy" from the seven dwarfs!

Everyone burst out laughing, but Sammy was not amused!

At the end of the game, we had wrapped really nice gifts for the other couples and of course they opened theirs before we handed out the "Consolation" gift to Matt and Sammy. Sammy was in such a foul mood at this point, that she refused to open it, and threw it at Matt. When Matt saw the title and car keys, he began to connect the dots, and realized they had been set up. When he told Sammy they were getting a new car, she was in such a bad mood that she didn't truly hear him, and made a caustic comment about; "What does she need with a toy car?" Matt said "No honey, we won a real car. We've been set up!"

We had a friend drive the car up to the windows at that very moment! When she saw the car, and the big bow we had put on top, she just broke into tears.

She hugged us and confessed that she was "Grumpy" with me for "ruining" her plans for the party. I told her, I could tell you were upset, but our plans were more fun.

All too often in life, we just simply don't have all the information. Sammy didn't have the information. She had misread all the facts. Remember; The known facts are not ALL the facts! This happens so often with God in our lives. He knows all the facts, and asks us to trust Him. Many times I have considered a life circumstance to be a bug, yet it turns out to be a feature. What I deem a virus, often times is God's blessing. It just looks like a tiny box.

Rope

When we interviewed at Elko, we had a bitter encounter with a woman I will call Jezebel. She ran the church with an iron fist. She controlled everything. The Church was made up of almost all woman. Most of these women had attended another church with Jezebel, and when she left that church, they had followed her. The previous pastor was a passive personality and she ran over the top of him. He called me and warned me about her.

Jezebel was on the board. She ran the music team, and was the only adult Sunday school teacher.

When we sat down with the board, it was made up of nearly all woman. Jezebel ran the show. They complained that the church needed men. They asked me if I thought I could bring in more men? I told them that to attract men, they might have to change the culture of the Church. Thirty minutes of singing hymns that were written in the 1700s would have to change. If you want to reach men of our day, they would have to be willing to make concessions. That set Jezebel off!

When we went to lunch after the interview, Jezebel confronted us and these were some of the things she told us. First off, we needed to understand, that this was her church! Pastors come and go, and she wasn't going to allow someone to come in and destroy the church and then move on. Secondly, she told me, that she wanted to see my messages before each Sunday. There were other demands but these two stuck out.

She also informed us that prostitution was legal in Elko, and she was all for it, because the girls got full medical.

When I got in the car, I turned to Michelle and told her "That church needs protection from her!" I felt that God was asking us to take the church, and protect the souls. I called the District Superintendent, and told him I would take the church, but we had a problem. I explained that I could foresee a conflict with Jezebel. He said that he was aware of the woman, and that because she was the influencer in that church, that if she left, she could take the rest of the congregation. If that happened, they would be forced to close the church.

The church board extended a unanimous call. I can only guess that Jezebel thought to herself that she had me under control. When the District Superintendent came for the induction service, he attended Jezebels Sunday school class. Afterword he took me aside and said, you are right, she has to go, but you need to be extremely careful, or this could end the church. They are loyal to her. If you can, give her enough rope to hang herself."

I felt that Jezebel saw herself as a mother bear, and the woman of the church as her cubs. She would fight me all the way.

I went to prayer and asked God to give me wisdom. I wanted Him to work this out and protect His church. I had no answers. The Perry part of me wanted to stand up against this bully, and tell her to hit the highway. But She would have taken 90% of the woman with her.

I had been there only a few weeks, and she was angry with me for not cowing to her demands. She miscalculated badly. She may have run over the previous pastor, but she had zero influence over me. She could see that, so her anger began to brew.

It was a Sunday night service. The service was over and I was sitting in the pew chatting with Jezebels husband. He lived in Indonesia, working as a miner, at one of the mines there. He just happened to be visiting the states that weekend. Jezebel saw an opportunity, and came up to the pew in front of me. She just started leveling accusations against me. The blowup that I was dreading, was upon me. I knew it was coming, but I was not prepared.

I felt Gods prompting to "keep silent! Let her rant! Don't say a word! Just sit there and endure this!"

Everyone in the parking lot, could hear her screaming at me, so they returned. This is just what she wanted, and it emboldened her. The sanctuary began to fill up. She had me just where she wanted me. A large

254

crowd surrounded us. She was snarling and spitting out all kinds of accusations. Calling me a woman hater, a cult leader, a domineering bully, and a number of other things. After she had ranted for a few more minutes, I could see she was out of control and so full of anger, that I felt the prompting to reach up and take hold of her hand. When I showed her a compassionate gesture, she started to accuse me of placating her.

Finally, Terry, a woman who was standing near, interrupted the tirade and dared to scold Jezebel, and said "He can't have done all that, he has only been here a few weeks!" Jezebel snapped her head around and blasted Terry for daring to open her mouth. Jezebel told her to keep her mouth shut, and speak only when spoken to. Then Valorie spoke up and came to Terry's defense. Jezebel told her to shut up as well. Then threatened to tell everyone in the room the sin Valorie was struggling with.

Some of the other woman came to Valorie's defense. Jezebel found herself attacking her own audience.

Exasperated Jezebel grabbed her coat and yelled, "OK I am leaving this church for good; Lets go ladies." She stomped to the back of the sanctuary and slammed the doors on exiting. It was totally quiet in the sanctuary for a few awkward moments. Valorie turned to me and quietly asked, "Are you, ok Pastor? "A number of them put their hands on my shoulder. I watched God transfer all the loyalty from Jezebel to our ministry in an instant.

Just then the doors flew open and Jezebel screamed; "I SAID WHO IS COMING WITH ME?" but no one moved. Then one of the women spoke up, "This is my church I'm not going anywhere."

This whole time, Jezebel's husband is still sitting at my side. I still haven't said anything. Then Jezebel screamed at her husband to grab his coat, they are leaving. He stood up, kind of sheepishly and apologized and slowly walked out. They are the only two who left the church.

Several Sundays later, just before service, someone stood and asked the entire church, "Have the rest of you noticed the dark spirit of oppression is no longer here? I hadn't even realized that it was here, until it was gone. I walked in this morning and felt my heart was at peace." To my astonishment a number of people stood and acknowledged that a spirit of joy had returned to the church.

It is extremely hard not to defend yourself when you are being falsely accused. Everything inside you wants to shout back "That's not true! I never said that! That's a lie! But God had told me not to get in the way, and let her hang herself. In the process, God, in the Divinely orchestrated exit, had endeared Michelle and I, with the wonderful women of that church. I am convinced that if I had started to defend myself, it would have digressed into a shouting match, and I would have looked like a bully, yelling at a woman. The church would have imploded. But I had learned to listen to that inner voice of God!

There's Something Wrong

I had to return to Sacramento, to testify in a court case. When the trial was over, we were faced with a difficult decision. We needed to get back to Elko, because there was no one else to preach on Sunday. Unfortunately, a powerful winter storm was moving into the western United States. The I-80 freeway was open, but for how long, was anyone's guess. So, we decided to take our chances and try to get over Donner Pass before they closed the freeway.

The snow was coming down hard and accumulating on the road. It took longer than expected to reach the summit, and it was getting dark. I was thankful that I had made it, but I had hoped that when we made it over the Sierra Nevada range, the snow would let up. It did not. In fact, it was coming down so hard that I was only able to travel at fifty miles an hour.

A trip that would normally take six hours was taking much longer and it was nearly ten o'clock before we arrived in Winnemucca Nevada. We fueled up and decided to keep going, and try to make it to Elko by 1:00 AM.

The snow was coming down so hard it was difficult to see the road. I was grateful for the reflectors on the side of the freeway. I had slowed down to around 35 miles an hour. We seemed to be the only ones, brave enough to travel in these conditions.

The snow falling in the headlights was mesmerizing. Suddenly I could see that something was in the left lane. It turned out to be a tire, and my first thoughts were that it had fallen out of a pickup truck. But there was something that didn't seem right. The tire and wheel still had the tie rods sticking up out of the center. As I crept along, I kept thinking about the tire. I turned to Michelle and explained that I was going to turn around and go back and look at that tire more carefully.

Who would remove a tire and wheel with the tie rods still connected? Common sense told me that it had to have been ripped from the frame.

I found an emergency turnaround and headed slowly back in the other direction in the West bound lanes. I asked Michelle to keep her eyes peeled for any sign of an accident. We could barely see but continued backtracking. After several miles, I saw tracks leaving the freeway. I couldn't see any vehicle, but there shouldn't be tracks leading off the left side of the freeway.

I stopped and grabbed my flashlight. I told Michelle to stay put, and I would follow those tracks and see where they led. I walked through the snow and suddenly the tracks stopped and there was a large divot out of the snow. I kept walking and came across a crater in the snow where it looked like a vehicle had come crashing down. I intuitively reasoned that the tire I had seen, had been ripped off the car and thrown into the oncoming lane.

I still couldn't see any vehicle, but it was obvious that there was an accident. I knew it was fresh, because the snow had not fully covered the impact areas. It had obviously flipped several times. I kept walking and finally got a glimpse of a reflector in the flashlight beam.

I ran up to find a van that was upside down. It was missing the driver's front wheel. It was eerily quiet as the snow floated down. There was no traffic and I could hear someone moaning. The front driver's door was open and I found a young woman wandering in the snow.

I asked her if she was all right and she mumbled something, but it was clear she was in shock. I asked her if there was anyone else in the vehicle and she told me no. I flashed my light into the van and it was filled with junk.

I asked her what had happened and she told me she must have fallen asleep. She had no coat on, so I took off my coat and put it around her, and led her back to our SUV. We wrapped her in a blanket and tried to warm her up. We called out on our cell phone and told them to send an ambulance. She was really disoriented and not making much sense.

We kept asking her questions and she couldn't tell us where she was from, or where she was going. I realized then that if she didn't know these simple answers that I couldn't trust any of her answers. I told Michelle that I was going to search around to make sure no one else had been thrown out of the vehicle. I grabbed my coat and flashlight and went back out into the storm.

I walked back and forth looking for any evidence of another victim. I didn't see any, so I returned to the van. I took the flashlight and shined it into the back, and to my shock I found a baby. It was hanging upside down, still in her car seat. She hadn't made a sound. She was not crying, so at first, I thought she might be dead. But she was staring at me. I crawled into the back of the van and unbuckled her and wrapped her in my coat. I ran back to my SUV and handed the baby to Michelle.

I was never so happy that we kept extra blankets in our vehicles, for just this reason. Michelle and I have always had an emergency kit in all our vehicles, since my horrible experience driving to Pendleton, I have always had extra blankets in the trunk. I almost froze to death that night. I made it a priority to have a full emergency kit, just in case we ever came upon an accident or broke down. We always have two blankets as part of the kit. We have bottled water and first aid packets as well.

I returned again to the van and did another thorough search. Not finding anything I came back to the SUV and we waited for the Ambulance and police.

She had left the freeway and flipped a number of times. I can only imagine what would have happened, if the tire had not ended up on the roadway. The vehicle was completely out of sight, and the tracks leaving the roadway were all but invisible under the snow. The only reason we saw them is because we were looking specifically for them. Once again God ordained a Divine appointment. Two lives were saved that night.

The ambulance transported them to the hospital, and we never heard how it all turned out.

Bo

One of the families in the Church, Bo and Jane, had a child with severe brain damage. He was alive, but since he was a newborn, he had never had any brain function. He had been kept alive, but the strain on Jane was overwhelming. When at age eleven, the boy died, the church was packed in support of Bo and Jane. Jane sobbed and cried through the whole service.

Shortly thereafter, Bo came home and found Jane's dead body, she had taken her own life. As hard as the first funeral was, Janes funeral was devastating for Bo. He was almost inconsolable.

A month later in the dead of winter, I was still counseling with Bo, when he asked me if I would like to go snowmobiling, in the Ruby's. The Ruby Mountains tower above the horizon over eleven thousand feet. I love the outdoors and had snowmobiled a number of times, but not in the Ruby's. I jumped at the chance.

I met Bo at his house, and we left early in the morning, and drove to the entrance of Lamoille canyon. When we arrived, there was a Sheriff's deputy and he approached us. "Gentlemen, I wonder if you could do us a favor. We have two missing men, who have been missing since yesterday. We are in the process of forming a search party, but we won't get the team together for at least a couple more hours. Could you take a run into the mountains and see if you can locate them?"

The high temperature for the day was forecast to be zero. He told us that the temperature that night had been 20 degrees below Zero. He warned us that we were probably looking for bodies. Even in the best of conditions, with the best clothes, the chances of surviving the night were remote.

My first thought was, "Oh, NO!" We had come up here to try and escape the memory of death. Now we were headed to find more corpses. What was this going to do to Bo? I prayed silently, oh please Lord, protect Bo. Don't let him come across more dead bodies.

Of course, Bo was eager to help. So, we unloaded the machines and headed up the canyon. It was beautiful and haunting at the same time. The air was so cold that Crystals were floating in the air. We hadn't been gone more than a half an hour, when we spotted them. They were alive and waving at us. We put them on our sleds and headed back to base camp.

When we arrived, the ambulance was there and a number of law enforcement vehicles. Bo became the hero that day. They interviewed him, and his picture was on the front page of the paper the next morning. God knew what he was doing. That did more good for Bo, than years of counseling.

The men we found had experienced a breakdown, and had survived the night in a snow cave. They went to the hospital, but they were fine.

Kelly

I was taking a team from Elko to the Celebrate Recovery ministry conference in San Jose. It would be the first time back in the area since Mindy was born. Mindy was now 13 years old.

I asked Michelle, if it would be appropriate to see if I could contact Kelly, Mindy's birth mom. Michelle was so utterly confident in her role as mother by then, that she thought it would be a wonderful idea. Michelle had known from the beginning, that this day would eventually come. Michelle had purposely been scrapbooking since Mindy was an infant, for just such an occasion. Michelle knew that someday the birth mother would want to see the life of her baby. Michelle filled an apple box full of scrapbooks of Mindy, to share with Kelly. That is if Kelly wanted the contact. We weren't sure.

It took almost a month to finally get Kelly's cell number. I dialed the number and waited as it rang. No one answered, and I didn't want to leave a message, so I hung up. A few seconds later, my phone rang and I said, "Hello." The voice on the other end said; "I just received a call from this number, I couldn't answer because I am at the theater."

I asked, "Is this Kelly?"

"Yes." She replied

"This is Perry Arbogast do you have a moment to talk?"

"Absolutely!" she said excitedly.

"I am coming to San Jose, for a church conference with Celebrate Recovery in a few weeks and wondered if you would like to get together and look over some albums Michelle has of Mindy?" I asked.

Kelly couldn't speak, she was so overcome with emotion, I could hear her crying. Eventually she said, "Yes, Yes, Yes." She apologized and told me she was caught off guard, and had been waiting all these years, and feared that if it ever did come, it would be after Mindy turned 18.

We agreed to meet at a restaurant near her place. A few days later she called and asked if it would be all right to bring the birth father? I was thrilled. In the ministry you try to avoid any awkward times, where you are alone with a women, and now Jeff would be joining us.

When I arrived, I asked the manager if they had a booth far from people, so we could visit. We were ushered into a portion of the restaurant that was closed. We spent nearly six hours looking through all the albums, and catching up on life. They wanted to know everything about Mindy. It was a wonderful time and I grew to love both of them.

A few weeks after I had returned to Elko, I received a call from Kelly. She asked if I would officiate at her upcoming wedding. I agreed.

A few weeks after that call, she called again and asked if it would be possible to bring Mindy? I said I had already planned on it. I then asked her, if she would like to talk to Mindy? "She is sitting right here, if you want, I can hand her the phone." So, the two of them chatted for the first time.

A few weeks after that call, Kelly asked me if it would be possible to have Mindy as one of her brides' maids. Once again, I handed off the phone and the girls started chatting. When she got off the phone, Mindy told us, talking to Kelly, felt like talking to a sister.

Just before we arrived at Kelly's house, Mindy just blurted out; "I can only imagine how awkward Kelly must be feeling! I want to put her at ease, so when we arrive, I am going to run up to her and give her a big hug. I need to break the ice, and help put her at ease!"

I was bursting with pride; my little girl had become pretty wise for her age.

It probably ranks up there with the most amazing reunions, but my daughter met her birth mother, as her bride's maid.

It was summer, so we agreed to have Mindy, stay a couple weeks with Kelly, and another couple of weeks, with Jeff and his family. We also got to meet Mindy's biological grandparents, and even a half-sister.

Mindy and Kelly have been a part of our family ever since. We found out at the wedding, that Kelly's dad Perry, had passed away a few years earlier. So, we just adopted Kelly as well.

Newmont

When we returned to Elko we planned the launch of our Celebrate Recovery Ministry in earnest. We had developed a team, and decided to launch on 9-11, in honor of the first 9-11. We used the 911 logo and our leadership team was raring to go. We had the strangest group of people as a part of that leadership team. I am going to list their names and you're going to think I'm making this up. But look at the charter and you will see this is fact. We had Carri, Carry, Sherry, Terri, Terry, Terrie, Berry, Perry, and Lisa. We threatened to make T-shirts with just the first letter of our names, we chided Lisa for ruining a perfect plan.

Just before we were to launch, one of the church board members confronted me, and told me that he had reconsidered the prospect of Celebrate Recovery, and insisted we pull the plug on the idea. I held my ground, and implored him to reconsider his stance. He threatened to leave the church, and take the rest of his family members with him, if we launched. He reminded me that his family was the financial backbone, and without it the church would collapse. It was true that his daughter and her husband lead the youth group, he himself was head of the Church board.

I felt very strongly that God was behind reaching people through this amazing ministry. I was not going to be threatened, by the prospect of losing their financial support. It was Gods church after all!

So, on 9-11 we launched CR and was blindsided by the loss of many in the church. The finances of the church collapsed. It got so bad that the board approached us to consider going on half salary. The following month we began living on a thousand dollars a month.

Elko is a mining town. Specifically, it is a gold mining town. I have been told that if Elko were a country, it would be the third largest gold-producing nation in the world. I never fact-checked that, but with all the gold mines in the area, I can believe it.

There were two big companies that owned the majority of the mines. Newmont and Barrick. Most of the people in our church worked for one of these two. Newmont came up with an incredible and generous offer. They called it the Newmont Legacy fund. They gave their employees the option to donate to any nonprofit organization, and Newmont would match it dollar for dollar. Every quarter they would send a check to the organization.

They specifically encouraged their people to give to the local church and Newmont would double the tithe. Newmont realized that a strong church presence meant a better community. A better community meant higher quality employees. It was a win-win!

Almost everyone on the church board worked for Newmont. This would be an unprecedented boost for the church. The church board members calculated, that if only the church board tithed just 10% and Newmont doubled it. The board alone could support, all our ministries, and get Michelle and I back at full salary. In fact, the board made plans to pay off all our back pay as well. Most of our board members, were making nearly $100,000 a year. Some were in management, and making even more.

My neighbor was the head of the Newmont Legacy fund. She walked me through all the steps to get our church registered. She told me that not only my church would tithe, but anyone of the thousands of employees, could also choose our church, as a recipient of their donation. We had three streams of income, the board members, the church body, and any other employee in Newmont. The payoff was that Newmont doubled the entire amount. If people gave $50,000 then the check would be for $100,000

Now all we had to do was wait the three months, and receive the biggest financial boost the church had ever experienced. Things were extremely tight those three months. Michelle and I were hit the hardest of course. By taking half salary, we were carrying the bulk of the financial weight. One family, ours, was suffering the hardest blow.

The board members were constantly apologizing for the financial position the church was putting us in. They told us how awful they felt. They told us they wished they could do more to relieve the pressure. They encouraged us to wait it out and when that quarterly check came in, all our problems would be over.

At the end of the quarter, we received the check in a sealed envelope. We decided to open the check that night at board meeting. When I opened the check, my jaw dropped. The grand total, which was not only the board but everyone in the church, that worked for Newmont, was represented in the grand total of 150 dollars! And that was after Newmont doubled the amount. So, someone had been donating 25 dollars a month.

They were exposed as "Posers."

The ramifications were obvious. No one was supporting the ministry. Not even the leadership board. Not one person in Newmont was tithing! They all assumed that everyone else was giving and it would hide the fact that they were just giving lip service. All their words of empathy, were empty.

People were looking at each other as if to say, how could you?

When I left the church that night I walked slowly back home, emotionally empty. I did not want to tell Michelle, that we were not going to be paid.

We lost every Newmont employee in our church, when the news came out, they never showed their faces in church again.

The financial situation didn't change, because everyone who left were not supporting Gods work anyway. So, we remained on half salary.

FedEx

I truly believed in Celebrate Recovery. It was a God based, 12 step program, that changed thousands of lives across America. I was not sorry I started the ministry. I would do it again, even if I knew how bad it would impact our lives. Even one changed life made any inconvenience worth every penny.

Every year we had a campout for CR. One year I was walking by a building when someone grabbed my arm and pulled me between the buildings. In those first few seconds, I was terrified I was being mugged, but the gentleman started talking rapidly. "Listen" he said, "I can't get caught talking to you, or the consequences could change my life. I am an elder for the Jehovah witnesses. I have come to believe they have been lying to me all my life. I've been studying and I need to talk to someone. Will you pick me up after it is dark at this address? If I get caught talking to you, my wife and family are obligated to disfellowship me. We are forbidden to talk to an evangelical pastor. I am only here to support my son who is a part of your CR program."

I quickly agreed, and later that night I drove to the location, and he came out of the shadows and jumped into my truck. Over the next six months, I met often with Chris, but only at night. I quickly garnered the help of another pastor Dan Dusoliel, who is an expert with those caught in a cult. Between the two of us, and hours of intense academic study, Chris accepted Christ as his savior.

Chris and I became friends. His wife did not leave him, but the Jehovah witnesses disfellowshipped him. His parents called and told him he was dead to them. But Chris began to attend our church. When he found out that we were on half salary, he approached me with an idea. Chris was a contractor for FedEx. He owned routes all over the northeast corner of Nevada. He was the sole contractor for the terminals in Wendover, Ely, and Winnemucca. He also owned the majority of Elko as well. His territorial area was 100 times the size of New York City. New York is 450 square miles; his territory was over 450,000 square miles.

His proposition was that the church could continue paying me, but he would hire me to work for him. So I went to the board, and they agreed wholeheartedly. I worked for Chris for several years, and we recovered all our back pay. Then Chris and Yvette, his wife, came to Michelle and I, with a proposition. They asked us if we were willing to invest in their FedEx company. In exchange, he would pay me a solid amount of interest. We prayed about it, and we felt very good about the prospect.

That decision changed the direction of our lives.

Just weeks later Chris disappeared. They assumed he had been murdered because they found his vehicle open, boxes still inside. He had simply disappeared, vanished. They put a nation-wide APB out on him. For the next few weeks, we did everything we could to help Yevette keep the company running.

Law enforcement finally found Chris, living as a mountain man in the Appalachian Mountains in the eastern United States. He had suffered some sort of mental breakdown. He had not broken any laws, so they could not detain him, but Yvette and her two children were thrown into a nightmare.

She eventually called me and gave me the devastating news. FedEx had decided to exercise their right, according to the contract, to take all the routes and hand them to other contractors free of charge. She was about to lose everything.

Chris and Yvette had paid more than 80,000 for each of the twelve routes. She told Michelle and I, "You are about to lose everything!"

Michelle and I had spent a lifetime, saving our money, and now we were about to lose most of it.

Yvette told me she had tried to sell the routes, but the other contractors, won't pay for something, they can get for free. "They are sitting like vultures on a fence post, for the free handouts from FedEx," She complained.

She then told me she had an idea. She would sell us the company, if I would be willing to pay off all the vehicles and her credit cards.

I went to the board, and proposed to them, that I would continue to pastor the church, but my weekdays would be spent getting the company back on its feet. The only other option is to lose my life savings. They were wholeheartedly in favor of Michelle and I taking on this challenge.

One of the board members, made a statement that stuck with me. He said, "God seems to have given you a second church to pastor. Another congregation to love and lead."

Another board member looked at me and said; "You didn't go looking for this, God dropped it into your lap. He is up to something!"

I asked them to pray with me. As a group we would have to make this decision. We must consider all the ramifications. I told them it might take up to five years. I would not be at their beck and call. Would they be willing to lose that ability?

The following week, we met again and it was unanimously agreed, that God was up to something, and Michelle and I should take the challenge.

FedEx accepted Michelle and I as contractors, and we took ownership of a FedEx franchise. I took the rest of our investment monies and we purchased all the trucks. We paid off Yvette's credit cards and she moved away.

Michelle and I took the next two years and invested 100% of the business income back into the company. By doing this we were able to get it back in good stead with FedEx. At the end of the two years, we had hired managers, and the business was turnkey ready.

During those two years I never missed a week of preaching, and the church actually flourished. Because Michelle and I were not available, others in the church stepped up and filled in. The congregation, as a whole, took more responsibility, and instead of relying on the pastor to do everything, everyone shared in the ministry.

It had also gotten me out of the church and back into the work a day world. It helped me to appreciate, what the people in my congregation, were dealing with every day of their lives. God reminded me that for salt to be effective, it must leave the salt shaker. I had spent 30 plus years in the church, and had lost touch with the world. I needed to leave the church walls, and enter the lost world. I had impact in lots of people's lives, that would never have ventured into our church.

We contacted a FedEx broker and sold the entire business in a matter of weeks. The day the sale finalized, I was taking the men of the church on retreat, and we were all gathered in the parking lot. We formed a circle to pray and Michelle implored the men, "Remember you're on retreat, don't allow the Pastor to mention the "F" word all weekend." I was put on restriction not to mention FedEx. The entire group laughed heartedly; they had their pastors back.

God had taken our life savings and multiplied it in just two years.

F-350

During the sale of the business, I took the buyer on all the routes. We spent days in my personal FedEx truck. I had purchased a white F-250 and put thousands of miles on it over its short life span. Some of our routes were six hundred miles long.

The new owner asked me why this particular truck, was not on the manifest. I told him, even though it was fairly new, it had been driven hard. Over 50,000 miles in just one year. It was my personal delivery truck.

He begged me, to put the truck on the list of vehicles he was purchasing because he needed it. It was already in the FedEx system, it already worked with the scanners, and it already had all the appropriate FedEx logos. Besides he complained, it would take him months to get a new truck into the system.

He offered me a deal; If I was willing to put this truck in the deal, he would buy me any truck I wanted.

I went home and shared with Michelle the offer, and told her I felt it would be utterly unjust, to trade a used, high mileage, truck for a brand-new truck. God had taught us that we should treat others, as we would want to be treated. So, we simply put the truck on the manifest and decided to buy an old used F-150.

We hated that old truck from the beginning. First of all, it only had a 27-gallon tank. (We had not been told that when we bought it, we just assumed all trucks had a 40-gallon tank!) Secondly, it was only getting 7 miles per gallon. Thirdly It was not diesel, it was gas. It also was a short bed, and the truck I had given up was a long bed. Worst of all I hated the color.

One day, after hearing me complain about the truck for the hundredth time, Michelle turned to me and said, "We hate this truck, I don't want to live with regret, let's just bite the bullet and trade it in on something we can live with."

We drove up to Nampa, Idaho, to Corwin Ford to see my friend Jeff Moffis, a delightful believer in Christ. I had been working with him for several years, purchasing some fleet vehicles for our FedEx company.

I told him I was looking for a nice used truck, and I told him of our utter frustration with the Ford truck I was trading in. He tossed me his car keys and told me to go to lunch in his car, leave my truck with him, and come back in three hours.

When we drove up to the front doors, I saw this absolutely beautiful burgundy F-350, long bed, with the full crew cab. The biggest pickup Ford sells. When I hopped out of the car, I happened to glance in the windows and it was all leather interior. It was their top-of-the-line truck, it also had a top-of-the-line price! The sticker price was $83,000 dollars. "Wow," I said to Michelle, "Can you believe someone would pay that kind of money, for a pickup? That's more than we paid for our first house!"

I walked in the entrance and Jeff was standing near the door, and said, "I saw you looking at that truck, what do you think?" Suddenly my heart froze, Jeff must have misunderstood what I was looking for!

"It's absolutely beautiful," I said, "But...," Jeff abruptly cut me off, and threw me the keys and said "It's yours!"

I said, "I'm sorry Jeff, but I can't afford something that nice..." and he cut me off again and said; "No Perry, were giving it to you!"

I was trying to process what he was saying and he continued; "We sell over 350 vehicles a month, and the Ford corporation gives us three "Star vehicles" a year to give away. You have to meet some pretty stringent guidelines, but you meet them all.

First of all, you have had to buy a number of vehicles from us in the past. You purchased a number of them. Secondly, you have to be bringing in a Ford you're not happy with. You brought in a Ford 1-50. There must be something mechanically wrong with the vehicle, and I had your truck test driven, and something is definitely wrong with that truck. I talked it over with the owner Mr. Corwin, and we are giving you the truck."

There were some extra costs involved, but we drove away that day, with a brand-new Diesel F350.

I am convinced, that God saw into my heart, and that I had not taken advantage of the new FedEx owner, and blessed me with a new truck anyway.

All 50 States

In the Nazarene church, they allow a pastor a sabbatical, every seven years. A sabbatical is several months off of pastoral duties. We had always been too poor to take advantage of a sabbatical. Yet while we were in Elko, we decided to take our first sabbatical. We wanted to make it a trip of a lifetime. We wanted to take Mindy to see the United States. We started in the west. Then the southern states. Moved to the eastern states and spent several weeks in Washington D.C. We ended the adventure by coming back across the northern states. After the 48 states, Michelle and I flew to Hawaii and Alaska on separate trips. God has opened many doors of travel for us over the years.

We have had the privilege to visit Mexico, Canada, England, Israel, Brazil, China, Nepal, and all 50 states.

Seven years after that first sabbatical, we were offered a second.

On our second sabbatical, I asked Michelle what she would like to do? She was firm that she did not want to sit in a car, and travel twenty thousand miles again. She wanted to rest, truly rest, on a tropical island. I reminded her, that would cost far more, than we could afford. Yet I told her I would see what I could do. I prayed and told God, I knew it was frivolous, but if it were possible, would He help me to find someplace to fulfill Michelle's dream.

I called up delightful friends from my seminary days, Martha and John Martin. I knew at one time, their daughter and son-in-law pastored in the Hawaii Islands. Martha informed me that they still lived there and pastored the church on Kauai.

Martha gave me Lori's number and I called. I asked Lori if anyone in her church rented out their homes or had a bed and breakfast. She told us her best friends, were in that very business, and she gave me their number.

I called, and they told me they rented out homes for $2,500 a week. My heart sank. That was way over our budget. Then she asked me when I was planning the sabbatical? I told her April, May time frame. She said "Well in that case, I have a brand-new home you can stay at for free! I couldn't believe.... did she just say free?

She went on to explain that her parents were retiring to the Islands, but they wouldn't be there till August. The home had just been built, and no one had lived in it yet. We could have the entire place to ourselves. We could stay there for the whole two months for free. Just after that call, another couple called and told us not to rent a car, that they had an extra vehicle that we could use while we were there.

I bought two round-trip tickets for $1,200. When we arrived at the airport gate, they informed us that the flight was overbooked and offered us $2,800 and a free night stay at a resort hotel that night, with meals, transportation, and other extras for free. If we would be willing to postpone our flight till the next morning. Since we were going to be staying for two months we agreed immediately.

The bottom line is God worked it out, so we spent nearly two months in Kauai, in a new home, with a vehicle, and got paid $1,600! We actually had money left over after the two months. That $1,600 paid for all our food and fuel. Who but God could work it out, so that we could stay two months in an Island paradise and make money doing it? As an added bonus we could walk from our house to the beach in a matter of minutes. And because it was April and May, we had the beach to ourselves for the most part. It was beyond our wildest dreams!!!

Mom Sheets

We were much closer to Michelle's parents than mine. We loved the two of them and they came up to visit many times.

One day her parents called us to ask a favor. They were looking to move and were asking if we could help them buy a place. They needed a loan for the down payment. We agreed and sent them the check. They were thrilled and the sale went through.

Unfortunately, shortly after, dad passed away. Mom was left in a financially difficult position. She complained that she was finding it hard, to make it to the end of the month. Michelle and I had just recently sold FedEx, and I felt Gods leading us to honor, and care for momma Sheets.

I told Michelle, that God was prompting me to buy moms house for her. She agreed and we purchased the house and told mom she could live there the rest of her life. Since mom no longer had a monthly mortgage, she was free to travel, eat out, and enjoy the golden years.

Just as Travis told us all those years ago, when he welded the trailer, pass the blessing on.

Jury Duty

I have always been interested in our judicial system. So, whenever I had been called for jury duty, I would come eager to help. The problem was, that if you are in law enforcement or clergy, you are immediately dismissed. Every time I was called, I was dismissed.

So, when I received a summons to appear yet again, I lamented to Michelle that I didn't know why they kept calling me to serve, I couldn't even serve on a traffic case. I went down to the courthouse and sat with about a hundred other people. I filled out the customary jury forms, and waited to be dismissed. To my shock I was actually called into the room for jury selection.

The judge told us, that the case was a murder trial. I couldn't believe my good fortune. Not only a trial but a murder trial. I knew I would never be called, but the prospect was exciting.

One by one people would be called, and excused. Some wanted out due to hardship, but most were simply excused by either the prosecution or defense. The room began to empty out and the jury box slowly filled. There were still a couple seats left to be filled, when I was finally called to the stand. I fully expected to be excused, as soon as they realized I was clergy. Yet again I was amazed, as they actually started asking me questions.

But I was floored, when both sides agreed and I was placed in the jury box. Now they still had the opportunity to find others that they would prefer, and excuse me from the pool, so I half expected to be released later. At the end of the day, they had the jury fully selected and I was still in the jury box. They selected some alternates, and we went home.

I couldn't believe my good fortune. I was genuinely excited. I was going to be a part of a murder trial.

We were not allowed to say anything to anyone, but we were not sequestered either. Each night we were able to go home, but were warned every night, not to read the paper, or watch T.V. I couldn't even talk to Michelle about the case.

The case lasted a couple of weeks. It was based on complicated forensic evidence. Scientists from all over the United States were flown in to testify. Experts on both sides were examined and cross-examined. At the end of the closing arguments, the judge gave us our instructions. We were led to a deliberating room. The first order of business was selecting a Jury Foreman. To my utter amazement, I was selected.

I was humbled. I found myself as a jury foreman in a murder trial. Yet another amazing chapter in my already Miraculous life.

The case was a disaster from the beginning. The normal homicide investigator, was gone on vacation, when the murder occurred. The lead detective had never done a homicide investigation before. Turns out the lead detective was also sleeping with the victim. The body was not sent for autopsy in a timely manner. The coroner made some gross errors, and assumed the victim died of asthma. Much of the critical evidence, had accidentally been thrown away. It was a mess. Not only did the prosecution have to prove, "Who the murderer was", but "that there WAS a murder" in the first place.

We were left with only one choice, to find the defendant not guilty.

After the trial, the district attorney asked me if I would be willing to come to his office, and discuss my perspective, and why the verdict had come down the way it did. He interviewed me for about three hours. During that interview I asked him, how I had made it through the vetting process, and found out that the reason I made it through the gauntlet, was because both sides were looking for highly educated people, that could understand and wade through the complicated scientific data. It was the only time in my life, that my degree actually had any influence what-so-ever!

Near Miss

I drove up to the hospital, and when I exited my truck, I was approached by a nefarious-looking individual. My Discernment meter was pegging! Something was amiss, and I could sense it.

It was in the middle of the winter, and this guy asked if I could help him out, and jump his dead battery. I asked him where his vehicle was located and he told me, that it was up a remote canyon road, near the hospital. He told me that his wife was waiting at their vehicle, and she was freezing.

I deal with scammers all the time at the church. I have learned over forty years of ministry to ask probing questions. Yet even then, sometimes I want to err on the side of mercy. His story seemed plausible, so I decided to take a chance. I told him to jump in the truck and show me where he was stuck.

I was making mental notes; Why were his shoes dry, if he had indeed, walked out of the canyon? Why would anyone be up the remote canyon, at this hour of the morning? If the battery was dead, the vehicle would be just as cold, why would he leave his wife? Why hadn't they walked out together?

I was just starting to drive out of the parking lot when I glanced up the canyon road he had just told me he had come down. I could see that there were no vehicle tire tracks, so in that instant, without letting on, I simply continued driving up to the entrance of the Emergency room. I told him to wait right there I would only be a moment; I grabbed my keys and ran into the hospital. I called 911 and told them I needed the police immediately.

Within just a minute or so a police car drove in the entrance. When he saw the cop, he jumped out and ran. By the time the cop got to me and I explained that I had just escaped an attempted carjacking, or worse, the guy was gone. If I had gone up that road, I may never have returned. He was desperately trying to get me into a secluded area.

Once again God's discerning spirit had possibly saved my life. I have often wondered what would have happened if I had driven, even another twenty feet.

Mohave Lake and Jeff Dunbar

I love people and I love crowds. The more the merrier. I have spent most of my life around people. My job, as a pastor, is wall-to-wall people.

A friend challenged me to take 40 days of alone time. He challenged me to travel to a completely remote place, and spend 40 days utterly alone. No human contact. Just like Jesus, who took 40 days in the wilderness, I was challenged to do the same. "Just you and God!" he said.

I have an adventurous spirit. I like a challenge. I enjoy trying something new. The thought of total isolation was intriguing. I had never considered that before, but the more I thought about it, the more appealing it sounded. I had been pastoring most of my adult life, and I needed a break, from people. I needed renewal and rejuvenation.

I talked with the church board and pitched the idea to Michelle as well. I would take my vacation that year and camp out all by myself. Michelle was all for it. The board encouraged me as well, so I took a full five weeks all at the same time.

In November, I packed my camp trailer and headed to the Mohave desert in southern Nevada. I drove 30 miles from the nearest small town and ten miles from the closest pavement.

I set up camp and sat under the stars that night. I was overwhelmed by the serenity and quietness. It was so quiet, all I could hear were my own ears. The stars were brilliantly clear. With my naked eyes, I could see Andromeda, our nearest galaxy.

I had decided, to spend every morning and every night, walking and talking with God. Just as Adam and Eve strolled through the garden, communing with their Heavenly creator.

I was a little self-conscious at first, talking out loud and chatting with God, but that self-consciousness, faded. Within three days it seemed as natural as talking to Michelle.

I found it utterly refreshing, not to have people vying for my attention. I would sit for hours, and watch a bird dart around, and God would whisper, that is you, Perry, constantly darting around and never lighting. Your thoughts are always flittering from this thought to that. Let your mind be quiet.

One afternoon I took a lawn chair and walked up to the top of a nearby bluff. The view from up there was spectacular. I was sitting in the lawn chair, with the wind at my back. I had placed myself right on the edge of the bluff. The wind was blowing hard enough, that a crow was able to hover without moving its wings. I was perfectly still and it glided up to me. It was looking into my face. It kept coming closer and closer, but I remained utterly still. That silly crow was so curious and came so close, if I had wanted to, I believe I could have reached out and touched it. I almost half expected it to start talking to me.

During those quiet weeks, I could understand the stories of David in a different light. He was alone, out in the wilderness, tending sheep, just communing with his God. I could understand Jesus's desire to escape to a remote place to pray and spend time with His Heavenly Father. I felt closer to God during those weeks than at any time in my life. And it felt as normal and natural as breathing.

One morning, I woke up and I sensed that God said, "I want you to get up and police the area!" this struck me as odd. First of all, why did He use the word "Police" the area? That's a military word or law enforcement word. I had never been in the military. Why hadn't He just said, "clean up the area?"

Secondly, why police an area so completely remote? I had seen evidence of people, and there was some trash. But why, way out here?

Yet, I had learned long ago, to simply obey. I cleaned the area of all trash and found pieces of half-burned wood. I was parked next to Mohave Lake, and there was evidence of old campfires. In the sand there were old rusted-out nails, so I began running my hand through the sand along the beach, to remove all the old nails. I was surprised by just how many hundreds of nails I found.

I had a thought run through my mind that this would be a lot easier if I had a magnet. I searched everywhere and couldn't find one. Just then my

271

quiet world was interrupted by the sounds of a vehicle. As it came into view, I could see it was a Park Ranger. My first instinct was to leave and not have human contact, but it occurred to me that perhaps he might have a magnet.

He pulled up to my trailer and jumped out. He had a puzzled look on his face, and I could tell he was wondering, what in the world was someone doing in the middle of nowhere, in the off-season?

I walked up to him and asked if he had a magnet. Suddenly I felt a powerful sense of the Holy Spirit overwhelm me. I felt a sense of strength, and a boldness swept over me. I asked him if I could share something with him. I was about to do something I had never done in my life. It only happened one time in my life and it was that morning. Unfortunately, it has never happened again. I will try to explain it, but it is as miraculous to me now, as it was then! It was completely out of character for me.

In a quiet, gentle, but firm and authoritative voice I began to tell him, nowhere in the bible is Heaven called a reward. Rewards are earned, Heaven is always called a Gift. There are rewards "IN" heaven, but heaven and eternal life are always called a gift.

I was listening to myself talk, but it was as if I were experiencing an out-of-body phenomenon. I was telling him, but at the same time, I was listening to myself speak. I was just as amazed at my actions as you are reading this. But I assure you that if you had been there, you would have felt it was as natural, gentle, and smooth as if I had practiced it all my life.

I told him the story of Bobby and Bruce that I've shared in this book.

I shared the story of a Bridgman, that is faced with lowering the bridge and killing his son, or leaving it up and killing everyone on the train. God sacrificed his son so that we might live. If we came face to face with the Bridgman, we would tell him we are so sorry, and yet so thankful for saving our lives. That sorrow and thankfulness are two sides of the same coin. It's the same way for Christians, we are so sorry that Jesus had to die for us, yet so thankful he did. We are humbled and grateful at the same time.

The idea of spitting in the Bridgman's face would never occur to us. This helps to explain how the desire to sin is taken away. We COULD spit in his face, but when we know the sacrifice he made, that thought doesn't even come to our mind. When Christians truly understand that Jesus died in our place, the desire to sin against him is taken away. Could we continue to sin? Of course! But for those who truly appreciate his sacrifice, we simply don't want to anymore.

The ranger's eyes were filling with tears, and he took a step back, and he spoke; "Who are you? Are you an angel?"

"Why do you ask that?" I wondered out loud.

This is what he shared; "I just lost my best friend. I am about to lose my wife and my marriage. I have been an alcoholic my whole life. Several months ago, I became sober for the first time in my adult life. I decided this morning to come and police this area. On the drive out, I did something I have never done in my life!" he said. "I screamed out in my truck, 'God I don't know if you exist, but if you do, I have three things I have never understood, if those things ever made sense to me, it would make it a lot easier to know you are real.' Then I stepped out of my truck and there shouldn't be anybody here. You walk up to me, and before I can even speak, you answer all three questions. Are you an angel?

I assured him I was not, and with tears, standing right there he accepted God as his savior.

I told him that God had spoken to me earlier, and He told me to police the area. I know now it was so we would have time to talk. We went into my trailer and because I had policed the area, we took three hours and studied scripture. I showed him everything I had spoken to him about. He asked many more questions and I showed him the answers in the bible.

The next day he drove the 120-mile round trip a second time, to bring me a magnet on a stick. We studied for another few hours, and with tears, he thanked me for the amazing Divine appointment.

Jeff became a new man and began attending a church in the Vegas area. His wife Gloria was so amazed at the change, she joined him.

And as a fascinating caveat, Mindy's birthmother, Kelly, had moved to the same area and was attending the same church! What an amazing moment it was, the first time Michelle and I sat with them all, in their church. Jeff and Gloria have remained friends ever since.

Coincidence? Not a chance!

Conclusion

Life is a quest! The purpose of life is to discover how to turn a temporary life, into an eternal life. How to turn a dot into an eternal line. We are just a dot on an eternal line. Within that dot, we have a quest. Life's journey is to find out how we can turn that dot, into an eternal line. The answer to the quest is so simple, a child can understand it.

God is perfect. He is utterly Pure. He is perfect love. He is in a dimension, that we call heaven. No evil is present there. Not one atom of impurity exists there. The entire Bible can be summed up in a few words. It is a story of how a Perfect God worked out a formula so that soiled humanity can be washed pure and be considered perfect as well.

God is so perfect; His character can't overlook our impurity. If he overlooked our sin, that would be unjust. He would be considered an unjust God. Pure justice requires vindication. A loving God simply tells his created children, I love you so much, I will take your punishment.

The first part of the Bible is the story of how God required every family to sacrifice a lamb, once a year, and God would forgive them of every sin committed by any family member for that given year.

The New Testament is the story of how God himself became the sacrificial lamb. The good news is it was for a lifetime, not just one year. He forgives every sin, for every family member, for their entire life. The rest of the Bible is just God inviting us to be a part of His family. He will be our Father and we will be His children.

It's as simple as **A.B.C.**

Admit were sinners. Admit we are not pure, or perfect! Remember that Christianity is different from any other religion on earth. In all other religions, the people themselves have to be good enough, and then perhaps God will be happy with them, and give them heaven as a Reward. Other religions treat you like a performing circus animal. The Bible does NOT teach that. The Gift of Heaven is given to those who admit they are NO GOOD. God is DELIGHTED when we tell him we're no good. He already knows that; WE are the last ones to that party.

Believe Jesus died in your place. True justice requires a payment for sin. God is Just. He is a God of Justice. In the Old Testament, God allowed a lamb to be sacrificed once a year, to pay for the immediate family's sins. Then God told the world, I will provide the Lamb. My Son Jesus, will be the Lamb, and will cover all our sins for our entire lifetime, for anyone in My family. He writes the name of everyone who admits they are a sinner and is relying on Jesus as their payment, in the Lamb's book of life. The book of Life is simply a list of family members.

Confess, and let your heavenly Father know, that from this time forward, He is your king. He is your Heavenly Father. Let Him know that from now on, you are comfortable letting Him reparent you. Tell Him "You're the boss of me!" And determine now to obey Him when He starts the reparenting process! God is crazy in love with you.

Made in the USA
Monee, IL
25 January 2025

10952357R00157